The Economics of Cooperation

East Asian Development
and the Case for
Pro-Market Intervention

The Economics of Cooperation

East Asian Development and the Case for Pro-Market Intervention

EDITED BY

James A. Roumasset
and Susan Barr

Westview Press
BOULDER • SAN FRANCISCO • OXFORD

This Westview softcover edition is printed on acid-free paper and bound in library-quality, coated covers that carry the highest rating of the National Association of State Textbook Administrators, in consultation with the Association of American Publishers and the Book Manufacturers' Institute.

Copyright © 1992 by Westview Press, Inc.

Published in 1992 in the United States of America by Westview Press, Inc., 5500 Central Avenue, Boulder, Colorado 80301-2847, and in the United Kingdom by Westview Press, 36 Lonsdale Road, Summertown, Oxford OX2 7EW

A CIP catalog record for this book is available from the Library of Congress.
ISBN 0-8133-0454-7

Printed and bound in the United States of America

The paper used in this publication meets the requirements
of the American National Standard for Permanence of Paper
for Printed Library Materials Z39.48-1984.

10   9   8   7   6   5   4   3   2   1

Contents

Preface

The role of government in market economies has been at the core of economics since Adam Smith wrote *The Wealth of Nations*. As we move toward the "Pacific Century," this question has been given renewed impetus. The success of East Asian economies in the face of extensive government involvement in the economy has called into question the free-market slogan "privatize and get the prices right." Even in the U.S., there is increasing interest in having an industrial policy, not to direct commerce but to facilitate cooperation in increasing global competitiveness. Socialist countries seeking to liberalize their economies are now asking how government policies can best align private incentives in order to decentralize economic cooperation. In an effort to contribute to the better understanding of these issues, studies of investment coordination in the Asia-Pacific region were undertaken which have, in turn, given rise to the present volume.

We wish to thank President Albert Simone, former Vice President Anthony J. Marsalla, the School of Hawaii, Asian and Pacific Studies and the Department of Economics of the University of Hawaii for helping to sponsor the discussion of these issues. Special thanks to Cynthia Wood for her creativity and patience in the technical editing and electronic typesetting of this volume, Trent Bertrand, Christopher Clague, James Mak, Seiji Naya, Calla Weimer, and Raeburn Williams for helpful discussions and Lee Endress for comments on a previous draft, and Benton and Brian Roumasset for their inspiration and good cheer.

James A. Roumasset
Susan Barr

1

Introduction:
The Role of Government
in Economic Development

James A. Roumasset

Economists have long been divided, in formulating policy advice, along the lines of the political right and left. Economists leaning towards the left have advocated government intervention as a corrective for a wide variety of market failures and to correct the allegedly unjust distribution of income that results from capitalism. Politically "right" economists have resisted such intervention, arguing that so-called market failures could be more effectively managed by voluntary action than by coercive government edicts. These "free market" economists also maintain that justice is more a matter of protecting liberty than taking from the rich and giving to the poor.

In this contrast between the economics of the right and left, government intervention is assumed to be anti-market, and the promotion of markets is thought to be anti-government. "Pro-market government intervention" thus sounds like a contradiction in terms.

A number of recent developments have contributed to a challenge to the conventional government versus market paradigm. First, there has been a widespread disillusionment with the ability of government planning to replace voluntary exchange. Discussion of "government failure" has become commonplace. Journalists as well as economists speak of the "iron triangle" between government bureaucracy, lawmakers and special interests in the private sector. The iron triangle tacitly colludes to establish regulations, economic policy, and public programs that redistribute income towards the influential coalition instead of promoting the common good. At the same time, the market success stories of Japan, Korea and Taiwan appear to have been stimulated and accelerated by government facilitation. Apparently, government intervention does not necessarily detract from economic development.

The theory and practice of economic planning has traditionally focused on the amount and composition of government spending and on "picking the winners," choosing new products that the government will promote in order to stimulate economic growth. An alternative view is that government policy should be focused on improving the performance of private markets, i.e. that government intervention should be "pro-market." In order to explore further the role of government in promoting economic development, this chapter begins with a review of the role of government policy in the theory of economic development. The next two sections explore lessons for the role of government that are suggested by recent development success stories in East Asia. The last sections provide an overview of the rest of the book.

The Evolution of Development Theory

Economic development theory has undergone a number of stages of fad and fancy in the last 30 years. Economic planning and development policy prescription have correspondingly swung from one panacea to another. It has not always been clear whether the policy-makers were following the ideas of economics or whether the economic ideas that became popular were those that rationalized what policy-makers wanted to do. In any case, it is time to take stock. What have we learned about government's role in economic development? What do lessons about the development of Asia suggest about the role of government?

In the 1960s, the predominant strategy for economic development was to transfer resources from the "backward" and "traditional" agricultural sector to the modern manufacturing sector. Popular policy instruments for effecting the resource transfer were tariff and non-tariff barriers against foreign competition, credit subsidies and other fiscal incentives.

The experience of the 1950s and 60s in many developing Asian countries suggests that subsidizing import-substitution does indeed lead to an initial period of rapid manufacturing growth but only in the finishing stage of the industry (e.g. assembly). Since protection of one economic activity indirectly discriminates against other activities and sectors, the initial period of growth is followed by stagnation. Forward and backward integration, diversification, export promotion are all stifled by the very policies conceived to stimulate growth.

In response to this experience, the 1970s witnessed a change to a new strategy. International development agencies such as the World Bank dubbed the 70s as the "employment decade." Developing countries were encouraged to invest in promoting new agricultural technology, and to build infrastructure such as bridges, roads, communication facilities, electrification and irrigation works. Governments also invested in subsidizing agricultural inputs, rural credit, land reform, crop insurance and other programs designed to compensate for perceived inefficiencies of the private sector.

While these policies achieved some degree of success, especially in boosting agricultural yields and employment, overall performance failed to live up to expectations. Infrastructure was often poorly designed, mismanaged, and improperly maintained. Irrigation systems, for example, were incapable of delivering reliable water supplies and depreciated much faster than had been projected. Subsidy programs also failed to achieve benefits that were commensurate with their total economic costs.

The disappointing achievements of government intervention in the seventies led to widespread claims that the "government failures" associated with these programs were worse than the "market failures" which they were designed to correct. In the 1980s, the World Bank, the International Monetary Fund, the U.S. Agency for International Development and other international agencies pressured developing countries to adopt conservative monetary and fiscal policies, to privatize public enterprise, and to liberalize trade policy in order to "get the prices right."

Again, the performance of these programs did not live up to their promise. Attempts to privatize public enterprise often resulted in the mere substitution of a private monopoly for a public one. Tariffs were substantially reduced on consumer items in many countries, but the nontariff barriers continued to shelter "infant industries" that had somehow never managed to grow up and compete in the world economy. Not only did import-substituting industries mount political pressure to continue protection, but attempts to remove protection often caused temporary disruptions that made the maintenance of economic liberalization politically untenable.

Lessons from Recent Experience and the East Asian Success Story

Much attention has been paid in recent years to the "economic miracle" of Japan and the East Asian "gang of four" (Korea, Taiwan, Hong Kong and Singapore). These countries are said to have succeeded by strategies of "outward orientation" and "export-led growth." Exports of manufactured goods from Korea, Taiwan, Hong Kong and Singapore grew at an annual rate of 28% from 1950 to 1971. Many observers have argued that it was the lack of protectionist policies, which allowed the export sectors in these countries to respond to the accountability and discipline of international competition, that accounts for the rapid economic growth.

More recently, however, it has come to light that the outward orientation of Japan, Korea and Taiwan has been accomplished in large measure by active government involvement in targeted sectors. In particular, MITI and other government agencies in Japan have provided "administrative guidance," organized "deliberation councils" and facilitated "discussion groups" (Lee & Naya 1988). Similar institutions for coordinating interdependent enterprises have also been documented in Korea and Taiwan. All three countries are known to have used subsidized credit to promote priority industries (Wade 1990).

While economic theory explains how the "invisible hand" of free markets leads to an efficient allocation of labor under some restrictive conditions, it does not imply that markets can achieve an efficient coordination of interdependent investments. In a world where information is both crucial and costly, where many enterprises are highly interdependent, and where agreements among enterprises are sometimes costly to achieve and difficult to enforce, private markets may fall well short of possible expansion and growth. While government in the U.S. is often portrayed as adversarial to business, government in East Asia has played more of a partnership role with the private sector.

These lessons suggest a new role for economic planning and policy analysis. In the past, planners have often been asked to make economic forecasts and to designate which sectors of the economy are the most promising for investment promotion. The experience discussed above suggests that the appropriate role of government is not so much in controlling the future as in facilitation.

Economic development experience also suggests that protectionism and other "rent-seeking" restrictions of competition are politically resilient. By facilitating the coordination of new investment, government can lower political resistance to liberalizing the restrictive economic policies that have led to stagnation. Economic protection tends to insulate the private sector from the discipline of competition and to create incentives for entrepreneurs to seek subsidies instead of innovations. There are many ways that the government can support coordination in the private sector without distorting incentives. Communication and transportation infrastructure facilitate the market's ability to direct resources into their highest and best use. Market information, including the support of research and design, and liberal banking policies can make market opportunities available to many potential entrepreneurs. These policies complement the market's ability to select the organization or organizations best suited to exploit a particular market niche.

In addition to playing a partnership role with the private sector, government can also go a long way towards promoting efficiency in the public sector. Most of the rapid expansion in public spending in developing countries in the last twenty years has been financed from borrowing and general tax revenue. The heavy subsidies to individual projects such as irrigation create perverse incentives for design, operation and maintenance. Typically we see a pattern of over-construction (high capital-intensity) and undermaintenance. New methods are needed to provide adequate incentives to the public sector for efficient performance. In particular, decentralization, cost recovery, and local finance will be needed to provide better incentives and smaller budget deficits. There also are substantial improvements possible in the composition of taxation in most countries. High taxes on various sources of income and spending blunt economic incentives and impair efficiency. Some "fiscal drag" is inevitable, but a number of reforms are possible which keep tax friction to a minimum.

Some of the other patterns of economic development which have become more apparent in recent years have particular relevance for economic development strategy. One such pattern characterizing a modern and rapidly growing economy is that the service sector grows faster than either the agricultural or manufacturing sector, largely because as individual countries and the world economy in general become both more specialized and more interdependent, the coordination of economic activity takes up a larger and larger share of the value of total production. It is important to note that product design, marketing and coordination are no less important in creating value added, employment opportunities, and increasing standard of living, than are production activities. Another pattern is that the export and import accounts grow more rapidly than total economic activity. This is also related to the growing specialization within economies and between economies. The principal reason for expanding exports is to finance the importation of goods that are more efficiently produced in other countries. Striving to simultaneously increase exports and decrease imports does not necessarily contribute to economic development.

Another important pattern of economic development is that economic expansion and diversification evolves from existing strengths of an economy. It is typically not the case that development is characterized by dramatic shifts to new product types for which the economy has not previously developed some expertise. Thus for example, Honda gradually built up its market share from 20% to 80% of the domestic motorcycle market in Japan during the 1950s before beginning a phase of rapid export expansion of motorcycles in the 60s, then turned to the production of very small automobiles, and gradually to higher and higher quality cars (Halberstam 1986).

Another lesson from the Honda case is that competition is helpful in stimulating the product quality and excellence that is a prerequisite to rapid growth in international markets. In competition to become number one in the motorcycle industry, Honda focused on quality improvements that enhanced the reputation of their product and market share. To the extent government is helpful to Japanese companies in promoting their exports, it is typically after these companies have survived the rigors of competition and passed the test of market excellence. This strategy is diametrically opposed to infant industry arguments for protection and the use of antitrust mechanisms to discriminate against companies which are successful in achieving major increases in market share.

The East Asian experience suggests that economic development is best facilitated by creating a healthy economic environment, not by attempting to direct and control. "Picking the winners" and trying to subsidize them is a prescription for building dependence not excellence. The winners of East Asia were selected and perfected in the crucible of competition. It was only when successful companies emerged with quality products that East Asian governments provided additional incentives in order to promote exports.

Implications for Developing Economies in the Asia-Pacific Region and the Prospects for Exporting Cooperation

Apparently, governments can do a great deal to increase the competitiveness of their economies' exportables. Moreover, the government's role extends beyond the provision of the physical structure of coordination such as transportation and communication facilities to the institutional prerequisites of exchange and the coordination of investment. Government policies and programs are also critical for the dynamic research and development needed to achieve and maintain areas of excellence. Competitiveness is not well served, however, by subsidies, protection, and regulations that decrease competition. Indeed, the degree of competition is an important indicator of the performance of the exportable sector. But competition should not become an end in itself, lest anti-trust institutions and other regulatory instruments are used to increase the balance of power among domestic firms by penalizing industry leaders.

It is also clear from the the experience of economic development elsewhere that developing new products is not necessarily crucial to economic development. There has been a rapid growth of intra-industry trade such that market niches have become increasingly narrow. It is possible, for example, for the U.S. to expand the value of its garment industry while moving the physical production of garments to other countries and specializing instead on the design and marketing stages of product development.

Many of the coordinating activities of government may be handled in partnership with the financial sector. Coordination of investments is the natural province of financial intermediaries, and investment banking provides a useful model of coordination. In order to stimulate domestic banks to play more of a coordinating role in particular countries and internationally, however, some liberalization of financial regulations that limit entry into the banking sector and limit bank operations may be needed.

Much of economic planning in the Asia-Pacific region, however, remains oriented to the old "pick the winners" approach to identifying new products. Economic coordination increases value added and promotes a higher standard of living just as does the physical production of goods. Market information, processing, packaging, advertising, finance, legal services and other forms of intermediation all serve to create value by directing diverse resources, talents and creativity into their highest and best use by serving the various wants of disparate and distant consumers.

For example, Hawaii has a potential for facilitating economic coordination in the Pacific region. Hawaii is closer to East Asia in distance, time and culture, and thereby has a natural advantage as a bridge between East and West. Numerous dialogues are taking place about how to foster better cooperation between the U.S. and East Asia, how to minimize conflict, and how to appropriate synergy out of diversity. Hawaii and other Pacific Island economies can play an important role in facilitating such coordination. Moreover, the values of many Pacific Island cultures may help to facilitate economic coordination. The Hawaiian word, *ohana*, means community, and is understood as an institutional basis for appropriating synergy from diversity. *Ohana* means being open in the face of conflict and employing such Hawaiian practices as *ho'oponopono* and *kukakulea* to restore harmony and to discover win-win resolutions. After evaluating alternate dispute resolution methods for many years, the Harvard Negotiation Project recommends these same methods for international negotiations and resolution of commercial disputes. Cooperation is not only a socio-political objective; it is good business. And coordination is an economic good.

Economic policy in many developing economies stands at a crossroads. There are two basic approaches to economic policy. One is the policy of fear and protectionism. Under this policy, the idea is to regulate so many aspects of development that little change can take place without the explicit permission of government authorities. The other approach is to take the leap of faith into the international economy knowing that the businesses that flourish will be those whose entrepreneurs believe can survive the rigors of competition.

The latter approach does not imply an uncontrolled *laissez faire* posture of government regarding foreign investment. Government can still find policies that protect the environmental and cultural heritage of a nation without having to second-guess the economy's future comparative advantage. To the extent that liberalizing regulations that currently constrain growth will increase the demand for new investment, new business taxes and foreign investment taxes can be imposed and still maintain investment demand at a desirable level. The new tax revenue thus generated will permit lowering existing tax rates.

The role of government in the new view of planning is to act as the facilitator of development. To the extent to which planners provide information about future prospects it should be more in the spirit of providing a menu instead of controlling the direction of progress. Government agencies can also facilitate agreements within the economy and between economic interests inside and outside the economy's political boundaries.

While cooperation thus becomes the recommended mode of development policy, cooperation is also what development policy should promote. The traditional values of many indigenous cultures may prove to be instrumental in achieving the mutual respect that is the source of genuine cooperation. In this way, diversity may pass from being an obstacle to a source of abundance.

The book is organized into two parts. Part I discusses the nature of institutional development as it promotes market growth. Particular attention is paid to financial institutions, intellectual property rights, and industrial restructuring policies. Part II reviews the successful experience of East-Asian countries, especially Japan and Korea. Particular attention is focused on government's role in promoting industrial conglomerates, the *Kieretsu* and *Chaebol*.

Overview of Part I: Institutional Aspects of Market Development

Apparent ideological differences between economists manifest themselves not only in policy recommendations but may creep in to positive (i.e. explanatory) economics as well. Economists favoring market solutions tend to interpret the East Asian "economic miracle" as a triumph of free markets. Economists who lean more towards government intervention, on the other hand, tend to see a much larger positive role having been played by government planning and incentives.

Part of the problem is the tradition, at least among American economists, that the existence of both markets and government is to be taken as given. This perspective leads to the view that a central problem in the formulation of economic policy has to do with the scope of government policy, that is, with the designation of which activities should be within the sphere of government and which should be left to markets. An alternative view is that markets evolve as property rights become more sharply defined. In order to facilitate and enforce a system of the contractual exchange of rights across diverse agents who are separated by space, social status, economic condition, and heritage, a system of centralized control and justice is required. The growth of these institutional prerequisites to market exchange may therefore be warranted in order to facilitate economic development. This type of growth in governmental institutions is apparently pro-market.

The unifying theme of the following four chapters is that both property rights institutions and markets are endogenous. Chapter 2, by Joseph Stiglitz, applies this perspective to financial institutions. From the perspective of economic development, one can think of banks as the formalization of the highly personalized money-lending industry. In this view, banks are an intermediate institution between the informal money lender and in personal capital markets. Banks rely more heavily on third-party enforcement through the government justice system than do private moneylenders, but still base much of their decision making on idiosyncratic information about individual borrowers. Capital markets can then be thought of as the further depersonalization of lending. In the limit of capital market development, the identity of traders becomes irrelevant.

Chapter 3 continues the analysis of financial markets. Banks provide personalized services of financial intermediation. To the extent that specific services to borrowers and lenders can be defined in terms of objectively identifiable contingencies, then banking services can be replaced by tradable financial instruments. Brian Wright and David Newbery suggest that commodity bonds can perform such a service for the exporters of primary commodities.

One of the principal ways in which government can actively promote productivity growth is to stimulate and coordinate investment into research and development. Chapters 4 and 5, by Robert Evenson and Sumner La Croix, explore how patent policy and other instruments of intellectual policy rights (IPR) protection may be used to improve R&D incentives. The design of patent law poses a central dilemma. On the one hand, "loose" IPR protection will help firms in an economy to be "good pirates." Professor Evenson suggests that the economic success of the rapidly growing East Asian economies is highly correlated with the ability of those economies to borrow technology from abroad. On the other hand, a more protective IPR system will encourage inventive activity within the domestic economy. One way out of the dilemma may be through a system of "petty patents" whereby firms can essentially borrow technology from abroad and then obtain patent protection on numerous adaptations of the technology. Professor La Croix suggests that, historically, countries have switched to more protective policies as the political influence of the inventive sector has increased. From an international perspective, the existing situation is clearly far from optimal. There is considerable scope for institutional reform that would allow the benefits of new technology to be widely appropriated while simultaneously preserving the incentives to invent and develop it.

There has been a call by politicians, business leaders and academics (including, e.g., Paul Tsongas, Lee Iacocca and M.I.T.'s Paul Krugman) for an American industrial policy. One way of viewing the creation of industrial policy is from the perspective of constitutional design. That is, what collective institutions and governance structures can best facilitate the coordination of investments and commercial enterprises for mutually beneficial outcomes? Chapter 6, by Ira Lieberman, provides grist for just such a constitutional mill.

Overview of Part II: The East Asian Experience and Pro-Market Planning for Economic Development

Part II is concerned with the nature of and the prospects for pro-market development planning, especially in East Asia. As already noted, the anti-market government intervention in developing countries over the past thirty years contrasts sharply with the more successful pro-market policies in East Asia. Anti-market policies have the effect of inhibiting mutually beneficial transactions. Pro-market policies have the opposite effect and enhance economic cooperation.

In Chapter 7, Louis Putterman examines 25 years of economic development policy in China, contrasting periods of maximum suppression of market allocation with periods in which decentralized decision making was given greater sway. He also contrasts China with the market-oriented and high-growth East Asian success stories. While the state apparently played a strong coordinating role in Japan, Taiwan and South Korea, government action was in the context of a property system and enhanced market development. In China, on the other hand, government planning and control substituted for markets and thereby inhibited market development.

Chapter 8 concentrates on two under-appreciated aspects of Japanese and South Korean industrial policy: the promotion of industrial conglomerates, and industrial sector targeting. In Japan, industries were organized in bank groups *(Keiretsu)*, which descended from the old *Zaibatsu* trading companies. In the Korean case, *Chaebol* were promoted through government-controlled credit institutions. Mukesh Aswaran and Ashok Kotwal show that government promotion of such industrial conglomerates may in fact be efficiency-enhancing despite the popularity of the opposite argument among Western economists.

Chapter 9 provides additional description of the nature of the South Korean government's industrial policy. Chung Lee particularly emphasizes the role of government in coordinating investments. Chapter 10 is addressed to the apparent poor communication between Japan and the United States regarding foreign investment and trade. Keizo Nagatani argues that the level of communication is due in large measure to different economic doctrines. He then explores some specific differences in "Japanese Economics."

References

Halberstam, D. 1986. *The Reckoning*. New York: Avon.
Lee, C. H., and S. Naya. 1988. "Trade in East Asian Development with Comparative Reference to Southeast Asian Experience." *Economic Development and Cultural Change* 36 (3): S123-152.
Wade, R. 1990. *Governing the Market: Economic Theory -- the Role of Government in East Asian Industrialization*. Princeton: Princeton University Press.

PART ONE

Institutional Aspects of
Market Development

2

Banks Versus Markets as Mechanisms for Allocating and Coordinating Investment

*Joseph E. Stiglitz**

The relationship between finance and economics is a curious and tortuous one, which has changed dramatically during recent years. I begin my chapter with a thumb-nail sketch of the history of that relation, because I hope, by doing so, I can provide some insights into current thinking about the role of financial markets in economic growth, and the role of government in financial markets.

The Relationship Between Finance and Economics

In the nineteenth century, finance (or "credit") was very much at the center of economic concerns. What we today call business cycles was typically referred to, in those days, as credit cycles, associating the fluctuations in the economy with perhaps their most marked feature, the fluctuations in credit, and the generally identified cause of the onset of many of these fluctuations, the panics in financial markets.

To whom should we give credit for the demise of the central role of credit in economic analysis? Some, no doubt, should be assigned to Walras and the development of general equilibrium theory. Finance or credit -- whatever it was -- was not so easily incorporated into that framework. Like other aspects of the economy which could not easily be accommodated within that powerful paradigm, finance was dismissed as little more than providing institutional details. This view was reinforced by the classical dichotomy, which argued that money simply determined price levels: everything *real* (that is, out-puts and relative prices) were determined by *real* factors.

Keynes, too, must share some of the blame: he erred on two accounts. First, his analysis, aggregating long term bonds and equities together, seemed to suggest that the details of how finance was provided to firms made little difference. Second, his emphasis on money led a whole generation of economists to focus on that financial instrument to the exclusion of others. This is not the occasion for an enquiry into why Keynes took the tack he did. I suspect there may have been an element of attempting to differentiate his product from his rival, Professor Robertson.[1] Keynes did not so much as attack the loanable funds theory as provide an alternative theory: he claimed, in effect, that interest rates were determined in the money market. It was left to his reader to figure out how the two theories might be reconciled.

Not long after the publication of the General Theory, Joan Robinson developed the notion that there were multiple related markets, with slightly different interest rates, determined within a general equilibrium model. This developed into one of the two major strands of work on the role of finance in macroeconomics. Tobin formalized Robinson's general equilibrium approach, focusing on the special case of mean-variance models. In this approach, it appeared that debt and equity were markedly different financial instruments. To which market, then, was investment to be related, the debt market (as implicitly suggested by Keynes) or the equity market? Tobin, in later work, suggested it should be the equity market: investment was related to the price of the firm in the equity market (Tobin's Q).

The second strand was perhaps more in keeping with Keynes' ignoring of finance: Modigliani and Miller (1958) argued that the firm's financial structure was irrelevant. Jorgenson and succeeding generations of students of investment took them seriously, and banished, as a matter of faith and theory (or should I say, faith in theory) rather than evidence, financial variables from their investment functions.[2]

A Re-examination of the Irrelevance Propositions

Less than fifteen years after Modigliani and Miller published their results, a major assault on the validity of the proposition that financial policy was irrelevant was begun. First, Stiglitz (1969, 1974a) showed that while in the *absence* of bankruptcy, their proposition was much more general than they had asserted; with bankruptcy, it was false. While bankruptcy may occur relatively rarely, the pervasiveness of concern with bankruptcy is reflected in the persistence of substantially higher interest rates for corporate bonds than for government debt. Furthermore, even if bankruptcy is rare, it may be because firms have responded to the concern about it, and this has affected their choice of financial structure. Subsequently, Stiglitz (1974b, 1982a), Stiglitz and Weiss (1981), Leland and Pyle (1977), Ross (1977), Myers and Majluf (1984) and Greenwald, Stiglitz and Weiss (1984) brought forth a variety of arguments, based on adverse selection and moral hazard concerns, for why the firm's financial structure matters.[3] They argued that there may be credit rationing and equity rationing; that the firm's choice of financial structure might convey information from the firm to potential purchasers of shares, and thus might affect firm's market value; that the differences in the obligations of firms under debt and equity contracts might affect managerial incentives.

Financial structure was not only important because it (a) affected the probability of bankruptcy; (b) affected the beliefs of outsiders -- potential purchasers of firm's shares -- about the firm's profitability, or at least about the managers' beliefs about the firms profitability; and (c) affected managerial incentives. It also (d) affected tax liabilities (see Stiglitz 1973); (e) affected how the firm's managers were monitored (see Stiglitz 1985); and (f) in some instances, affected who controlled the firm.

Finally -- and this is the topic to which I shall return in this essay -- it affects the flow of funds to the firm under different exigencies.

Difficulties in Testing the Alternative Theories

Testing the alternative theories -- in particular, testing for the importance of "finance" -- is not as simple as it might seem. The financial structure of the firm is an endogenous variable, and hence naive tests, relating investment to the debt equity ratio of the firm would seem to be inappropriate. An increase in cash flow would, in a finance constrained model, lead to increased investment; but since increases in cash flow are likely to be highly correlated with increases in profitability, how can one tell that the increased investment is not primarily the result of increased profitability rather than increased cash flow. But of course, the converse is also true.

Consider Tobin's Q. Tobin argued that what was relevant for determining investment was the value of the firm's shares in the stock market. Of course, what he really argued was that it paid a firm to invest a dollar, raised say by issuing a dollar's worth of new securities, if that extra dollar increased the value of the firm by more than a dollar. Put this way, the proposition seems unexceptional -- and in fact was no more than a restatement of the standard theories in the literature (Diamond 1967; Stiglitz 1972b). Empirical implementation went further, for it identified the incremental value/investment ratio with the average value/capital ratio. (This was perhaps surprising, for even by then, it was recognized that when markets for risk were incomplete, the two could differ markedly. See, for instance, Stiglitz 1972b or 1989a.)

In empirical testing, Tobin's Q has not fared too well. (See Abel and Blanchard 1986.) But what success it has had may largely be the result of a spurious correlation. It is not that firms' managers look to Q at all in deciding their level of investment, only that the information on which they make their investment decisions is correlated with the information which investors use in evaluating securities; and both are correlated with the cash flow of the firm.

The facts that firms make so little use of new equity issues (see Mayer 1989) and that there appears to be so much noise in stock market prices lends support to the view that investment is not driven by Q. Surely, managers of a steel firm do not look to the judgments of the dentists in Peoria or the retired stock brokers in Florida to obtain information about the prospects within their industry. Moreover, firms do not simply invest in "steel," they invest in specific projects; firms have to evaluate specific projects, and even if it were thought that the stock market price were informative, the information it conveys is too coarse to be of much use in evaluating any particular project.

The fact that firms by and large do not resort to new equity issues to finance investment, but rather (when they must turn to outside finance) to debt, suggests that perhaps Keynes was right, after all, in focusing on the interest rate. But standard theories have argued that what is relevant is the real interest rate, and for long periods of time -- say from the mid 1950s to the mid 1970s -- real interest rates[4] simply did not vary much. (See Figure 2.1.[5]) Variations in the real interest rate simply could not account for much of the variability in investment, and if monetary policy was ever effective during this period, it surely was not through its effects on real interest rates.

The Re-examination of the Keynesian Monetary Theory

The recognition of this has come at the same time that the theoretical foundations of traditional Keynesian monetary theory have again been called into question: the opportunity cost of holding

Movements in Real Interest Rate: 1952-87

1 - Year Real Rate

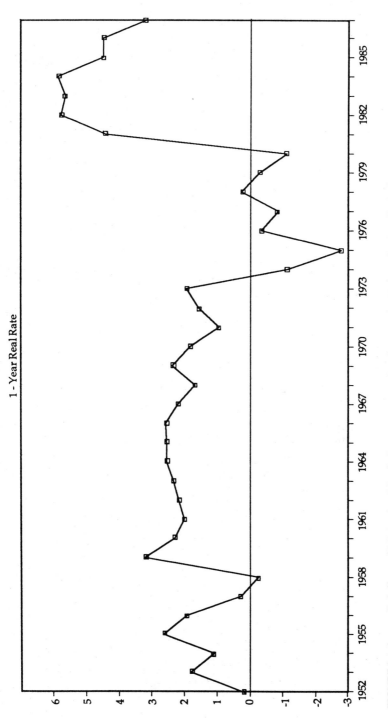

FIGURE 2.1 *Source:* D. Jaffee and J.E. Stiglitz, "Credit Rationing," in B. Friedman and F. Hahn, eds., *Handbook of Monetary Economics.*
Pp. 837-888. Amsterdam: Elsevier Science Publishers. Reprinted by permission.

money (taking as M_1^6 as our definition of money, and recalling that
most of M_1 consists of demand deposits, not currency) is the difference
between the return on money and the return on other short term interest
bearing assets; this difference is small, probably driven more by technological considerations than by anything else, and even less related to
investment than the real rate of interest. Moreover, the transactions
motive for holding money (the only motive that distinguishes money
from other short term assets) is not related to income in a simple way:
money is not required for most transactions (credit is); and most
transactions are exchanges of assets, and thus are not directly related
to income generation. Moreover, there are theoretical reasons why one
should not expect that the relationship between asset exchanges and
income generating transactions to remain unchanged with business
fluctuations. (See Stiglitz and Weiss 1989.)

The New Theories: Capital Markets with Imperfect Information and a Role for Financial Institutions

In the last few years, Bruce Greenwald, Andy Weiss, and I have
been developing a set of theories which we believe provides a
consistent explanation both of firm behavior, e.g. with respect to
investment, and of why, when, and how monetary policy is effective.
It recognizes the distinction between capital markets and the markets
for chairs, tables, and other conventional commodities. The capital
market is not an auction market. The bank does not simply allocate
credit to those who are willing to pay the highest interest rate. Doing
so would not necessarily maximize the bank's expected return.

At times, there may be credit rationing. Even when there is not,
the admittedly imperfect judgments made by banks about the risks and
returns associated with different investments and investors has significant effects on how society's resources get allocated. We have,
moreover, explained why it is that firms make so little use of equity
markets for raising new capital. For simplicity, we say that there is
equity rationing.[7] The consequence of equity and credit rationing are
that (a) firms act in a risk averse manner; (b) changes in the firm's net
worth and cash flows may have real effects; (c) similarly, changes in
risks (that is, say, in the variance of returns, holding mean returns
constant) have real effects; and (d) changes in credit availability may
be far more important in affecting investment than changes in the real
interest rate. In our theories, for the most part, neither the real
interest rate nor Tobin's Q drives investment.

A natural consequence of this shift in views concerning how capital markets function is that attention is drawn to the institutions and mechanisms by which capital is allocated. If capital were allocated as if in an auction market, these institutional arrangements would be mere details, the kind that good theory ignores. On the contrary, we have shown that it makes a great deal of difference whether capital is raised by equity or debt, and if by debt, whether by short term debt or long term debt. The efficiency with which economic institutions are able to screen loan applicants (either by examination or self-selection devices) and monitor how funds are used affects the extent to which other mechanisms for allocating and controlling the use of capital have to be used. The extent and even the presence of credit rationing depends on the nature and magnitude of the residual variability in the quality of the applicant pool, after the screening is completed. At the extreme, if there were perfect screening, there would never be credit rationing.

This chapter represents another step in our investigation of these institutions and arrangements. Here, we focus on the use of markets versus banks as allocative mechanisms.

Three Hypotheses

There are some marked differences across countries and over time in the reliance placed on markets versus banks for raising funds. In the United States, recent years have witnessed a significant increase in securitization of mortgages, allowing mortgages to be written by brokers rather than banks. The commercial paper market has grown enormously as a source of short term credit for large firms. Many Japanese firms seem to have reduced their reliance on their traditional banks as a source of funding, and turned to the market instead.

What are the causes and consequences of this shift? There are several alternative hypotheses, each with its own implications. The effects upon which each of the hypotheses focus undoubtedly play a role in what has happened. The question is, which effects predominate?

The Efficient Markets Hypothesis

The first hypothesis is that markets are more efficient than banks in allocating capital. Transactions costs are lower. Accordingly, firms that can raise capital on the market -- large firms with national and international reputations -- do so. In this view, banks are, for these large corporations, an unnecessary intermediary. The kind of screening that is required can be done just as well by the analysts at a bond mutual fund. These large institutions can also provide to their "depositors" (share owners) the same risk diversification services that banks provide. And if they invest in government backed securities, they can provide the same security that a FDIC insured account does.

This view, then, sees banks as specialized intermediaries. They specialize in screening smaller firms, firms that are too small to attract widespread attention. Banks have a comparative advantage in going inside the firm, examining its books, making judgments about the quality of the management, supervising the loans, etc.

Advantages of Banks. There is one puzzle. Bond mutual funds can be viewed as "banks" without deposit insurance. Conventional banks with government deposit insurance (at what appears, ex post, to be more than actuarially fair terms) should thus have an advantage over these mutual funds. Could the failure of the banks to take advantage of this advantage be attributed to some inefficiency on their part, in which case the relative growth of the importance of the market is to be attributed not to the efficiency of the market, but to the lack of efficiency of banks?

There are other reasons why one might have thought that banks are at an advantage vis-a-vis the market:

Long term relationships. Banks can establish a long term relationship with their clients, a relationship which is distinctly different from that between a borrower and the "market." In general, in markets with imperfect information and incomplete contracting, long term relationships often enhance economic efficiency. In this case, the long term relationship has some reciprocal advantages. The lender can accumulate more information (and it pays for it to do so) than if it were a short term relationship. The threat by the bank to terminate the relationship in the event of extremely bad performance has positive incentive effects.[8]   At the same time, the "implicit contract" between the bank and the borrower can be used to provide insurance to the borrower, that he will continue to be funded through at least certain types of hard-times.

Better monitoring. The fact that firms typically obtain funding from a limited number of banks (or that there is a "lead bank") reduces the "public good" problem associated with monitoring the loan.[9] This should enhance the returns obtained.

Greater flexibility. Banks may be more flexible. It is hard to design "credit lines" using market mechanisms. Ideally, firms would like to have a variety of contingent contracts, which would provide capital to them in different amounts at different terms in different circumstances. Though many financial contracts are indeed fairly complex, they are still less "contingent" than most firms would ideally like. For instance, few contracts are very indexed.

Bank loans often appear to have a kind of flexibility which is missing in market based finance. The credit line is one instance of this. Beyond a fee for maintaining the credit line, firms only have to pay for the credit they actually use.

Of course, in a world with perfect capital markets, this would make no difference. Whenever a firm wants to go to the market, it simply does so, paying the prevailing market rate of interest at the time. If a firm was concerned about the risk that this imposed on it, it could insure against this risk. But firms cannot buy this insurance, and in particular, they cannot buy insurance against the risk that their credit rating will be decreased, and they will have to pay a much higher interest rate to obtain funds (or that they will find it essentially impossible to raise funds.)[10]

Alternatively, the firm could borrow more money than it needed. This, too, has its problems. First, there is frequently a marked difference between lending rates and borrowing rates, so that it is costly to borrow more than one needs. Secondly, lenders may worry about the uses to which the extra funds might be put. Borrowing more funds than is immediately needed can be interpreted as demonstrating the borrower's lack of confidence in the short run returns on the project: the additional borrowed funds are used to pay the interest due in the first few years of the bond. (This was evidently true of many junk bonds. In addition, some of the extra money was used to buy junk bonds in other firms, thus helping to support the market.)

Disadvantage of Borrowing from Banks. All of these factors mean that bank-finance is a more flexible form of finance than market-finance. And these seeming advantages of banks over markets make the decline in the role of banks all the more puzzling. On the other side, banks face one disadvantage: the amount of funds which banks can or wish to lend can be affected by the actions of the monetary authorities. The effect of their actions is not spread evenly throughout the financial market, but is concentrated in the banking sector, and accordingly, on those who are dependent on banks for the sources of funds. Indeed, credit crunches have contributed strongly to the growth of the commercial paper market.

If it were costless to move in or out of the commercial paper market, then the variability in bank finance might make little difference. Large firms that have their credit restricted would simply turn from bank to commercial paper as a source of finance. Indeed, to the extent that this is true, the effectiveness of monetary policy may be greatly reduced.

In the case where the switch in and out of bank lending and market finance is easy, of course, the reduced *share* of bank lending may portend little for how capital markets function.[11] Banks may perform their role in monitoring and screening almost as effectively: the market, for instance, may rely on the certification provided by a bank loan, and firms may accordingly pay close attention to what their bankers say.[12, 13]

Markets versus Banks: Self Selection

The fact that there are differences between bank and market finance implies that there are opportunities for self-selection mechanisms to work.[14] On the one hand, firms that feel that being put on the short tether of bank finance -- the potential at least for close supervision and monitoring -- imposes little cost will be the most likely to accept it. In that case, choosing to use the market, and particularly, choosing to raise funds by long term debt, may serve as a signal of lack of credit worthiness.

On the other hand, as we have noted, bank finance provides greater flexibility (apart from the periods of credit crunches). For a firm to say that its financial strength is so great that in can dispense with that kind of flexibility serves as a signal of credit worthiness. In that case, turning to the market may increase the firm's market value.

It is, by now, well recognized that there may be multiple signalling equilibria (Spence 1974). Perhaps the increased reliance on markets as a source of finance, particularly by larger corporations, can be seen as a movement from one signalling equilibrium to another. Since the "best" firms resort to market finance, not to use market finance signals financial weakness, requiring the flexibility of bank finance.

Even if there were a unique signalling equilibrium, three factors could have contributed to the change in the signalling equilibrium. First, the transactions cost of using the market has been reduced; second, the credit crunches of the monetary authorities, particularly that of the Volker years, has reduced in borrowers' eyes the advantages of bank finance; and thirdly, the overall success, in the post-World War II era, of stabilization policies reducing the magnitude of cyclical fluctuations may have reduced the necessity of flexible access to funds.[15]

A Market Inefficiency Interpretation

There is a third interpretation of the change in the sources of finance which I want to put forward. It is based on the hypothesis that markets and banks are both remarkably inefficient (in a sense to be explained below), suppliers of capital are remarkably myopic, and firms (borrowers) are run not in the interests of the shareholders so much as in the interests of managers.[16] The confluence of these imperfections has resulted in a shift in the institutional form in which funds are raised, a shift which does not necessarily mean that society's scarce investment resources are being allocated and used more efficiently.

The evidence of the incompetency of banks is, by now, bountiful: a series of disasters -- real estate loans in Iowa, Florida, the Southwest, Texas, and most recently in the North East, loans to Third World countries, oil and gas loans -- provide a convincing case of incompetency. This string of failures could, of course, simply be bad luck, but that seems an unlikely explanation. *Some* of this may be related to the peculiar incentives associated with high leveraged firms operating in an environment in which deposits are guaranteed. Yet the pervasiveness of the problems, not only in S&Ls but also within more conventional banking circles, suggests that there is more to it than that.[17] At the very least, the banks have demonstrated an ignorance of two very basic aspects of risk: (a) The importance of correlation. The fact that country risk was a common component in all loans to a single country should have led banks to limit their exposure in loans to any single LDC.[18] (b) The possibility of price declines. Though students in old-fashioned Keynesian courses may have been taught about downward price rigidities, bankers should have paid more attention to the historical record than mere theorists: the decline of prices by a mere third during the early years of the Great Depression may be evidence of rigidity -- relative to what was required to clear markets -- but to a lender holding an 80% mortgage it spelled disaster. And the last century has been marked by many other periods in which particular assets have faced even greater price declines.

By now, the discrepancies between the interests of managers and those of the shareholders is also widely recognized. There is both a theoretical literature explaining why this should be so,[19] and a growing body of empirical evidence documenting important instances of these discrepancies.[20] Since banks have the capacity for closer monitoring, managerially run firms may prefer to use markets rather than banks simply because it enhances their managerial discretion. If banks exercise their monitoring in an incompetent fashion, then it enhances the argument for the use of markets: bank monitoring may be value reducing rather than value enhancing. Instances of incompetent bank interference would strengthen management's case for reducing the potential interferences from banks by raising funds from the market.

At the same time, lenders may be even worse than banks in assessing risks. The success of the junk bond market provides ambiguous evidence. Asquith, Mullins, and Wolff (1989) provide evidence that the average returns, taking into account default rates, on junk bonds which have been out for several years is little higher than on safer bonds; certainly not enough higher to compensate for the risks. Total default rates have been low simply because most of the junk bonds are newly issued: it takes a while for these loans to go sour. Indeed, many newly issued junk bonds raise more capital than is "required" for the investment; the extra capital is used to make the interest payments during the first couple of years. Accordingly, the absence of a failure during the first few years of the bond means absolutely nothing concerning the viability of the enterprise.

The success of these bonds depends to a large extent on a belief in the absence of the kinds of cyclical fluctuations that have marked capitalist economies for the past two centuries. True, those fluctuations may be less marked than before the advent of Keynesian economies (though even here, as we noted earlier, the evidence is controversial). Still, even a moderate downturn in the economy can result in *marked* reductions in profit levels, to levels below that which would enable these firms to meet their interest obligations. Thus, the viability of the junk bonds requires that no such downturn occur during the period two to six years after the junk bond is issued (there being a two year cushion provided by the initial finance; and a series of say five profitable years enabling the firm to reduce its outstanding debt.) Any statistical model based on the past history of the economy would predict that during the required period, there is a fairly high probability of a downturn of sufficient magnitude to cause a problem. Luck may be with these firms: there is sufficient variability in the periodicity of the cyclical fluctuations that defaults may not be widespread. But luck may not be with these firms, and the entire economy may suffer as a result. But the point I wish to emphasize here is that it is hard to believe in the "rationality" of a market which seems, on the basis of no sound evidence, to discount the possibility of a major recession during the decade following the issuance of the junk bonds![21, 22]

The success of other financial markets may be equally problematical. For instance, the increased securitization of mortgage markets can be looked at in two different ways (ignoring, for the moment, the effects of government provided insurance). On the one hand, it could be the result of lower transactions costs for nationally marketing this class of assets, providing greater opportunities for risk diversification. Since the default rates within a community or region are correlated, there are benefits from investors holding a portfolio of mortgages, consisting of mortgages from all the regions in the country (and from abroad as well).

On the other hand, when banks retained the mortgages which they issued, they had greater incentives to screen loan applicants. The brokers who write the mortgages often receive commissions on the loans they write, with little or no accountability on their efficiency in screening. Their incentives are thus only to ensure that the loans meet (on paper) the requirements of the loan. For instance, there may be a requirement that the ratio of the value of the land to the total value of the property be less than one third (intended to limit the use of funds for land speculation, which is undoubtedly highly risky); the broker has an incentive to find an appraiser who will appraise the property accordingly.

The question is, has the growth in securitization been a result of more efficient transactions technologies, or an unfounded reduction in concern about the importance of screening loan applicants? It is, perhaps, too early to tell, but we should at least entertain the possibility that it is the latter rather than the former.

Economic Development and the Evolution of Financial Markets

The switch that we have been observing, from banks to markets, is only the latest stage in the on-going development of capital markets. The fact that it is the latest stage -- combined with the widespread belief that market institutions are superior to non-market institutions -- has lent support to the view that these are developments which enhance the efficiency of the economy, and, in particular, its ability to allocate resources efficiently. The discussion of the previous section should at least serve to dispel some confidence in that conclusion.

Three observations concerning the evolution of financial markets are worth making. First, earlier transformations involved a similar switch to greater specialization in lending activity, but too may have involved a reduction in monitoring capacity. In many more primitive environments, there is an interlinking between lending activity and other activities (landlord, provision of inputs, processing of output). It has been argued that this interlinking facilitates economic efficiency in the presence of moral hazard problems.[23] The early development of capital markets entailed the displacement of these interlinked contracts by lending institutions, who were more specialized; the specialization allowed greater risk diversification (just as markets allow greater risk diversification, at least than local banks); but the lenders have less ability to control the actions of the borrower than was afforded by the interlinked contracts.

Second, we note that the development of formal financial institutions in many LDCs has not displaced local money lenders, in the way that was widely anticipated, in spite of the greater ability to diversify risks beyond the bounds of the village, and despite the often preferential access they have to government provided funds. Local money lenders have survived, and indeed, there seems little evidence that the high interest rates which they charge have been substantially reduced.[24]

Finally, we emphasize the important distinction between improvements in the secondary market for securities -- the markets in which already issued securities are traded -- and the primary market, the market in which new funds are raised from savers and transferred to firms. Much of the focus, both in developed and less developed countries, has been with improvements in the secondary market; whether these improvements have led to substantial reductions in the costs of raising new funds for investment remains problematical.[25] Indeed, Summers and Summers (1989) argue persuasively that viewed as institutions for raising new capital, even American capital markets entail enormously high transactions costs; that is, the costs of running the market, relative to the value of the new capital raised in those markets, is extremely high.

Interactions Among Financial Institutions

In the preceding section, we noted that the evolution from banks to markets has led some observers to conclude -- not necessarily convincingly in our judgment -- that since markets are later arrivals in the "evolutionary" process, that they therefore are necessarily superior. Or at least, *given* the information and other characteristics of modern economies, markets dominate, and we should accordingly expect the eventual withering away of non-market institutions.

There is another view, however, which sees the two institutional arrangements as being at least partly complementary, rather than substitutes; in this view, the success of the market institutions depends, to some extent at least, on the non-market institutions. We have already encountered one instance of this perspective: in our signalling equilibria, it is the differences between the institutions which serve to distinguish among borrowers.

In earlier work (Stiglitz 1985) I noted the interdependence among all the stakeholders in the firm.[26] Equity holders benefit from the monitoring services provided by banks. By the same token, bondholders (those who lend through the market) benefit from the monitoring and screening services provided by banks. Indeed, the willingness of banks to extend credit to a firm is an important positive signal. If it were believed that the reason that the firm was trying to raise money from the capital market was that it could not obtain further funds from its banks, then that would have a markedly adverse effect on the terms at which it could obtain funds on the capital market.

One of the reasons that borrowers turn to the capital market to raise funds is the presumably lower costs associated with doing so. The lower costs are partly, probably largely, related to the lower costs of monitoring and screening loans. But these costs, like information costs more generally, are largely fixed costs, independent of the scale of borrowing (though, to be sure, the magnitude of the exposure of the lender will affect his incentives for engaging in monitoring/screening). Accordingly, as a matter of economic efficiency, so long as there is some borrowing from banks, the "savings" from borrowing from the market, and thus avoiding the higher screening/monitoring costs of banks, is spurious. Thus, it may be that banks, not recognizing the fixed cost nature of these expenditures, do not design lending charges appropriately; or alternatively, it may be that borrowers, not recognizing the fixed cost nature of these costs, fail to take into account that if they borrow less from their banks, the "transactions" charges made by the banks, per dollar borrowed, will have to increase. In either case, there is a market inefficiency. The failure to recognize the interdependence among financial institutions and the fixed cost nature of information expenditures -- rather than any real resource savings -- may be what underlies the switch from banks to market institutions.

Some Consequences

The consequences of the switch from banks to markets as sources of finance depend on the interpretation one places on the causes of that switch.

If the switch is the result of reduced transactions costs and facilitates greater risk diversification -- and that is all that there is to the matter -- then the switch is welfare enhancing. The potential for greater risk diversification reduces the risk premium, which will mean that projects with higher returns, which were not undertaken before because of the undiversified risks associated with them, will now be undertaken.

If the switch is the result of a change in the signalling equilibrium, the effects are more ambiguous. Some of the gains are largely redistributive,[27] though correctly ascertaining the risks associated with different investments does affect how resources are allocated.

On the other hand, there may be serious social costs. Greenwald and Stiglitz (1988, 1989a) have attributed much of the cyclical variability in the economy to certain aspects of the capital market. The inability to diversify out of risks (equity rationing) makes firms act in a risk averse manner, leading to cyclical fluctuations in both demand (investment) and supply. In their earlier models, debt involves fixed obligations, and there are high costs (both to the firm and its managers) from failing to meet those obligations. Whether, of course, an unmet loan obligation results in bankruptcy depends on the actions of lenders (See Eaton, Gersovitz, and Stiglitz 1986). Thus, a flexible lending arrangement with a bank may result in less risk averse behavior than an inflexible market arrangement. If this is true, then the magnitude of the cyclical fluctuations may be increased as a result of the switch from bank to market finance.

Finally, if the switch from bank to market finance is based on myopic investors underestimating the importance of the screening and monitoring functions performed by banks, and managers who see the opportunity provided by market finance to increase their managerial discretion, then the switch may actually lead to less efficient utilization of capital resources.

If, as we have suggested, the evolution of financial institutions has entailed a movement from more to less control of borrowers (with control being greatest within interlinked contracts in less developed countries, and with control under banks being greater than under markets), and if markets are not necessarily efficient (as we have suggested), this *may* suggest a potential role for government intervention, though the design of such intervention is not an easy matter. On the other hand, markets -- and prices -- *may* be more effective in coordination than banks, which suggests that the switch from banks to capital markets may imply that the role of institutions, such as MITI/Ministry of Finance in Japan, in coordination may be less important.

Regardless, however, of the reason for the switch from banks to markets, it may have serious implications for the conduct of monetary policy. Monetary policy exercises its influence most directly on those parts of the economy which rely on bank finance. In earlier days, these included home construction and businesses. As mortgages are increasingly securitized, home construction may be less affected. As large businesses increasingly rely on commercial paper, they too may be less affected. The impacts will increasingly be concentrated on small businesses. Is it desirable that the first round impact of attempts to control economic fluctuations should be imposed on this group of firms, perhaps those who are least able to bear the costs?

On the other hand, if many firms can easily switch from bank to market finance, restricting bank finance will merely result in a switch in the form of finance: monetary policy will be less effective. In either case, this change in the institutions by which capital is allocated raises important questions concerning how the government should attempt to stabilize the economy.

Conclusions

The institutions of our capital markets -- including banks -- serve important functions in allocating capital, choosing among alternative investment projects and firms to manage capital, and in monitoring how capital is used. How funds are raised and distributed affects how, and how well, those functions are performed. In this chapter I have asked how do we explain the increased use of markets and the corresponding reduced reliance on banks, and what are its consequences. I have put forward three hypotheses:

(a) Markets represent a more efficient way of providing funds, lowering transactions costs and increasing the potential for risk diversification.

(b) There are some important differences between markets and banks, which serve as the basis of a signalling equilibrium. Better firms have switched to use market finance because it indicates their ability to dispense with the flexibility afforded by bank loans.

(c) Banks in the 1970s and 1980s have demonstrated a remarkable level of incompetency. This, combined with the greater opportunities for managerial discretion provided by market loans and the market's myopic undervaluation of the monitoring and screening services which banks are *supposed* to provide has provided the impetus for the switch.

The switch has consequences for the efficiency with which resources are allocated and used, for the magnitude of the economy's economic fluctuations, and for whether and how monetary policy affects the economy. Whether the switch is efficiency enhancing or decreasing -- with respect to the manner in which funds are allocated -- depends on whether one believes the predominant explanation of the switch is hypothesis (a) or (c). But whether there are positive or negative microeconomic effects, the macroeconomic consequences may be deleterious.

The evidence as to which explanation is most convincing is far from in. Believers in efficient markets will, I am sure, continue to believe in hypothesis (a). Yet I find the evidence in support of the second and third hypotheses sufficiently convincing that we should at least give some attention to the questions: if the switch is not welfare enhancing, is there anything the government should do about it? If so, what? These are questions which will have to be addressed in a sequel to this chapter.

Notes

*   This chapter is part of a larger research project with Bruce Greenwald and Andy Weiss. I have benefited greatly from conversations with David Scharfstein and Mark Wolfson. Financial support from the Olin Foundation, the Hoover Institution, and the National Science Foundation is gratefully acknowledged.

1   Relics of the antipathies between Keynes and his disciples, and Robertson and his, survived through the days when I was a student at Cambridge, in 1965-1966. There was a weekly secret seminar of Joan Robinson, Lord Kahn, and other Cambridge notables, to which "wrong thinking" colleagues, in the earlier days, Robertson and his disciples, in the 50s and 60s, "conservatives" such as Michael Farrell of Gonville and Caius College, were not invited. The fact that I had studied under Samuelson and Solow and was a colleague of Farrell at Gonville and Caius College tainted me, and I was never invited to the secret seminar. This tradition of a third of a century was broken in 1969-1970, when a counterseminar, including several American visitors (besides myself, Arrow, Scarf, and Radner visited that year) was organized.

2   Before Modigliani and Miller, Myer and Kuh (1955) had shown that cash flow (profit) variables affected investment. This work was dismissed more because it was not based on "sound theory" than because of faults in the empirical analysis. Subsequent empirical work has provided further support to the finding that cash flow and balance sheet variables are relevant for investment. See footnote below.

3   For a brief survey, see Stiglitz (1988).

4   A problem encountered in calculating real interest rates is ascertaining expectations concerning price changes. The figure is based on realized rates of inflation. During most of the period in question, rates of inflation were relatively stable, so that there should not have been much difference between anticipated and realized rates of inflation.

5   For long periods of time, the real interest rate exhibited relatively little variability.

6   Similar results hold using M_2, etc.

7   Although, to be more precise, our argument is that firms choose not to issue new equity, because of the strong negative effect that doing so has on the value of its shares.

8   In Stiglitz-Weiss (1983), we show that the threat of termination is a more effective threat than simply raising the interest rate charged, and that in fact such threats will be employed in market equilibrium contracts. Arnott and Stiglitz (1985, 1989) spell out more generally the role of intertemporal interdependence in the presence of moral hazard.

9   See Stiglitz (1985).

10   It should be emphasized that the arguments put forward by Stiglitz and Weiss concerning credit rationing apply not just to banks, but also to loans made on the market. Investors may worry that the expected return to a bond issued by firm which promises to pay too high an interest rate will actually be lower, because of the increased probability of default. To put it another way, assume the firm fixed a nominal interest rate on its bond, and put them up to a Dutch auction. As the price became lower, not only would the fact that no one else was willing to buy the bonds convey information which might decrease demand (lower reservation prices) for the bond even more, but since the amount received by the firm was less, the chance that it could fulfill its commitment would be lowered. At low enough prices, of course, the firm would not be willing to issue the bond.

11   Similarly, firms may rely on banks for "flexibility" -- turning to the market for their "infra-marginal" funds. In this case too banks will exercise considerable influence over the firms to whom they loan funds.

12   A. Berle (1926) argued more than a half century ago that banks play a vital role in the control of capital: in firms where ownership was highly diversified they were more effective in doing so than the shareholders who "nominally" control the firm. Stiglitz (1985) has shown why this is so, based on considerations of imperfect information and the public good associated with management.

13   The fact that banks have less a stake should, however, affect the efforts that they put into selection and monitoring, and hence the quality of their certification signals.

14   Other examples of such self-selection mechanisms include the issuance of equity (Greenwald, Stiglitz, and Weiss 1984; Myers and Majluf 1984),

the retention of shares by the original owners (Ross 1977; Leland and Pyle 1977; Stiglitz 1982a); and the multiple issuance of equity (Gale and Stiglitz 1990).

15   It should be noted, however, that there is some controversy about the extent to which stabilization policies have been successful in reducing the magnitude of cyclical fluctuations. See Roemer (1986).

16   I thus have in mind here a broader sense of inefficiency than just that entailed by "constrained Pareto efficiency." The fact that markets with imperfect information are not, in general, constrained Pareto efficient is, by now, well established. See Greenwald and Stiglitz (1986), or, for applications to the capital market, Stiglitz (1972b, 1982b, 1989b).

17   To be sure, there are still other interpretations of what has happened: given the lack of credibility that government would not bail out the banks, in the event of a disaster, it was rational for them to engage in the kind of risk taking which they did. Managerial incentive schemes in which managers' rewards depends (implicitly or explicitly) on relative performance may result in equilibria in which it pays all banks to imitate each other: if all other banks are making risky loans to third world countries, it is still safer from the perspective of the bank manager to do the same. His performance will be no worse (though no better) than the others. On the other hand, if he decides not to follow the pack, *and* their gambles turn out successful, then his bank will look like a poor performer, and he will be judged accordingly. See Nalebuff and Stiglitz (1983a, 1983b).

18   Though the change in real interest rates during Volker's years might reasonably have been assigned a low probability, the disastrous potential consequences of such a change, were it to occur, should have led to greater caution on the part of banks.

19   This is one of the central lessons of the principal-agent literature (Ross 1973; Stiglitz 1974). For a discussion of why alternative control mechanisms are only partially effective, see Stiglitz (1981).

20   Including the evidence concerning "tax paradoxes" (Stiglitz 1981) and evidence concerning behavior in take-overs (Shleifer and Vishny 1988).

21   Since these paragraphs were written, in late 1989, the American economy entered a major recession, and, as one would have predicted, there have been a number of defaults of junk bonds.

22   Some of my colleagues have suggested that I have overestimated the cost of default. If default were costless, then junk bonds provide corporations a tax favored way of raising capital, because interest payments are tax exempt. However, I argued (Stiglitz 1973) that if one takes an *integrated* -- personal plus corporate -- perspective on the consequences of taxation, though debt has some advantages, they are relatively slight, given the tax advantages of capital gains. The higher corporate tax rates beginning in 1986 combined with the higher tax rates on capital gains have enhanced the advantages of bond finance. The revision of the bankruptcy laws has, no doubt, lowered bankruptcy costs.

Still, as the experience with the S&L's demonstrates, there are large agency costs as firms approach bankruptcy. One interpretation of the junk bond market has it that Milliken had established a reputation equilibrium: he had the incentive to monitor the firms for which he had issued junk bonds and to make sure that when defaults were imminent, the financial restructuring was done efficiently. In that interpretation, even if it should turn out that the junk bonds yield a low return, it is not evidence of myopia on the part of investors, only the realization of one of the "rationally" expected outcomes, the unravelling of the reputation equilibrium.

[23] See Braverman and Stiglitz (1982).

[24] See Hoff and Stiglitz (1990) and the other papers in the *World Bank Economic Review* symposium on rural credit.

[25] See Stiglitz (1989c).

[26] In that article, I suggested the firm should be viewed as a multiple-principal agent problem.

[27] That is, the point of signalling equilibrium is that those whose risk has been overestimated can convincingly indicate such to the market; their gains are at the *expense* of others. See Hirschleifer (1971) and Stiglitz (1975).

References

Abel, A. B., and O. J. Blanchard. 1986. "The Present Value of Profits and Cyclical Movements in Investments." *Econometrica* 54: 249-274.

Arnott, R., and J. E. Stiglitz. 1985. "Labor Turnover, Wage Structure & Moral Hazard: The Inefficiency of Competitive Markets." *Journal of Labor Economics* 3 (4): 434-462.

_____. 1989. "The Welfare Economics of Moral Hazard," in Henri Louberge, ed., *Risk, Information and Insurance: Essays in the Memory of Karl H. Borch.* Pp. 91-122. Norwell, Mass.: Kluwer Academic Publishers.

Asquith, P., and D. W. Mullins. 1986. "Equity Issues and Stock Price Dilution." *Journal of Financial Economics.*

Asquith, P., D. Mullins, and E. Wolff. 1989. "Original Issue High Yield Bonds: Aging Analysis of Defaults, Exchanges, and Calls." *Journal of Finance* 44 (4): 923-52.

Berle, A. 1926. "Non Voting Stock and 'Bankers' Control." *Harvard Law Review.*

Braverman, A., and J. E. Stiglitz. 1982. "Sharecropping and the Interlinking of Agrarian Markets." *American Economic Review* 72 (4): 695-715.

Diamond, P. 1967. "The Role of a Stock Market in a General Equilibrium Model with Technological Uncertainty." *American Economic Review* 57: 753-776.

Eaton, J., M. Gersovitz, and J. E. Stiglitz. 1986. "The Pure Theory of Country Risk." *European Economic Review* 30: 481-513.

Gale, I., and J. E. Stiglitz. 1989. "The Informational Content of Initial Public Offerings." *Journal of Finance* XLIV (2): 469-478.

Greenwald, B., and Stiglitz, J. E. 1986. "Externalities in Economies with Imperfect Information and Incomplete Markets," with B. Greenwald, *Quarterly Journal of Economics.* Pp. 229-264.

_____. 1988. "Financial Market Imperfections and Business Cycles." NBER Working Paper No. 2494.

_____. 1989a. "Financial Market Imperfections and Productivity Growth." NBER Working Paper No. 2365.

_____. 1989b. "Information, Finance and Markets: The Architecture of Allocative Mechanisms." Paper prepared for International Conference on the History of Enterprise: Finance and the Enterprise in a Historical Perspective, Terni, Italy.

Greenwald, B. C., J. E. Stiglitz, and A. Weiss. 1984. "Informational Imperfections in the Capital Markets and Macro-economic Fluctuations." *American Economic Review* 74 (1): 194-199.

Grossman, S., and O. Hart. 1980. "Takeover Bids, the Free Rider Problem, and the Theory of the Corporation." *Bell Journal of Economics* 35 (2): 42-64.

Hirschleifer, J. 1971. "The Private and Social Value of Information and the Reward to Incentive Activity." *American Economic Review* 67: 561-574.

Hoff, K., and J. E. Stiglitz. 1990. "Imperfect Information and Rural Credit Markets: Puzzles and Policy Perspectives." *World Bank Economic Review.* Pp. 235-250.

Jaffe, D., and J. E. Stiglitz. 1990. "Credit Rationing," in B. Friedman and F. Hahn, eds., *Handbook of Monetary Economics.* Amsterdam: Elsevier Science Publishers.

Jensen, M., and Meckling. 1976. "Theory of the Firm: Managerial Behavior, Agency Costs and Ownership Structure." *Journal of Financial Economics* 3: 305-360.

Kennedy, W. P. 1987. *Industrial Structure, Capital Markets, and the Origins of British Economic Decline.* New York: Cambridge University Press.

Leland, H. E., and D. H. Pyle. 1977. "Informational Asymmetries, Financial Structure and Financial Intermediaries." *Journal of Finance* 32: 371-387.

Mayer, C. 1989. "Myths of the West: Lessons from Developed Countries for Development Finance." CEPR discussion paper, London.

Meyer, J., and E. Kuh. 1959. *The Investment Decision, an Empirical Study.* Cambridge, Mass.: Harvard University Press.

Modigliani, F., and M. Miller. 1958. "The Cost of Capital, Corporate Finance and the Theory of Corporate Finance." *American Economic Review* 48: 261-297.

Myers, S. C., and N. S. Majluf. "Corporate Financing and Investment Decisions When Firms Have Information that Investors Do Not." *Journal of Financial Economics* 11: 187-221.

Nalebuff, B., and J. E. Stiglitz. 1983a. "Prizes and Incentives: Towards a General Theory of Compensation and Competition." *Bell Journal of Economics* 14 (1): 21-43.

_____. 1983b. "Information, Competition and Markets." *American Economic Review* 72 (2): 278-284.

Romer, C. D. 1986. "Is the Stabilization of the Postwar Economy a Figment of Data?" *American Economic Review* 76 (3).

Ross, S. A. 1973. "The Economic Theory of Agency: The Principal's Problem." *American Economic Review.* Pp. 134-139.

_____. 1977. "The Determination of Financial Structure: The Incentive Signalling Approach." *Bell Journal of Economics* 8: 23-40.

Shleifer A., and R. Vishny. 1988. "Managerial Entrenchment: The Case of Manager-specific Investments," paper presented at Olin Conference on Economic Organizations, Princeton.

Spence, A., and Michael. 1974. *Market Signaling: Information Transfer in Hiring and Related Processes.* Cambridge, Mass.: Harvard University Press.

Stiglitz, J. E. 1969. "A Re-examination of the Modigliani-Miller Theorem." *American Economic Review* 59 (5): 784-793.

_____. 1971. "Perfect and Imperfect Capital Markets." Paper presented to Econometric Society Meetings, New Orleans.

_____. 1972a. "Some Aspects of the Pure Theory of Corporate Finance: Bankruptcies and Take-Overs." *Bell Journal of Economics* 3 (2) 458-482.

_____. 1972b. "On the Optimality of the Stock Market Allocation of Investment." *Quarterly Journal of Economics* 86 (1) 25-60.

_____. 1973. "Taxation, Corporate Financial Policy and the Cost of Capital." *Journal of Public Economics* 2: 1-34.

_____. 1974a. "On the Irrelevance of Corporate Financial Policy." *American Economic Review* 64 (6): 851-866.

_____. 1974b. "Incentives and Risk Sharing in Sharecropping." *Review of Economic Studies* 41: 213-255.

_____. 1975. "The Theory of Screening, Education and the Distribution of Income." *American Economic Review* 65 (3): 283-300.

_____. 1981. "Ownership, Control and Efficient Markets: Some Paradoxes in the Theory of Capital Markets," in K. D. Boyer and W. G. Shepherd eds., *Economic Regulation: Essays in Honor of James R. Nelson.* Pp. 311-341. Ann Arbor: Michigan State University Press.

_____. 1982a. "Information and Capital Markets," in W. F. Sharpe and C. Cootner, eds., *Financial Economics: Essays in Honor of Paul Cootner.* Pp. 118-158. Englewood Cliffs: Prentice Hall.

_____. 1982b. "The Inefficiency of the Stock Market Equilibrium." *Review of Economic Studies* XLIX: 241-261.

_____. 1985. "Money, Credit and Banking Lecture: Credit Market and the Control of Capital." *Journal of Money, Credit and Banking* 17 (1): 133-152.

_____. 1988. "Why Financial Structure Matters." *Journal of Economic Perspectives* 2 (4): 121-126.

_____. 1989a. "Monopolistic Competition and the Capital Market," in G. Feiwel, ed., *The Economics of Imperfect Competition and Employment: Joan Robinson and Beyond.* Pp. 485-502. Houndmills: Macmillan Press. (originally IMSSS Technical Report No. 161, Stanford University, February 1975).

_____. 1989b. "Using Tax Policy to Curb Speculative Short-Term Trading." *Journal of Financial Services Research* 3 (2/3): 101-115.

_____. 1989c. "Financial Markets and Development." *Oxford Review of Economic Policy* 5 (4): 55-68.

Stiglitz, J., and A. Weiss. 1981. "Credit Rationing in Markets with Imperfect Information." *American Economic Review* 71: 393-410.

_____. 1983. "Incentive Effects of Termination: Applications to the Credit and Labor Markets." *American Economic Review* 72: 912-927.

_____. 1986. "Credit Rationing and Collateral." *Recent Developments in Corporate Finance.* Pp. 101-135. New York: Cambridge University Press.

_____. 1989. "Banks as Social Accountants and Screening Devices and the General Theory of Credit Rationing." *Essays in Monetary Economics in Honor of Sir John Hicks.* New York: Oxford University Press.

Summers, L. H., and V. P. Summers. 1989. "When Financial Markets Work Too Well: A Cautious Case for a Securities Transactions Tax." Paper presented to the Annenberg Conference on Technology and Financial Markets, Washington D.C.

Taggart, R. A., Jr. 1985. "Secular Patterns in the Financing of U.S. Corporations," in B.M. Friedman, ed., *Corporate Capital Structures in the United States.* National Bureau of Economic Research Project Report, Chicago: University of Chicago Press.

Tobin, J. 1958. "Liquidity Preference as Behavior Toward Risk." *Review of Economic Studies* 25: 65-86.

Tobin, J., and Brainard, W. 1977. "Asset Markets and the Cost of Capital," in B. Balassa and R. Nelson, eds., *Economic Progress, Private Values and Public Policy: Essays in Honor of William Fellner.* Amsterdam: North Holland.

3

Financial Instruments for Consumption Smoothing by Commodity-Dependent Exporters

*Brian D. Wright and David M. G. Newbery**

Introduction

Loans and other investment contracts are widely perceived as legally enforceable in lender countries but not in debtor countries. In that context, this chapter shows how novel financing arrangements using commodity bonds with put options for the seller can be used for stabilization of risks associated with export prices.

Given the substantial instability in all primary commodity markets, one would expect countries that depend on a single primary export for most of their foreign earnings (for example, Mexico, Nigeria, Zambia, New Guinea and most OPEC countries) to experience especially sharp fluctuations in export earnings and their underlying wealth. To the extent that these fluctuations affect consumption, they are costly; and we would expect such countries to seek ways of managing these fluctuations and reducing their costs.

In many countries the nature of the resource endowment and its comparative advantage rule out production diversification as a significant near-term strategy, and we assume it away here. In addition, we rule out diversification via exchange of equity investments with foreigners. In this chapter we consider the cost of export risk and show the potential contribution of commodity bonds in this context. We show that, in theory, appropriate commodity bonds can achieve optimal smoothing of i.i.d. export price disturbances -- if that is what countries really want or need.

Commodity bonds ("c-bonds") are bonds whose principal repayment (and perhaps dividend payments) may be made in units of physical commodity (or the terminal value of some appropriate futures contract). Typically, the bond buyer has the option to receive the nominal face value or the commodity bundle. In the finance literature, studies of the pricing of c-bonds (Schwartz 1982; Carr 1987; Priovolos 1987) do not distinguish bonds issued by foreign governments from private corporate bond issues. However, the literature on foreign borrowing recognizes that the distinction is crucial.

Sovereign Borrowing and Default Prevention

The main distinction between corporate and sovereign borrowing, described in masterly fashion by Keynes (1924) and incorporated in the seminal work of Eaton and Gersovitz (1981), is that collateral is generally unavailable to creditors of a sovereign borrower since the assets of the latter are located within its borders. Only in exceptional cases can they be attached by lenders in the event of default.

The absence of a final distribution of assets to creditors as seen in domestic bankruptcy also changes the nature of default. It arises in the context of a sequence of strategic moves by creditors and the sovereign debtor who retains (and, in fact, cannot credibly foreswear) the power to make subsequent decisions that affect the interests of creditors.

Here we focus on income-smoothing financial transactions between investors in developed countries (DCs) and a less-developed country (LDC) heavily dependent on a single commodity subject to substantial revenue fluctuations. The default penalty is enforcement of debt seniority clauses in the courts of all potential borrower-lender nations so that a defaulter's foreign investments or servicing of new debt would be subject to seizure. Default means permanent elimination of foreign borrowing or lending opportunities.

The Costs of Income Variability

Consider a country that has economically unresponsive production ("zero supply elasticity") and seeks to maximize the expected utility of its representative consumer

$$(1) \quad V_t = E \sum_{t=0}^{\infty} (1 + \delta)^{-t} u (c_t)$$

where E is the expectation operator, c_t is consumption in period t, and u is felicity, $u' > 0$, $u'' < 0$. There is no storage. Output and price are each subject to one discrete i.i.d. random disturbance per period.

To dramatize the issues, assume that exports from a single commodity account for 33% of GNP on average, and suppose that the coefficient of variation (CV) of output and price of the commodity are both 30%, and that the correlation between output and price can be ignored. Suppose also that all other income is nonstochastic and that the country optimally shares risks internally. There is, however, no saving or borrowing or other intertemporal income smoothing. Using the standard formulas[1] for the cost of risk, if the coefficient of relative risk aversion is R (defined for one-period variations in consumption), and if the CV of consumption is s, then the annual cost of risk, ρ, is defined implicitly by $u(c - \rho) = Eu(c_t)$, where a bar over a variable indicates its expected value, and the relative cost, $p/\bar{c}$ is approximately (exactly if utility is quadratic in income per period) $Rs^2/2$. If consumption must be equal to income each year, then $s = 0.33e$ where e is the CV of export revenue (and 0.33 is the average share of exports to GNP). If output and price are independently normally distributed, then $e^2 = 0.19$ (and this will hold approximately even if output and price are not normal). In this case, if R has the not unreasonable value of 2, the cost of risk is approximately 2% of average income, the amount representative consumers would be willing to forego each year in return for a stabilized consumption stream of c.

Consumption Smoothing by Borrowing and Lending

Can a country optimally smooth consumption by borrowing and lending from overseas sources? If the utility function is quadratic, then δ can be interpreted as the rate at which future consumption is discounted; and if this is equal to the rate of interest abroad, r, then the country would have no motive for saving or borrowing other than to smooth consumption. We make this assumption here to focus on the consumption smoothing aspect of international borrowing. We continue to assume that exports are subject to random i.i.d. price disturbances. Then the optimally "smoothed" consumption of a borrower committed to borrowing and lending only for smoothing and to meeting his interest payment obligations is $c_t = E_t(c_{t+1}) = \bar{y} - rL_t$ (Newbery and Stiglitz 1981:201-202). Under the scheme accumulated debt, L, follows a discrete random walk with increment equal to the difference between income y_t and its mean, $\bar{y}$. For permanent operation, there must be no limit on L. But in finite time, L will pass the value at which repudiation becomes more attractive than continued interest payments, even if all borrowing and lending opportunities are then cut off.[2] Thus, competitive lenders will not make unlimited loans. Any feasible loans would offer at best only suboptimal and/or impermanent smoothing.

The nature of the evolution of general obligation loan contracts for sovereign borrowers is a currently active research area.[3] At this stage it seems clear that consumption smoothing by sovereign borrowers using conventional borrowing and lending is infeasible if the contract is not renegotiated. If so the quest for a better instrument makes sense. Accordingly we now turn our attention to c-bonds.

Commodity Bonds Issued by Sovereign Lenders

To simplify the discussion, assume that the c-bond under discussion is a zero-coupon bond with payment upon maturity consisting only of a completely specified commodity bundle. We assume the issuer is competitive and market risk-neutral with respect to this bond (see O'Hara 1984, for analysis of the demand side of the market for c-bonds under other assumptions). As above, assume initially that all contracts are always honored.

Under these assumptions, if the country issues c-bonds (which in this model need only be one-period bonds) and if these can be issued (and indefinitely re-issued) at the present value of the expected price for next period, then their risk-reducing properties in the steady state are exactly the same as those of an optimal forward or futures hedge at the same price. Newbery and Stiglitz (1981:186) show that, in the case of stationary, uncorrelated output and price disturbances, the ratio of income variance with and without optimal forward hedging, is roughly $1/(1 + k^2)$, where k is the ratio of the CVs of price and output. In our numerical example above, k equals 1. If there is no other means of consumption smoothing by lending and borrowing, then c-bonds will halve the steady state costs of the risk -- to 1% of GNP in our example. If the CV of income were the same, but only price were stochastic, then c-bonds eliminate risk, worth 2% of GNP.

Assume, henceforth, that no other borrowing is possible and that all income variation is due to price. Then with credible commitment, complete smoothing is achieved by selling c-bonds for the whole (deterministic) output. The country then has constant income and consumption and delivers all output of random value to the lender.

In low-price states the smoothing raises income, so there is no incentive at all to default. But in high-price states, delivery to the lender reduces current income, y_t, by $(y_t - \bar{y})$. This, plus the expected present value of autarkic future consumption, may in some high price states exceed the maximum expected present value of the consumption path given default does not occur now. Then in those states default *will* rationally occur; a no-default commitment is not credible.

The credibility of a no-default commitment by a c-bond issuer depends on the parameters of the model. Consider the simple case with a two-point probability density for the multiplicative income disturbance which is i.i.d., $u = \pm v$ with probabilities of outcomes $+v$ and $-v$ equal to one-half. Assume mean income is unity and utility is quadratic over the consumption range, $1 - v$ to $1 + v$. Then the annual cost of risk in the stochastic steady state (and the value of access to c-bonds) is in this case with all uncertainty due to price: $\rho^* = Rv^2/2$ and the present value is $\rho^* / \delta = Rv^2/2\delta$. Now consider the stochastic steady state in which a fraction $(1 - a)$ of output, $0 < a < 1$, is delivered each period in payment for c-bonds issued one period earlier, and all consumption is financed from current sales of c-bonds and the uncovered fraction (a) of output. If the income draw is high at v, then default is the expected-utility-maximizing decision if and only if the current period gain, $v - av$, exceeds the present value of the risk cost incurred. If the c-bonds cover a fraction $(1 - a)$ of output $0 < a < 1$, the change in per period risk cost is $Rv^2(1 - a^2)/2$. The one-shot gain from default is $v - av$. Default occurs if $\delta \geq Rv (1 + a)/2$, so full coverage is feasible if and only if $\delta \leq Rv/2$; some fractional coverage is feasible if and only if $\delta < 1/2\,Rv$; some fractional coverage is feasible if and only if $\delta < Rv$.

As the CV, v, the relative risk aversion, R, or the uncovered portion a increases, the minimum δ consistent with default rises. Default on full coverage is not a problem in this case if income is risky enough and/or risk aversion is high enough.

Optimal Dynamic Smoothing Strategies

Default Constraint Nonbinding

We have seen above that the c-bonds may be default-free in the stochastic steady state with an i.i.d. price disturbance in which consumption equals the mean value of output discounted one period. If so, one description of the optimal infinite horizon smoothing plan for implementation in period 0, given current income, y_0 (assumed for this exposition to be entirely from export of one commodity at price p), and the discount rate equal to the interest rate is as follows: Invest βy_0, where $\beta \equiv 1/(1 + r)$, overseas for a certain periodic rate of return of r, issue a c-bond to cover all output, with current sale price $\beta \bar{y}$ and consume $r\beta y_0 + \beta \bar{y}$ in each period 0, 1, 2.... Full consumption smoothing is immediately achieved forever. (A short forward contract plus a loan on the anticipated proceeds could replicate the c-bond contract. So could a short futures contract, with an additional line of credit to cover initial and variation margin.)

The opportunities for overseas investment at the (certain) market interest rate and for sale of c-bonds at unbiased prices are all the financial facilities needed for this plan. Furthermore, note that, if the initial income, y_0, is invested where it can be collateralized for the c-bond loan (for example in the lending country), the default constraint is relaxed relative to the comparative static analysis above that assumed all income was from sales of c-bonds and none of the current income in the period in which c-bonds were introduced was saved. So, even if full c-bond coverage seemed infeasible in that analysis, the above strategy may work.

If one ignores transactions costs, as we do here, a number of different combinations of contracts could replicate the above arrangement, given the assumption of a nonbinding default constraint. One example is a short forward contract plus a loan on the anticipated proceeds of the contract. Several commentators have inferred that a combination of a futures contract and a loan would also be equivalent. If one takes seriously the assumption of one discrete decision instant before the later maturity date, then they are equivalent if the loan is adjusted to cover initial margins. But in a more general context the futures contract is marked to market as price varies over the time between commitment and maturity, and this leads to additional uncertain increases or decreases in credit requirements on the part of the hedger. In practice this can result in serious complications, especially if trading is obstructed by price move limits for significant periods, and/or interest rates move substantially and are not themselves hedged.

If the default constraint binds on hedging with commodity bonds or forward contract, the full smoothing described above is infeasible. The alternative of using futures markets is precluded because the variation margin requirements that make default unattractive cannot be met by a liquidity-starved borrower. Nor will they be satisfied by a third party lender because of the induced incentive of the borrower to default on the margin loans.

Default Constraint Binding

If the default constraint binds, the immediate transition to full consumption smoothing is precluded. We ask what the optimal consumption smoothing contract is in such cases, following the analysis of Worrall (1987, and noting also Kletzer 1988), and then see if it can be replicated by existing financial instruments. Suppose the export price in any period t can take one of S values corresponding to S states of the world, $p_t(s) = p(s)$, $p(1) < p(2) < ...\ p(S)$, and associated with these values, the income of the country, valued at the spot price, is $y(s) = p(s)$ $\bar{q}$, $s = 1, 2, ..., S$. The optimal contingent borrowing contract is a level of borrowing, b, and a schedule for repayment in the next period, $M_{t,s} \equiv M(y_t - m_t, p_{t+1}(s))$, contingent on the price realization $p_{t+1}(s)$ which maximizes the borrower's utility subject to his not wishing to default. If the optimal value function is V, then V is the solution to the problem

(2) $\quad V(y_t - m_t) = \text{Max } u(y_t - m_t + b_t) + E[V(y(s) - M_{t,s})] / (1 + r)$

where y_t and m_t are the levels of income at current price p_t and debt repayment in the current period t, and consumption $c_t = y_t + b_t - m_t$. This is to be maximized by choosing $[b_t, M_{t,s}]$ subject to the constraint that the borrower does not wish to default in any state s, and consequently forego any future lending or borrowing opportunities:

(3) $\quad V(y_s - M_{t,s}) > u(y(s)) + E[U(y)]/r, \qquad s = 1,2, ..., S$

and subject to the zero profit constraint which, for risk-neutral lenders, is

(4) $\quad -b_t + \beta E[M_{t,s}] = 0.$

From the envelope condition, $u'(y_t - m_t + b_t) = V'(y_t - m_t)$, $V(\bullet)$ is strictly concave, implying existence of a unique optimum. The first-order conditions from this constrained maximization problem are

(5) $\quad u'(c_t) = (1 + \mu_s) V'(y(s) - M_{t,s}), \qquad s = 1,2, ..., S$

where μ_s is proportional to the multiplier on the default constraint in state s, which will be zero if the constraint does not bind.

It is possible to show (Worrall 1987:5-6, results 1-3) that, if the default constraint binds when the scheme is implemented in period t, with current repayment obligation m_t, then the optimal loan has a contingent repayment schedule that sets a floor on net income in the next period, $(y(s) - M_{t,s})$, equal to current net income, $(y_t - m_t)$, with repayment at higher income satisfying $V[y(s) - M_{t,s}] = u(y(s)) + E[u(y)]/r$. Consumption $(y(s) + b_{t+1} - M_{t,s})$ is nondecreasing in net income, $y(s)$.

Assuming the default constraint precludes complete smoothing, the optimal scheme could be operated using c-bonds as follows: In period t the lender issues to the borrower a loan b_t and a put option to cover fixed output $\bar{q}$ with strike price P_t^* equal to

(6) $\quad P_t^* \equiv (y_t - m_t + b_t/\beta + Z_t)/\bar{q}$

where the option premium, Z_t, is determined by the zero-profit condition for the writer of the put

(7) $\quad (y_t - m_t + b_t/\beta)/\bar{q} = E\left\{\min\left[p_{t+1}, (y_t - m_t + b_t/\beta + Z_t)/\bar{q}\right]\right\}$,

and b_t is the solution to the borrower's optimization problem given the associated values of P_t^* and Z_t from (6) and (7).

In period t + 1, the maximum repayment is $m_{t+1}^* = b_t/\beta + Z_t$. If the realized state s in that period is such that $p_{t+1} \le P_t^*$ and the option is exercised by delivery of $\bar{q}$ or equivalent trades, the borrower receives the option return less repayments, $P_t^*\bar{q} - b_t/\beta - Z_t$, and the lender is paid a net sum of $m_{t+1} = M_{t,s} = y(s) - y_t$ which may be negative. Income net of repayments is the same as last year, i.e., $y_{t+1} - m_{t+1} = y_t - m_t$. The smoothing arrangements of period t, $[b_t, P_t^* Z_t]$, are then replicated in period t + 1.

If, however, $p_{t+1} > P_t^*$, the borrower repays the lender m_{t+1}^*, sells $\bar{q}$ on the market, and retains net income $\bar{q}p_{t+1} - m_{t+1}^* = y_{t+1} - m_{t+1}^* > y_t$ where $m_{t+1}^* = \max M_{t,s}$. Then the procedure is repeated for period t + 1 and the new amount borrowed, b_{t+1}, is, in this case, less than b_t, but the strike price is higher to raise minimum net income to $y_{t+1} - m_{t+1}^*$.

If the default constraint is initially binding, the process thus evolves as follows. In the initial period (call it period 0), assuming no prior obligations, $m_0 = 0$, and $y_0 = p_0\bar{q}$. Consumption is raised by c-bond sales to $y_0 + b_0$. In period 1, if the state is j, $1 \le j \le S$, then $y_1 = y(j) = p(j)\bar{q}$, and $m_1 = M(y_0, p(j))$, so that consumption is $c_1 = y_1 + b_1 - m_1 \ge c_0$. Consumption never falls; assuming the maximum price p(S) has positive probability, in finite time (period w), it occurs, and $c_{w+i} < p(S)\bar{q}$ is constant for i = 0, 1, 2, 3. . . . (A longer maturity offers no additional advantage in our model). In each period an instrument that can achieve this is a zero-coupon, one-period c-bond payable in dollars or in a specified commodity bundle, at the *seller's* option. This instrument contrasts with the typical commodity convertible or commodity-linked bond which contains a *call* option for the *purchaser* rather than a *put* for the *seller*.

Such an instrument does not satisfy the default constraint. The latter also precludes full coverage by forward contracts, which would achieve immediate full smoothing in the absence of the default constraint.

Before closing this section, we note that the theory used here assumes that sovereign defaults are penalized by withdrawal of all lending and borrowing opportunities. But the historical record (Lindert and Morton 1987; Eichengreen 1987) does not clearly show the expected differentiation, in availability of loans and their terms, between countries that have defaulted several times and those that have never done so. On the other hand, despite the apparently lenient treatment of sovereign defaulters, the overall *ex post* rate of return has substantially exceeded the return on lending within the creditor countries themselves (Lindert and Morton 1987). Borrowers often appear to make net repayments in circumstances where it is difficult to demonstrate that their efforts are in their own self-interest, even where the latter is recognized as extending well beyond stabilization.[4] Resolution of these puzzles is currently an active area of empirical investigation.

Conclusions

Consumption smoothing could in principle be quite valuable to many countries in the absence of any other risk-reducing strategies. Commodity bonds (c-bonds) can achieve optimal consumption smoothing in the face of random export prices for commodity-dependent less-developed countries, dominating other international arrangements such as international buffer funds or attempts to create longer term futures markets.[5] Depending on initial conditions, the smoothing may be immediately complete, and use a straight c-bond, or it might involve a nondecreasing consumption path, which becomes constant if and when the highest income level is attained. In the latter case the bond could be constructed as a conventional loan with attached put for the seller; equivalently, a bond with a nominal face value at maturity and an attached commodity value, delivery of either to be at the *seller's* option. This type of c-bond contrasts with the observed forms, which generally offer the *buyer* a similar choice. The consumption-smoothing achieved reduces downside exposure of the seller, while leaving him a sufficiently large share of high realizations that he is not tempted to default.

Though we have shown this only in the case of pure price uncertainty with i.i.d. disturbances (and, hence, no interperiod storage), availability of a constant risk-free rate of return and market risk neutrality of lenders, our results suggest further investigation of the smoothing possibilities of these instruments in more general circumstances. If prices follow a random walk, it is easy to show that bond-option packages like those discussed here can smooth producers over a one-period production commitment under a default constraint. (Of course, eventual perfect smoothing is not feasible in such circumstances.) In a model with storage, prices tend frequently to be highly correlated over short intervals. Nevertheless, the price process is stationary, though complicated.[6] The optimal smoothing contract in such a model is an interesting topic for further investigation.

Whether the type of smoothing discussed here is what commodity exporters want or need is another question. But continued access to the benefit of income-smoothing is often identified as a major inducement for honoring loan contracts originally motivated by other objectives such as economic development (Eaton, Gersovitz, and Stiglitz 1986), though the observed procyclical nature of much borrowing raises questions about the smoothing objective (Gersovitz 1985; see also Fishlow 1987). Integration of this analysis with the extensive literature on swaps, renegotiation, and related matters is an obvious extension of this approach.

Notes

* This chapter is a revised version of "Financial Instruments for Consumption Smoothing by Commodity-Dependent Exporters" published in the *American Journal of Agricultural Economics* 71 (2), May 1989. This paper was also published in T. Priovolos and R.C. Duncan, eds., *Commodity Risk Management and Finance*. Washington D.C.: World Bank, 1991.

With the usual caveat, the authors thank Doug Christian for research assistance, Jim Vercammen for correction of a numerical error in a previous version, and seminar participants at the University of California, Berkeley, and Larry Karp, Ken Kletzer, Peter Lindert, Bob Myers, and Barry Eichengreen for helpful discussions, and two World Bank referees for useful comments.

1   If consumption c is a random variable with coefficient of variation s, $u(E(c)-\rho) = Eu(c)$. Expand both sides in a Taylor series: $u(E(c)) - \rho u'(E(c)) \approx u(E(c)) + 0.5s^2E(c)u''(E(c))$ or $\rho/E(c) \approx 0.5s^2R$.

2   If only borrowing opportunities are lost, but the country may invest the payments it saves overseas at the same interest rate, it can actually

achieve exactly the same consumption stream for periods beyond $t + k$ as if it did not default (or never borrowed at all); see Bulow and Rogoff (1988). The partial smoothing is like that achieved by commodity storage (Wright and Williams 1982).

3   See Eaton, Gersovitz, and Stiglitz for a recent survey. See also Kletzer (1988) and Bulow and Rogoff (1987). Alternative instruments are reviewed in Lessard.

4   There is a large literature following the pioneering work of Feder and Just on *estimation* (as distinct from *explanation*) of debt-service behavior.

5   See Finger and DeRosa (1980) for a cautionary analysis of the Compensatory Finance Facility of the International Monetary Fund. They find that, on average, it did not even stabilize the annual export incomes of participants.

6   See Wright and Williams (1982) for steady-state price distributions in a model of storage with rational expectations, and Williams and Wright (1991) for details of price behavior with storage.

References

Bulow, J., and K. Rogoff. 1988. "A Constant Recontracting Model of Sovereign Debt." *Journal of Political Economy* 97 (1): 155-178.

_____. 1988. "Sovereign Debt: Is to Forgive to Forget?" NBER Working Paper No. 2623.

Carr, P. 1987. "A Note on the Pricing of Commodity-Linked Bonds." *Journal of Finance* 42: 1071-76.

Eaton, J., and M. Gersovitz. 1981. "Debt with Potential Repudiation: Theoretical and Empirical Analysis." *Review of Economic Studies* 48: 289-309.

Eaton, J., M. Gersovitz, and J. E. Stiglitz. 1986. "The Pure Theory of Country Risk." *European Economic Review* 30: 481-513.

Eichengreen, B. 1987. "Til Debt Do Us Part: The U. S. Capital Market and Foreign Lending: 1920-1955." NBER Working Paper No. 2394.

Feder, G., and R. Just. 1977. "A Study of Debt Servicing Capacity Applying Logit Analysis." *Journal of Development Economics* 17: 25-32.

Finger, J. M., and D. A. DeRosa. 1980. "The Compensatory Finance Facility and Export Instability." *Journal of World Trade Law.*

Fishlow, A. 1987. "Lessons of the 1880s for the 1980s." University of California, Berkeley, Department of Economics Working Paper No. 8724. Pp. 26.

Gersovitz, M. 1985. "Banks' International Lending Decisions: What We Know and Implications for Future Research," in Gordon W. Smith and John T. Cuddington, eds., *International Debt and the Developing Countries.* Washington D. C.: The World Bank.

Keynes, J. M. 1924. "Foreign Investment and National Advantage." *The Nation and the Athenæum.*

Kletzer, K. M. 1988. "Sovereign Debt Renegotiation Under Asymmetric Information." Yale University Economic Growth Center, Discussion Paper No. 555.

Lessard, D. R. 1987. "Recapitalizing Third-World Debt: Toward a New Vision of Commercial Financing for Less-Developed Countries." *Midland Corporate Finance Journal* 5: 6-21.

Lindert, P. H., and P. J. Morton. 1987. "How Sovereign Debt Has Worked." Institute of Government Affairs Research Program in Applied Macroeconomics and Macro Policy Working Paper Ser. No. 45, University of California, Davis.

Newbery, D. M. G., and J. E. Stiglitz. 1981. *The Theory of Commodity Price Stabilization.* Oxford: Oxford University Press.

O'Hara, M. 1984. "Commodity Bonds and Consumption Risks." *Journal of Finance.*

Priovolos, T. 1987. *An Overview of Commodity Bonds: A Balance Sheet Management Instrument.* Washington D.C.: The World Bank.

Schwartz, E. S. 1982. "The Pricing of Commodity-Linked Bonds." *Journal of Finance* 57: 525-41.

Williams, J. C., and B. D. Wright. 1991. *Storage and Commodity Markets.* New York: Cambridge University Press.

Worrall, T. 1987. "Debt with Potential Repudiation: Short-Run and Long-Run Contracts," University of Reading Disc. Paper in Econ., Ser. A, No. 186.

Wright, B. D., and J. C. Williams. 1982. "The Economic Role of Commodity Storage." *Economic Journal* 92: 596-614.

4

Intellectual Property Rights for Appropriate Invention

Robert E. Evenson

Intellectual Property Rights (IPRs) are one of the oldest means by which "failures of the market" have been at least partially remedied in the United States. They are prescribed in the U.S. Constitution as the institutional means by which the "promotion of progress in science and the industrial arts" is to be achieved.[1] The new U.S. government passed the first Patent Act in 1790 and the Patent Office was one of the most important agencies in the U.S. government in its early years.[2] Over the years patent, trademark and copyright property rights have been sought by both U.S. and foreign inventors and writers.

IPR systems have evolved as institutions over time in response to changing prices, infrastructure and related institutional change. This evolution, however, has been slow and sometimes painful. By the end of the 19th century several international agreements were in place each calling for national IPR systems to provide "national treatment" to foreigners as regards IPR protection. Over the course of the 20th century, however, these international agreements, while nominally in place and binding, are clearly under great stress and conflict by different groups of countries.[3]

Those countries that today constitute the Developed Market Economies, i.e., the OECD countries, have generally been strengthening the scope, administration and general strength of IPR systems.[4] Furthermore, the various international agreements are generally respected by member countries and relatively few conflicts have emerged between these countries. This, however, is not the case for developing countries.

Twenty years ago developing countries mounted an effort to attain better terms of technology transfer between North and South countries. In practice this meant better terms for technology purchases by developing countries. Developing countries pursued several efforts to change the existing intellectual property rights framework in their favor. They argued that payments of royalties and license fees to foreign holders of patents and copyrights constituted "unfair" terms of exchange and that the holders of these rights in developed countries had no moral or "natural" rights to protection in developing countries.[5]

No new agreements or conventions regarding IPRs were developed as a consequence of the North-South debate, largely because the North resisted all changes. Many developing countries actually weakened their own IPR laws and the administration of those laws in the intervening years. Ironically, today the countries of the North, who resisted changes in IPR systems in the North-South debate, are now on a virtual "rampage" to force the countries of the South (at least a certain subset of them) to strengthen IPR protection for foreign inventors. The U.S. is leading a "war on piracy" using a provision of U.S. trade laws (sec. 301) as its chief weapon. IPR considerations have now become an integral part of the Uruguay round of the GATT.[6]

In spite of the increased demand for stronger IPRs by most developed countries, economists remain somewhat divided and inconclusive as regards the actual economic merit of IPRs in developed countries.[7] There is even less agreement as to their merit in developing economies where these economies have not exhibited a demand for stronger IPRs and have, if anything, been weakening their IPR systems.[8]

This divergence of interests and downright conflict raises a number of policy questions regarding IPRs. Do we have analytic and/or empirical studies that can explain why both national IPR systems and international agreements have been strengthened within the OECD "club"? Do we understand why this is not the case for developing countries and why there is growing institutional conflict? Should IPRs be strengthened? Would global welfare be improved if a strong international system of IPRs were in place and enforced? IPR systems are designed to provide stronger incentives for R&D (than afforded by trade secrets and monopoly) and to facilitate disclosure of inventions, and this disclosure facilitates follow on and inventing around (legal imitation) inventive activities.

In this chapter a review of relevant studies is undertaken. The review is undertaken from the perspective of developing countries and particularly the newly industrialized countries in Asia. The review begins with an institutional review of IPR systems (Part I). The usage patterns of IPRs are then reviewed (Part II). Part III examines empirical evidence on R&D spending with a view toward assessing whether developing countries are underinvesting in R&D. Part IV reviews studies of IPR incentives for R&D. The empirical literature reviewed in both Parts III and IV unfortunately is too limited to allow strong policy conclusions. The theoretical literature is also of very little policy relevance[9] for most of these questions. A summary of comparative international patterns of investment in R&D and related magnitudes is offered in the final part of the chapter as a basis for suggestions for some policy directions and for further work.

IPR Systems: An Institutional Review of IPR Systems[10]

Legal systems for securing private rights to inventions implement diverse types of protection: (i) seed and breed certification; (ii) copyrights; (iii) trade secret enforcement; (iv) invention patents; (v) utility models or "petty patents;" (vi) inventor's certificates; (vii) industrial design patents; and (viii) plant patents and variety protection. All of these systems provide some type of legally enforceable right to restrict the use of inventions by someone other than the inventors and their licensees/assignees.

The seed and breed certification systems normally require that seed and animals be marketed with sufficient labeling to identify the origin of the seed or animal and give its genetic heritage. Such certification operates like a trademark to prevent others from trading on the reputation that a breeder establishes with a new plant or animal variety.

A copyright prevents unlicensed copying of works of art or an author's writings. The "copyright" is quite literally limited to "copying" the publication and does not preclude the use of the information contained therein. For inventions which can be maintained in secrecy, such as manufacturing processes that are not readily apparent in the marketed product, trade secrets contracts prevent anyone (primarily ex-employees and collaborators) from disclosing secrets of manufacture and the like to competitors.

An invention patent system, which governs the usual type of patent, gives the inventor the right to exclude others from practicing the invention for a certain time period (usually 15-20 years). Invention patent systems traditionally require that an application for a patent must include an "enabling disclosure" which sufficiently describes the invention so that others skilled in the same technical field can reproduce it successfully.

An invention patent is not an exclusive right to practice a particular invention, but rather a right to exclude others from practicing the invention, within the scope of the exclusion defined by the claims which describe the novel contributions made by the inventor.

To be valid, an invention patent must disclose an invention that is novel, useful, and an improvement over the prior art. An invention must by novel in the sense that it has not previously been published, exhibited, or otherwise described, except within the period immediately preceding the application, and then only by the applicant. As to its utility, the invention must be capable of industrial or agricultural application, and not be purely ornamental.

The degree of "improvement over prior art" that an invention must exhibit defines the single most important attribute of a patent system. Also called the "inventive step" or "level of invention" requirement, this increment must be greater than what would be obvious to the average person skilled in the art. The height of this step varies from country to country.

Utility models or "petty patents" are similar to invention patents in that they give the inventor the right to exclude others from practicing the invention for some period of time. They differ from the invention patents in requiring only novelty and utility, without any "inventive step" above the prior art. Thus, petty patents preserve rights to minor variations of known devices rather than to major technical innovations having broad adaptability. Countries usually grant petty patent protection for a much more limited time than is the case for invention patents, and many grant petty patents only to their own citizens. Also, since the existence of an inventive step need not be determined, such systems cost less to administer than do most invention patent systems. In developing countries, minor adaptations of machinery and other inventions may be valuable in the local economy but may not be valuable abroad.

An inventor's certificate is a notice given in socialist countries that entitles an inventor to receive compensation for his invention, which as a matter of property belongs to the state. This non-market alternative to the standard patent aims to reward the inventor while removing his monopolistic control over the invention.

Industrial design patents provide protection to designs as opposed to inventions *per se*. They provide weak protection somewhat similar to that provided by copyrights.

The Role of International Conventions

In keeping with the treatment of inventions as "intellectual property," most countries of the world are party to at least one international agreement, the intent of which is to facilitate protection of an inventors rights to their inventions from country to country. The most widely held of these agreements is the International Convention for the Protection of Industrial Property, usually called the "Paris Convention" for the seat of its first formulation in 1883. This agreement, as subsequently amended at The Hague (1925), London (1934), Lisbon (1958), and Stockholm (1967), provides that any country belonging to the convention should grant to citizens of another convention country the same rights as those belonging to its own citizens.

The next logical step in providing uniform protection for citizens of different countries is to create a uniform application system under which a single application may be examined by designated member countries according to their particular laws. An agreement of this type was signed by 35 countries in 1978. Called the Patent Cooperation Treaty, its stated aims were "to make a contribution to the progress of science and technology," "to perfect the legal protection of inventions," "to simplify and render more economical the obtaining of protection for inventions where protection is sought in several countries," "to facilitate and accelerate access by the public to the technical information contained in documents describing new inventions," and "to foster and accelerate the economic development of developing countries through the adoption of measures designed to increase the efficiency of their legal systems...."

About half of the parties to the Patent Cooperation Treaty are developing countries: Algeria, Argentina, Brazil, Egypt, Iran, Israel, Madagascar, Malawi, North Korea, the Philippines, Sri Lanka, Syria, along with the following members of the African Intellectual Priority Organization: Cameroon, Central African Republic, Chad, Congo, Ivory Coast, Senegal, and Togo. The remainder comprises Western Europe, North America, Japan, and half of Eastern Europe. With the exception of the Philippines, North Korea, and Sri Lanka, underdeveloped Asia is missing entirely. Latin America, too, has few participants. We may ascribe the relatively strong rate of participation by African countries to the formation of the African Intellectual Property Organization (open to any country but presently comprising former French colonies), a group of countries which binds its members by a modern agreement modeled on French patent law.

Two other treaties have a more direct bearing on agricultural inventions: the International Convention for the Protection of New Varieties of Plants, and the Budapest Treaty on the International Recognition of the Deposit of Microorganisms for the Purposes of Patent Procedure. The first of these, the Plant Variety Convention, was amended most recently in 1978 and provides for patent or patent-like protection to breeders of new plant varieties who belong to member countries. These plants may be sexually as well as asexually reproduced (which gives protection to hybrid varieties), but member states may exclude hybrid varieties from protection at their discretion (on the grounds that the breeder retains control over the parents, which renders protection unnecessary). At present, no developing country belongs to this treaty, and only one, Argentina, has passed a law to give protection to new varieties.

The Budapest Treaty on Microorganisms was signed in 1977. It provides for an "international depository authority" in several nations, which keeps samples of patented microorganisms. This special arrangement takes the place of the usual written and/or graphic description that regular patent documents employ. The treaty aims to lower the cost and reduce the inconvenience of trying to deposit multiple samples in each country in which the inventor desires protection.

The treaty does not grant patent protection *per se*, but merely commits states to the system of recognizing deposits made in other countries as equally valid with those made in its own. Thus, the treaty leaves a considerable degree of freedom in the hands of the individual countries to decide what constitutes a patentable microorganism. Among developing countries, only Senegal, Korea and the Philippines belong to this agreement; the only other non-Western participant is the Soviet Union.

The degree of patent protection available to inventors in developing countries varies considerably, but is almost universally weaker than in developed countries. Several countries ban the patenting of chemical substances and the processes for making them; others ban only the substances; still others permit chemicals in general to be patented but do not allow chemical vaccines to be patented because they are medicines. Among Asian countries, India, Korea, and Taiwan do not allow chemical patents of any kind; Thailand excludes only chemical medicines. (Thailand is currently changing its laws.) As a group, Asia falls midway between Latin America and Africa in allowing chemical patents. In Latin America, half of all countries ban patents on chemicals of any type, and three-fourths of them ban patents on chemical medicines. By contrast, all the African countries permit some kind of chemical patent, and only two exclude chemical medicines from protection. In the Middle and Near East, all countries allow non-medicinal chemical patents, but most forbid patents on medicinal chemicals.

For minor mechanical-electrical inventions (those which do not meet the "inventive step" requirement of a regular patent, but which contain some adaptation or modification of existing technology), five semi-industrialized countries provide protection via a utility model system: Brazil, Uruguay, Korea, the Philippines, and Taiwan, as well as the parties to the African Intellectual Property Organization.

As to biogenetic inventions, most countries specifically exclude plant varieties and animal species from protection, either as such or by excluding foodstuffs. Among developing countries, only Argentina and Korea make provision for plants of any kind to be patented, and only Argentina permits sexually-reproduced plants to be patented. The U.S. has until recently not provided plant variety protection for the hybrid corn -- presumably because such protection is not needed, since corn breeders can effectively maintain control over the hybrid parents, and thus they already have so-called "genetic" protection. However, recent strengthening of the U.S. system allows the patenting of plants including hybrid corns.

As to microorganisms, the U.S., Argentina, Korea, and Israel specifically allow the patenting of microorganisms not occurring in nature; Argentina and Korea disallow the live-virus vaccine on the grounds that it is medicine.

India forbids the patenting of "a method of agriculture or horticulture;" "any process for medicinal, surgical, curative, prophylactic, or other treatment of human beings or any process for a similar treatment of animals or plants to render them free of disease or to increase their economic value or that of their products;" or any substance "intended for use, or capable of being used, as food or medicine or drug." Furthermore, "medicine or drug" includes "insecticides, germicides, fungicides, weedicides and all other substances intended to be used for the protection or preservation of plants."

The Indian law illustrates a general pattern in developing countries. The argument for such laws is that food and medicine products are "basic needs" and that citizens in less developed countries should not be vulnerable to the monopoly pricing associated with patents.

This argument suggests that a country like India would lower the total cost of producing technology were it to abandon its patent system.

In recent years the developed countries have taken steps to broaden and strengthen the protection afforded to intellectual property generally and to biotechnology in particular. The so-called "*Chakarbarty* decision" of the U.S. Supreme Court overruled the U.S. Patent Office by permitting microorganisms to be patentable subject matter. *Ex Parte Hibbard*, an Appeals Court decision, allowed plants to be patented even when they were subject to plant variety protection. *Ex Parte Allen* similarly allowed the patenting of animals.

Differences between the developed and developing worlds regarding IPRs parallel those that have emerged in many other contexts, notably in the Conference on the Law of the Sea Treaty, in which the developing countries took the position that the ocean seabeds represent part of the common heritage of mankind. The developed countries generally favor the possibility for private exploitation of resources on efficiency grounds and point to the public benefits that result. In more traditional areas of patent protection, developing countries are much more likely than developed countries to exclude medical and agricultural inventions from protection, on similar grounds.

Events indicate, however, that the developed world is prepared to press hard for protection in cases where piracy is a possibility, either because of indigenous adaptive capacity or because of infringing products exported to the market from other developed countries. For example, the United States recently completed a so-called "Section 301" action against Korea, in which it threatened trade sanctions if South Korea did not undertake an extensive revision of its intellectual property laws (covering copyright and well as patent laws). Among the results of the subsequent bilateral consultations was Korea's announced intent to accede to the Budapest Treaty on the Protection of Microorganisms and to grant and enforce protection for agricultural chemical and pharmaceutical patents. Under recently enacted amendments to U.S. trade laws, patent infringement is deemed a per se "burden or restriction on commerce" and sets in motion a series of events that culminate in trade retaliation. More generally, intellectual property protection has become a central issue at the current Uruguay round of talks of the GATT. The emerging conflict appears to be between advanced developing countries with significant adaptive capacity, such as Brazil and India, who argue that GATT is an inappropriate forum for the debate (they prefer WIPO), and the developed countries who claim to be losing billions of dollars a year to pirates.

IPR Use

Invention Patents

Tables 4.1 and 4.2 summarize the use of the invention patent in a number of countries for certain periods. Table 4.1 reports the number of patents granted to national (i.e., domestic) inventors, the number granted to foreign entities and the number obtained by nationals in other countries. Patent grants to foreigners reflect various forms of technology purchase by the granting country. The motive for obtaining a patent in a developing country include the use of the IPR to license technology in some form of technology sales contract. Most sellers of technology seek IPR protection in the buying country to prevent copying by competitors (although IPRs are not the only form of protection from competition). If the technology owner seeks to sell the invention in the form of a product he will also usually seek IPR protection against domestic copying and manufacture.

Table 4.1 indicates that some developing countries are significant markets for IPR protected technology. Of course, industrialized countries are also significant markets for technology. Indeed for most types of inventions these are the largest technology markets. This is borne out in Table 4.2 which shows patent trade data.

Technology buyers (from the perspective of the granting country) purchased most of their technology from industrial countries (with the U.S. being the major supplier). The Latin American countries do purchase a significant amount of technology from semi-industrialized and developing countries (also from Latin America). South Korea and Brazil, however, purchase 97 percent of their imported technology from industrial countries.

Technology sellers (from the perspective of the origin country) sell the bulk of their technology to industrial countries, although developing countries do find significant downstream markets in semi-industrialized countries and for recently industrialized countries.

The data in Tables 4.1 and 4.2 then portray the general features of international technology markets. Developing countries are primarily buyers of technology. Their IPR systems enhance technology purchase but do not stimulate large numbers of domestic inventions. As countries move up the scale they become larger purchasers of technology but they also begin to achieve more domestic invention. As they reach the recently industrialized stage they become significant sellers of technology and they find significant downstream markets for their technology.

Table 4.1. Invention Patent Summary

Country	Patents Granted to Nationals 1967	1976	1986	Patents Granted to Foreigners 1967	1976	1986	Patents Granted to Nationals Abroad 1967	1976	1986
USA	51,274	44,162	37,152	14,378	26,074	24,675	73,960	90,273	54,360
Japan	13,877	32,465	38,032	6,896	7,582	8,074	6,843	20,246	20,663
RECENTLY INDUSTRIALIZED									
Spain	2,758	2,000	1,485	6,827	7,500	7,739	627	766	1,180
Israel	178	200	305	935	1,200	1,419	219	145	316
Greece	975	1,343	1,114	2,302	1,285	942	61	81	691
Portugal	84	46	95	1,045	1,319	2,200	53	50	50
NEWLY INDUSTRIALIZED									
South Korea	207	1,593	2,580	152	1,727	1,161	20	50	50
Singapore	5	50	50	26	550	548	5	5	5
Brazil	262	450	349	684	1,500	3,494	63	88	50
SEMI-INDUSTRIALIZED									
Turkey	30	35	34	438	588	424	-	-	-
Philippines	16	108	82	498	767	755	-	-	-
Argentina	1,244	1,300	1,264	4,488	2,800	2,843	81	102	133
Mexico	1,981	300	174	7,922	5,000	1,831	149	181	171
Chile	80	60	60	1,237	514	514	-	-	-
DEVELOPING									
Egypt	48	16	10	873	511	317	-	-	-
India	428	433	500	3,343	2,062	2,000	72	73	57
Sri Lanka	7	9	5	148	156	36	-	-	-
Venezuela	41	50	55	954	514	408	-	-	-
Colombia	49	30	36	851	600	808	-	-	-
Uruguay	165	46	41	351	110	236	-	-	-
Kenya	1	5	-	104	98	-	-	-	-
Morocco	28	23	21	391	334	330	-	-	-

Source: Evenson, R.E. "Intellectual Property Rights, R&D, Inventions, Technology Purchase, and Piracy in Economic Development: An International Comparative Study," in R. Evenson and G. Ranis, eds., Science and Technology: Lessons for Development Policy. (Westview Press, 1990). Reprinted by permission.

TABLE 4.2 Patent Balance Data 1980

Country	Patents Granted to Foreigners	U.S.	Perspective of Granting Country Percent Form — Industrial-ized	Semi-Industrialized	Devel-oped	Planned	Patents Granted Abroad	U.S.	Perspective of Origin Country Percent In — Industrial-ized	Semi-Industrialized	Devel-oped	Planned
USA	24,675	.49	.94	.02	.01	.03	54,360	.35	.853	.098	.016	.033
Japan	8,074	.49	.91	.01	.00	.04	20,663	.35	.882	.093	.003	.022
RECENTLY INDUSTRIALIZED												
Spain	7,739	.25	.96	.01	.01	.02	1,180	.028	.893	.084	.016	.007
Israel	1,419	.46	.98	.001	.001	.01	316	.377	.930	.070	.000	.000
Greece	942	.21	.93	.02	.001	.05	691	.006	.982	.004	.000	.003
Portugal	2,200	.23	.93	.05	.01	.01						
NEWLY INDUSTRIALIZED												
South Korea	1,446	.26	.97	.002	.01	.02						
Brazil	6,228	.36	.97	.01	.01	.01	113	.204	.627	.336	.027	.009
SEMI-INDUSTRIALIZED												
Turkey	427	.29	.97	.01	.01	.01						
Argentina	4,479	.50	.97	.01	.01	.01	133	.211	.505	.412	.068	.015
Mexico	2,389	.62	.91	.02	.07	.01	171	.275	.701	.094	.176	.029
Chile	1,224	.46	.94	.04	.01	.01						
DEVELOPING												
Uruguay	236	.24	.83	.15	.01	.01						
Venezuela	408	.47	.88	.09	.02	.01						
India							57	.175	.737	.176	.069	.018

Source: Evenson, R.E. "Intellectual Property Rights, R&D, Inventions, Technology Purchase, and Piracy in Economic Development: An International Comparative Study," in R. Evenson and G. Ranis, eds., Science and Technology: Lessons for Development Policy. (Westview Press, 1990). Reprinted by permission.

Other IPRs

Table 4.3 reports a summary of the use of utility models, industrial design patents and trademarks in the countries of concern. The utility model or petty patent is utilized only in Spain, Portugal, South Korea, Brazil and the Philippines (as well as in Japan and West Germany). As the table indicates, most utility models are granted to domestic inventors and it does appear that they stimulate domestic invention, primarily of the adaptive type.

Industrial design patents are also provided primarily to national inventors and probably also serve to stimulate domestic invention. They are not used extensively in the older industrialized countries.

Table 4.3. Other IPRs: Summary 1980

Country	Utility Models To Nationals	Utility Models To Foreigners	Industrial Design Patents To Nationals	Industrial Design Patents To Foreigners	Trademarks To Nationals	Trademarks To Foreigners
USA			3,056	892	17,319	1,566
Japan	49,468	533	30,696	593	41,577	5,290
RECENTLY INDUSTRIALIZED						
Spain	3,845	1,131	2,239	407	11,119	12,822
Israel			266	56	255	863
Greece					1,260	1,800
Portugal	159	25	355	228	1,035	581
NEWLY INDUSTRIALIZED						
South Korea	1,315	438	3,917	154		
Brazil	500	13	136	81	136,808	42,821
SEMI-INDUSTRIALIZED						
Turkey					1,129	1,181
Philippines	465	3	151	19	1,125	1,031
Argentina			2,426	159	12,428	2,032
Mexico					8,637	8,292
Chile					1,986	1,735
DEVELOPING						
Egypt			166	27	145	408
India			723	29	3,019	640
Sri Lanka			8	10	160	376
Venezuela			77	16	2,360	1,961
Columbia			11	5	584	672
Uruguay					6,414	541
Kenya					443	747
Morocco					541	443

Source: Evenson, R.E. "Intellectual Property Rights, R&D, Inventions, Technology Purchase, and Piracy in Economic Development: An International Comparative Study," in R. Evenson and G. Ranis, eds., *Science and Technology: Lessons for Development Policy.* (Westview Press, 1990). Reprinted by permission.

Trademarks are also used quite extensively in developing and early industrializing countries. They are granted to foreigners in large numbers. Brazil granted huge numbers of trademarks in 1980 reflecting rapid growth in numbers of products in its rapid growth phase (since abated). Even countries with weak invention patent systems utilized trademark IPRs.

R&D and Returns to R&D

An International Comparison of R&D Investments [11]

OECD and UNESCO data on the scale of investment in R&D and basic science around the world show ratios of R&D to GDP in the 2 to 3 percent range in the industrialized countries. Among the more recently industrialized countries only Israel and South Korea approach this level; semi-industrialized and new industrialized economies generally fall within the 0.3 to 1 percent range. Among the developing economies India stands out with a relatively high ratio. Most middle- and low-income developing economies have R&D investment ratios of less than 0.3 percent. Expenditures on basic science are even more concentrated in the industrialized countries.[12]

Available estimates usually put the public sector as accounting for more than 80 percent of formal R&D expenditures in developing economies. An important exception to this pattern is South Korea, where in 1976 approximately 80 percent of R&D investments were financed by the public sector. By the late 1980s a complete reversal had occurred, and the private sector is now responsible for funding 80 percent of the total (Dahlman 1989:14). Estimates for Brazil suggest that the public sector is responsible for 70 to 90 percent of R&D-related expenditures. In the cases of Argentina, Mexico and India, comparable figures for 1982 were around 95, 90, and 86 percent, respectively. It should be noted, however, that some publicly funded research in these countries may, in fact, be conducted by industry. For further details see CNI (1988), Psacharopoulos and Saliba (1989), Evenson (1990b), and Deolalikar and Evenson (1990).

These statistics cover only formal R&D, that is R&D explicitly organized as such. Most firms, however, engage in informal invention activity, including "blue collar" R&D (meaning that workers and managers develop product and process improvements on the shop floor). Few estimates of the magnitude of such informal R&D exist.[13]

Developing countries are investing a higher share of GDP in agricultural than in industrial research. This can largely be explained by the fact that agricultural R&D has traditionally been performed in public-sector institutions, as few farms have been large enough to undertake, and profit from, effective R&D programs. The lack of protection for improved plants and animals in developing countries has contributed to the paucity of private R&D. In addition, studies have concluded that agricultural technology is highly location-specific (Evenson and Kislev 1975).[14]

Social and Private Rates of Return on Research Investments

Social returns accrue to the society at large, that is, to both producers and consumers. Private return is that portion of the social return captured by the producing firm.

Industrial R&D in Developed Countries. Surveys on returns to private R&D in developed countries show that investments in R&D, when evaluated ex post, yield returns to firms that are at least as high as returns to other investments (Griliches 1984). Mansfield et al. (1977) report on 17 case studies of innovation for which the median private rate of return was 25 percent. Griliches (1984) reports returns to R&D for large industrial firms in the United States ranging from 30 to 50 percent.[15]

Mairesse (1990) reviewed statistical estimates of the impact of research on a firm's productivity. He reviewed five economy-wide and four sector studies using cross-sectional, firm-level data to estimate research productivity elasticities (which approximate rates of return). His review covered seven U.S., five French, and four Japanese studies. All showed positive R&D elasticities of high statistical significance ranging from 14 to 42 percent, with a median of 27 percent. Through another set of firm-level studies in which rates of return were directly estimated, Mairesse confirmed his conclusion that for the three countries in question (including Japan during its imitation phase) private rates of return to R&D were at least as high as for other investments.[16]

Social rates of return may be considerably higher than private rates, because the individual firm is incapable of appropriating, or capturing, completely the benefits from conducting R&D. Even with strong intellectual property protection, the private firm's rent from licensing or product sales generally represents only a fraction of the real value of the invention to the economy, that is, of the invention's social return. In a study conducted by Mansfield et al. (1977), the median social rate of return from major innovations was 56 percent; the median private rate of return was 25 percent.

Industrial R&D in Developing Countries. Few studies have estimated returns to industrial R&D in developing countries. Pack (1990) has computed potential returns from productivity-enhancing R&D based on data for Philippine textile firms. He has shown that more than 80 percent of the firms in the industry would realize higher returns of R&D on factor demand but stopped short of computing returns to investment. Two studies of agriculturally related industrial R&D (see below) reported high rates of return as measured by their impact on agricultural productivity.

Agricultural R&D. On the basis of a review of 159 estimates of returns to agricultural R&D, most undertaken for developing countries, Evenson (1990b) concludes that returns to agricultural research are higher than those resulting from other public-sector investments and generally higher than from industrial R&D. These returns are inherently "social" and should be higher than private returns because they measure the full impact of agricultural research on productive efficiency, not just gains captured by farmers.

It is of interest to note that the distribution of rates of return reported in these studies is approximately the same for the 54 estimates reported for developed countries and the 73 estimates reported for developing countries. Returns to research conducted in the International Agricultural Research Centers within the Consultative Group for International Agricultural Research (CGIAR) are also high, reflecting the high degree of adaptation potential or location specificity of most agricultural inventions. Crop varieties, animal breeding gains, and agronomic practices are affected by soil and climate factors. Specific crops can only be economically produced over a specific range of sites, and many are strictly tropical crops where there is little or no scope for invention in developed countries. Accordingly, experiment stations, even with limited resources and research skills, can produce improved technology tailored to local conditions (Evenson and Kislev 1975).

Five of the studies, which focused on developing countries (Brazil and India), report social returns to private-sector R&D in agriculture. These studies estimated the benefits realized on inventions in the input-supplying industries (chemicals, machinery, veterinary medicine). Interestingly, these benefits remained largely "uncaptured" by the supplying firms.

Despite the widespread pattern of high returns to agricultural R&D, the connection between underinvestment in agricultural R&D and the presence or absence of intellectual property protection is difficult to establish (even in the OECD countries), precisely because the field in question is agriculture. The bulk of agricultural research is publicly funded; moreover, in developing countries patents have not been used to appropriate returns to research, except in the area of agricultural implements and agricultural chemicals.

Determinants of R&D: Does Protecting Intellectual Property Stimulate Inventive Activity?

Studies that attempt to determine the incentive effects of intellectual property on the decisions to innovate and imitate fall into two categories: (1) studies of behavior, either of firms holding patents or firms that conduct systematic R&D and may choose patenting as one option for appropriating returns, and (2) studies that try to establish for different sectors the intrinsic value of a patent (in comparison to the value of other rewards and incentives driving private R&D efforts).

How Firms Value Patents

Few studies have directly measured the incentive effects of intellectual property protection in industrial countries. Watanabe (1985), in a 1979-1980 survey of 2,390 Japanese firms, found that patents were viewed most often as the foremost incentive to industrial invention. Of these firms, 20.7 percent cited the patent system as the most important incentive, followed by 13.5 percent citing other financial incentives. With respect to the motivation of individual researchers within those firms, the possibility of patent protection was the third most important stimulus to invention, with 11.6 percent of researchers surveyed pointing toward it. This percentage trailed competition with other firms (22.9 percent) and academic or technical interest (16.8 percent).

A 1981 survey of United States firms in the chemical, drug, electronics and machinery industries (Mansfield, Schwartz and Wagner 1981) elicited related data and found that these firms would not have introduced about one-half of the patent innovations that composed the sample without the benefit of patent protection.

Economy-wide the evidence suggests that the benefits of a patent system are difficult to measure and vary widely across industries. Considering the issue historically, no evidence was found that the Netherlands or Switzerland were hampered economically during their patentless years (1869-1912 and 1850-1907, respectively, Schiff 1971:122). A survey in Canada, a major technology importer, concluded that patents were not greatly important to the decision to invest in a

Canadian subsidiary (Firestone 1971: ch. 7 and 10). Other surveys also rank patents as a low component of R&D investment determinants (reviews in Scherer 1986:446; Nogues 1990a:5-6). Grief (1987), however, shows that for the Federal Republic of Germany, R&D investments and patent applications are closely correlated, suggesting a role for patents in stimulating investment.

At the level of individual industries, the results are more supportive of patents, especially for pharmaceuticals. Taylor and Silberston (1973: ch. 14) attempted to simulate the effects of a weakened patent law in the United Kingdom. Their results indicated that the more affected industries would be pharmaceuticals and specialty chemicals, the two industries that use patents more intensively.

Despite the importance of patent protection implied by these results, there is also strong evidence that patents do not effectively deter imitation by rivals for very long. In part, this is because patents carry, in Schumpteter's words, "the seeds of their own destruction," in the sense that they disclose to rivals the means to reproduce the invention. A random 1985 survey of 100 U.S. firms (Mansfield 1985) in 13 major manufacturing groups yielded an estimate of the average time period between a firm's decision to commit to a new process or product and the point at which the detailed nature and operation of that new product or process is known to its rivals. According to the firms in the sample, such information with regard to products is in the hands of rivals within roughly one year; with regard to processes it generally becomes available in less than 15 months. These firms listed patents as one of the chief conduits through which this knowledge spreads.

Levin et al. (1987) interviewed over 600 R&D managers in major U.S. firms, asking about the relative efficacy of patent rights in appropriating the returns to R&D. The survey was conducted by "line of business." In most lines of business, patents were rated as being less effective than trade secrets and effective sales and service as a mechanism for securing the returns from R&D. The survey confirmed Mansfield's 1985 results in showing that imitation, even in the presence of a patent, occurs rapidly and the patents disclose a significant degree of information to competitors. Results varied by line of business, with pharmaceuticals and scientific instruments attaching particular importance to patent protection, whereas in most electrical and mechanical fields, patents were deemed less important.

Furthermore, it does not appear from Levin's research that patent protection prevented competitors from entering the market. Except in certain chemical-related areas, it is generally not difficult to devise a functional substitute for a successful new product that does not actually infringe the original inventor's patent. Firms participating in Mans-

field's 1985 survey believed that for about half of the sampled innovations patent protection postponed imitation by a matter of months
only. Within four years of the introduction of the innovations in the
sample, some 60 percent of those patented and profitable had been
imitated. For just 15 percent of the sample did patent protection delay
imitation by more than four years. And although patents increased
imitation costs across the board, these costs were not so substantial as to
markedly affect the speed with which imitators entered the market.

The studies discussed to this point do not allow us to draw
meaningful conclusions for the behavior of firms in developing countries. There are two important sides to R&D; the discovery of new
products and processes and the capability to quickly assimilate and
modify results of rivals' research (Cohen and Levinthal 1989). It is
this latter capability that is particularly important, yet lacking in
developing countries.

Studies on the incentive effects of intellectual property in developing countries are few, and their approach appears to be narrowly
focused. One survey that traces the interlocking nature of patent rights
with other rights, as well as the possible role that stronger intellectual property protection might play, was conducted by Sherwood
(1990a:115), who reported that in Brazil approximately 80 percent of
377 firms surveyed declared that they would invest more in internal
company research and would improve training for their employees if
better legal protection for trade secrets were available.

More recently it has been argued that because developing countries
have a comparative advantage in adaptive invention -- that is, in
assimilating and modifying the inventions of developed-country
firms they require intellectual property systems that facilitate access
to foreign inventions and stimulate adaptive or imitative domestic
invention. An important element in such a system is the utility model
(or "petty patent") because it is well suited to stimulating adaptive
invention.

This point is corroborated by two studies of the agricultural implements industry in Brazil (Dahab 1986) and in the Philippines
(Mikkelson 1985) which conclude that the utility model stimulated
adaptive inventions in these countries and enabled domestic firms to
increase their competitiveness with multinational firms whose inventions they imitated. Another study by Otsuka, Ranis and Saxonhouse
(1988) reports similar conclusions for textiles in Japan and India. All
three studies reported that much of this R&D was of the "informal" or
"blue-collar" type. Ranis (1990) discusses the relevance of informal,
blue-collar R&D in improving industrial productivity.

Synthesis of International IPR Data

Table 4.4 provides a comparative summary of the data reviewed in previous sections. Qualitative ratings are indicated, reflecting the author's judgment, for strength of IPRs, piracy, reverse engineering capacity and economic growth potential. Quantitative measures of investment intensities (GDP ratios) and patent ratios are also summarized. The groupings of countries are designed to reflect technological stages of development. Most developing countries are middle-income developing countries (see World Bank tables). The distinction between newly industrialized countries (NICs) and semi-industrialized countries is based on technical capacity and sophistication of industries but also reflects recent growth rates.

The fact that strong correlations between investment intensity and development success within the group of less than fully industrialized countries has been noted earlier. This is further illustrated in Table 4.4 which shows that when the data are aggregated, a somewhat more regular relationship between investment in R&D and development success exists. Table 4.4 also brings out several other differences between the newly and semi-industrialized countries and developing countries. Two of these are qualitative. The reverse engineering capacities are noted to be much stronger in the NICs than in the developing countries. The extent of piracy is similarly distributed. Three additional quantitative measures are pertinent as well:

First, technology purchase rises with the stage of development. Second, technology sales do not. Third, patents per scientist and engineer rise rapidly with development.

Technology purchase and sales are estimated from the proportion of foreign patents and the proportion of patents obtained abroad. (Data from India and the Philippines were used to scale foreign patents to reflect the R&D content of domestic patents. This is probably misleading for the patents obtained abroad.)

This rough evidence offers an explanation for piracy.[17] Pirates have high reverse engineering capacity, high technology purchases and low technology sales. Their domestic R&D, while adaptive and reverse engineering in character, is nonetheless highly productive, particularly as compared to less developed countries. When pirating countries begin to sell large volumes of technology abroad they join the Paris Convention "club." The notion that technology markets exist has been challenged by some. The terms purchase and sale as used here are meant to measure actual exchanges. This is not to suggest that these

Table 4.4 Comparative Summary of Type by Economy

		Indus-trialized	Newly Indus-trialized	Semi-Indus-trialized	Developing	Planned
I.	Qualitative Rankings (1-5)					
	Strength of IPRs	4-5	1-3	1-2	1	3
	Degree of Piracy	1	4-5	3-4	2	1
	Reverse Engineering Capacity	4-5	4-5	3-4	1-2	2
	Economic Growth Potential	3	4-5	3-4	1-3	2
II.	GDP Ratios					
	Science					
	Applied R&D 1986	.40	.15	.08	.05	n.a.
	Industry 1971	2.27	.56	.31	.15	2.61
	1979	1.96	.43	.30	.20	3.29
	1985	2.15	.50	.40	.25	3.10
	Agriculture 1960	.68	.29	.29	.15	.45
	1970	1.37	.54	.57	.27	.75
	1980	1.50	.73	.81	.50	.73
	Forestry 1970	.28	.10	.05	.02	.17
	1984	.27	.07	.06	.02	.15
	Agriculture 1960	.38	.29	.60	.30	.29
	(Extensive) 1970	.57	.51	1.01	.43	.33
	1980	.62	.59	.92	.44	.36
	Technology Purchase 1970	.67	.66	.37	.45	.27
	1984	.95	.67	.53	.75	.08
	Technology Sales 1970	1.95	.04	.02	.01	.13
	1980	1.23	.08	.06	.02	.10
III.	Patent Ratios[a]					
	$P_N/P_N + P_F$ 1967 - 1971	.53	.25	.17	.11	.76
	1983	.27	.20	.12	.93	n.a.
	P_A/P_N 1967 - 1971	1.79	.28	.10	.10	.15
	1981 - 1983	1.71	.47	.17	.10	.10
	$P_N/S + E$ 1967	.238	.998	.380	.053	.269
	1971	.258	.876	.337	.066	.218
	1976	.201	.494	.185	.055	.187
	1979	.200	.550	.154	.052	.243
IV.	World Shares (1983)					
	Invention Patents	.615	.033	.010	.044	.336
	Industrial Designs	.918	.046	.017	.010	.029
	Trademarks	.556	.309	.092	.036	.007

[a] P_N = patents granted to nationals; P_F = patents granted to foreigners; PA = patents granted abroad to nationals; S + E = scientists and engineers engaged in R&D.

Source: National Science Board, Science Indicators, Washington, D.C.: National Science Foundation.

markets are perfect. Nor does it suggest that the IPR systems are optimal. Piracy would probably not be an issue if they were.[18]

The treatment of technology as a marketable product is useful, however, even if markets are not perfect. The general principle of comparative advantage, for example, can be fruitfully applied to the data presented here. It should not be surprising that the big technology markets are in the industrialized economies. It should also not be surprising that firms (and individuals) located in these economies have a comparative advantage in producing technology for these markets. The "economic laboratories" for potential inventory outside these countries are best suited for the discovery of adapted or derivative inventions.

This adaptive and derivative invention (as reflected in the low patenting abroad and in the downstream patenting) suggests a kind of technology "drafting" phenomenon. Countries such as Korea have developed the capacity to copy and reverse engineer recently developed inventions from industrial countries. They are thus able to achieve technology that is of high value to them at low cost. An increase in investment upstream is quickly reflected in increased technology purchase (and pirating) and own R&D for firms in the draft.[19]

Most poorer countries are not in the draft. Their product (and process) markets are such that the value of slightly modified technology from the leaders is not high. They also lack the skills and experience to draft effectively. Indeed, many find that they must purchase technology in "turn-key" form, i.e. in large interlinked contract form. Their failure to be pirates is not for lack of will to pirate, but for lack of capacity.

The returns to R&D evidence for the NICs and for the poorer developing countries is quite limited. However, standard growth accounting calculations suggest that for the NICs investments in technology acquisition, including the investments required to pirate, i.e. to imitate illegally (from the U.S. perspective) as well as to imitate legally (pirating is probably hugely overstated because the charges cover both legal and illegal imitation) have been very high. They would have to contribute only a small part of realized productivity growth to generate very high returns.

For the "out of the draft" developing countries, the returns to R&D evidence is practically nil. These countries probably fall into two broad categories. Most poor countries simply have not created viable institutional infrastructures for technology exchange on a general basis. They do not have IPR systems of much relevance. They often do not have good contract enforcement systems. Many have very small and primitive industrial sectors. Some rely on "turnkey" type technology contracts with multi-national firms. These contracts are usually "inter-linked" and entail payments for IPRs and a number of other services. The returns to these purchase investments are probably quite variable, but in many cases are probably high and this investment enables some of the countries to develop improved institutions and infrastructures.

A number of "out-of-the-draft" developing countries -- notably India, but probably a few other countries -- have developed institutions and infrastructure to support significant investment in industries. They have not managed the package of institutions to achieve the high volume importation of technology at lower cost that characterizes the NICs. They usually do not have strong IPRs and they are usually obsessed with "dependency fears," vis-à-vis foreign technology. They have not developed incentives to achieve strong domestic R&D-pirating-imitation capacity. They invest little in R&D but it is probably highly productive. They are often characterized by tariff-protected and regulation-protected industries where competitive pressures are weak.

Further Research

The returns to R&D evidence, while scanty, indicate that there is probably widespread underinvestment in R&D and related activities in developing countries. For the NICs, returns to R&D, including imitative and adaptive legal and illegal (piracy) inventive activities are probably very high. The NICs are all expanding R&D investment rapidly. The out-of-the-draft developing countries generally do not have the institutional and incentive environments to invest in R&D optimally. For the poorer countries some of the problem is simply a basic problem of incentives and institutions working at cross-purposes.

This chapter has argued that the imbalance between buyers and sellers of technology promotes such a severe free-riding problem that Paris Convention rules will not prevent piracy. Is there an argument for alternative agreements? Do current pirates have a case for improved tariff treatment in exchange for giving stronger IPRs to foreigners? Can new IPRs instruments be developed to "tilt" incentives in favor of domestic technology activities in LDCs?

These matters all require analytic and empirical investigation. More return studies would be helpful. Empirical studies of domestic investment in technology activities (own R&D, technology purchase, even pirating imitation) and their responsiveness to international invention flows (i.e. to potentially imitable and adaptable technology) will be useful.

Modeling of invention and IPRs is less promising than empirical studies. This is a field where most theoretical models, while suggestive in many ways, have not had good testable implications that can guide empirical work. Returns to R&D empirical studies, for example, have not benefited greatly from theoretical models. R&D investment studies have benefited more. International studies have been even less informed by technology modeling, in part because the "foundations" of international trade modeling set aside technology. Nonetheless, there is much scope for further work. The policy relevance of technology transfer and of IPRs is not likely to decline.

Notes

1   Article 8, Constitution of the United States.
2   The Patent Office introduced the first public research activities in the U.S. and its statistical division was a forerunner to the U.S. Department of Agriculture.
3   Recent overviews of these conventions, and the North-South conflict regarding them, are provided by Lesser (1991) and Gadbaw and Richards (1988).
4   The 1985 *Ex Parte* Hibbard and the 1986 *Ex Parte* Allen decisions following the 1980 "Chakarbarty" decision (447 U.S. 303) are the major judicial changes in the U.S. These decisions opened the door to the patenting of multi-celled plants and animals.
5   See Viatsos (1976), Stewart (1977), OECD (1982), and Ranis (1979) for discussion.
6   See Bradley (1987), GAO (1986), Good (1985), IPO (1987), and Zalik (1986) for discussions.
7   U.S. Congress (1986), and (1984).
8   See Siemson (1987), and Obach (1987).
9   See Walker and Bloomfield (1988), especially chapters 9-13, for a sampling.
10 This section draws extensively on Evenson and Putnam (1986).
11 This section is based on Evenson (1990a).
12 Outside the OECD, definitions of scientists and engineers engaged in research and development are not standardized across countries. Caution is necessary because in some countries only scientists having Ph.D. and M.S. degrees are counted; in others, those with B.S. degrees may also be counted; similarly, an "engineer" may have graduate training or only a technical degree.

¹³ Mikkelson (1985) reports the manufacturers of agricultural implements
    in the Philippines undertake a significant level of informal R&D.
    Evenson (1983) reports similar findings for Indian manufacturers of
    agricultural technical degree.
¹⁴ The extension of intellectual property protection to biological and
    biotechnological discoveries in the developed world has been followed by
    an increase in private investment in agricultural research. See Chapter 6,
    section D. Private-sector R&D has been important in the fields of
    agricultural chemicals and implements. See Table 4.1 for estimates of
    returns to the investment.
¹⁵ Alam (1985) and Nogues (1990a) question the relevance of these results
    for R&D in developing countries.
¹⁶ It should be noted that conditions for invention may well have differed
    substantially in these periods from the contemporary setting.
¹⁷ Evenson (1983) provides a discussion of piracy and IPRs in developing
    countries.
¹⁸ See Stewart (1979).
¹⁹ The metaphor of auto racing where a vehicle drafts on a vehicle ahead of
    it is suggestive of technology drafting.

References

Alam, G. 1985. "India's Technology Policy and Its Influence on Technology
    Imports Development." *Economic and Political Weekly* 20: 2073-2080.
Bradley, J. A. 1987. "Intellectual Property Rights, Investment, and Trade in
    Services in the Uruguay Round: Laying the Foundations." *Stanford
    Journal of International Law* 23.
CNI. 1989. *Competitividade Industrial: Uma Estrategia para o Brasil*. Rio de
    Janeiro: Confederacao Nacional da Industria.
Cohen, W., and D. A. Levinthal. 1989. "Innovation and Learning: The Two
    Faces of R&D." *Economic Journal*.
Dahab, S. 1986. "Technological Change in the Brazilian Agricultural
    Implements Industry." Doctoral dissertation, Yale University.
Deolalikar, A. B. 1990. "Private Inventive Activity in Indian Manufacturing:
    Its Extent and Determinants." *Science and Technology: Lessons for
    Development Policy*.
Dahlman, C. 1989. "Impact of Technological Change on Industrial Prospects
    for the LDC." World Bank Industry Series Paper No. 12, Washington,
    D.C.: The World Bank.
Evenson, R. E. 1983. "Intellectual Property Rights and the Third World." *EIPR*
    12.
_____. 1984. "International Invention: Implications for Technology
    Market Analysis," in Z. Griliches, ed., *R&D, Patents, and Productivity*.
    Chicago: University of Chicago Press.

_____. 1985. "Review of Patents, Innovation, and Competition in Australia by the Intellectual Property Committee." *Prometheus* 3 (2).

_____. 1990a. "Survey of Empirical Studies," in W. Sieback, ed., *Strengthening Protection of Intellectual Property in Developing Countries.* World Bank Discussion Paper No. 112, Washington D.C.: The World Bank.

_____. 1990b. "Intellectual Property Rights, R&D, Inventions, Technology Purchase, and Piracy in Economic Development: An International Comparative Study," in R. Evenson and G. Ranis, eds., *Science and Technology: Lessons for Development Policy* . Boulder: Westview Press.

_____, and J. Putnam. 1986. "Institutional Change in Intellectual Property Rights." *American Journal of Agricultural Economics.*

_____, and Y. Kislev. 1975. *Agricultural Research and Productivity.* New Haven: Yale University Press.

Firestone, O. J. 1971. *Economic Implications of Patents.* Ottawa: University of Ottawa Press.

Gadbaw, R. M., and T. J. Richards. 1988. *Intellectual Property Rights: Global Consensus, Global Conflict?* Boulder: Westview Press.

General Accounting Office. 1986. *International Trade: Strengthening Trade Law Protection of Intellectual Property Rights.* GAO.

Good, A. H. 1985. "The Increased Protection of U.S. Intellectual Property Rights: A Commerce Department Priority." *Business America.*

Grief, S. 1984. "Patents and Economic Growth." *International Review of Industrial Property and Copyright Law* 18: 191-213.

Griliches, Z. ed, 1984. *R&D Patents and Productivity.* Chicago: University of Chicago Press.

IPO News. 1987. VII (1).

Kortum, S. A., and J. D. Putnam. 1987. "The Yale-Canada Industrial Patent Concordance: Its Construction and Use." Yale University.

Lesser, W. 1991. *Equitable Patent Protection in the Developing World: Issues and Approaches.* Christchurch: Eubios Ethics Institute.

Levin, R. A., A. K. Klevorick, R. R. Nelson, and S. G. Winter. 1987. "Appropriating the Returns from Industrial R&D." *Brookings Papers on Economic Activity* 3 (Special Issue on Microeconomics): 783-820.

Mairesse, J. 1990. *R&D and Productivity Growth: An Overview of the Literature.* National Bureau of Economic Research (U.S.).

Mansfield E. 1985. "How Rapidly Does Industrial Technology Leak Out." *Journal of Industrial Economics:.* Pp. 217-223.

_____, Rappoport, A. Romeo, S. Wagner and Beardsley. 1977. "Social and Private Rates of Return from Industrial Innovations." *Quarterly Journal of Economics.*

_____, M. Schwartz and S. Wagner. 1981. "Imitation Costs and Patents: An Empirical Study." *The Economic Journal.* Pp. 907-918.

Mikkelson, K. W. 1985. "Inventive Activity in the Philippines." Unpublished doctoral dissertation, Yale University.

Nelson, R. R., and S. G. Winter. "Neoclassical vs. Evolutionary Theories of Economic Growth: Critique and Prospectus." *Economic Journal* 84: 886-905.
Nogues, J. 1990. "Notes on Patents, Distortions and Development." Pre-Working Paper Series No. 315, Washington, D.C.: The World Bank.
Obach, S. 1987. "Recent Development of Industrial Property Rights in Chile." *California Western Law Journal* 17(2).
Organization for Economic Cooperation and Development. 1982. *North/ South Technology Transfer: The Adjustment Ahead-Analytical Studies.* Paris: OECD.
Otsuka, K., G. Ranis, and G. Saxonhouse. 1988. *Comparative Technology Choice: The India and Japanese Cotton Textile Industries.* London: Macmillan Press.
Pack, H. 1990. "Industrial Efficiency and Technology Choice." *Science and Technology: Lessons for Development Policy.*
Psacharopoulos G., and A. Saliba. 1989. *Brazil's Effort on Research and Development.* Human Resources Division LAC Technical Division, Washington D.C.: The World Bank.
Ranis, G. 1979. "Appropriate Technology: Obstacles and Opportunities." in T. Stanley and S. Rosenblatt, eds., *Technology and Economic Development: A Realistic Perspective.* Boulder: Westview Press.
_____. 1990. "Science and Technology: Lessons from Japan and the East Asian NICs." *Science and Technology: Lessons for Development Policy.*
Scherer, F. M. 1986. Innovation and Growth: Schumpeterian Perspectives. Cambridge, Mass.: M.I.T. Press.
Schiff, E. 1971. *Industrialization Without National Patents.* Princeton: Princeton University Press.
Schmookler, J. 1966. *Invention and Economic Growth.* Cambridge, Mass.: Harvard University Press.
Siemson, P. D., and Jose Antonio B.L. Faria Correa. 1987. "Recent Development of Industrial Property Rights in Brazil." *California Western Law Journal.*
Sherwood, R. M. 1990. "A Microeconomic View of Intellectual Property Protection in Brazilian Development." *Intellectual Property Rights in Science, Technology and Economic Performance.*
Stewart, F. 1979. "International Technology Transfer: Issues and Policy Options." World Bank Staff Working Paper No. 344. Washington, D.C.: The World Bank.
_____. 1981. "Arguments for the Generation of Technology by Less-Developed Countries," in A.W. Heston and H. Pack, eds., "Technology Transfer: New Issues, New Analysis." *Annals of the American Academy of Political and Social Science* 458:97-109.
Taylor, C. T., and Z. A. Silberston. 1973. *The Economic Impact of the Patent System.* New York: Cambridge University Press.

U.S. Congress, House Committee on Energy and Commerce, Subcommittee on Oversight and Investigation. 1984. "Unfair Foreign Trade Practices: Stealing American Intellectual Property -- Imitation is Not Flattery." Washington, D.C.: Government Printing Office.

Viatsos, C. 1976. "The Revision of the International Patent System: Legal Consideration for a Third World Position." *World Development* 4 (2):85-102.

Walker, C. E., and M. A. Bloomfield, eds. 1988. *Intellectual Property Rights and Capital Formation in the Next Decade.* Lanham, Maryland: University Press of America.

Watanabe, S. 1985. "The Patent System and Indigenous Technology Development in the Third World," in J. James and S. Watanabe, eds., *Technology, Institutions and Government Policies.* London: Macmillan.

Zalik, A. 1986. "Intellectual Property and GATT." *The Journal of Commerce.*

5

The Political Economy of Intellectual Property Rights in Developing Countries

*Sumner J. La Croix**

Intellectual property rights (IPRs) have recently been a contentious issue for the United States and some developing countries. Many developing countries have lower standards of intellectual property protection than the U.S., and this has led to charges by U.S. firms that foreign firms are "pirating" their intellectual property. A 1988 International Trade Commission study estimated that in 1986 U.S. companies lost between $43 and $61 billion in sales worldwide because of inadequate protection of intellectual property rights.[1] Many developing nations have also experienced losses due to inadequate IPR protection; one example is that religious books by Indonesian authors are reproduced in Singapore without permission or compensation of the authors (Nagara 1988).

The United States has recently pressured several developing countries in Asia (Malaysia, Thailand, Korea, Taiwan, Hong Kong, Indonesia) to reform their intellectual property laws and to increase their enforcement efforts. Reform has been pushed by the United States government's annual review[2] of the Generalized System of Preferences (GSP) benefits granted to developing countries and by the new "Super" 301 Section of the 1988 Trade Act. The U.S. government has suggested that continuation of GSP benefits be tied to the provision of a minimum level of intellectual property rights. In response, some countries (Indonesia, Korea, Taiwan) have strengthened their IPRs and

enforcement standards and retained GSP benefits. Singapore strengthened its IPRs but nonetheless lost GSP benefits. Thailand rejected
U.S. demands and has lost its GSP privileges.

Economists have consistently argued that IPRs are necessary if
economic development is to be dynamically efficient. Why then do
some developing countries refrain from adopting strong IPRs? This
chapter aims to illuminate the economic and political forces determining government policy in developing countries with respect to IPRs.
The economic rationale for and against IPRs is outlined in Section I. A
model of the political economy of property rights in small, open
economies is presented in Section II. Section III provides a concluding
summary of main points and an agenda for future research.

Economic Rationale for Intellectual Property Rights

Intellectual property rights (i.e., patents, copyrights, trade secret
rights, trade mark protection, and design registration) can be as important for economic development as property rights in more tangible
property.[3] Fully specified property rights in tangible goods provide
necessary conditions for individuals to use them efficiently. The Coase
Theorem tells us that in the absence of transaction costs and income
effects, private property rights in goods and in factors of production,
coupled with maximization by economic agents, are sufficient in a
competitive economy to establish efficient resource use regardless of
how the property rights are distributed.[4]

Positive transaction costs alter this strong result by limiting opportunities for the exchange of rights. As transaction costs increase,
exchange of rights is reduced and in the limit is eliminated. One
implication of costly exchange is that an individual's final allocation
will more closely resemble his initial allocation. Under the strict
assumptions of the Coase Theorem, the initial allocation of rights
would only affect the distribution of income, i.e., who pays who to get
to the optimal solution. As transaction costs increase, the initial
allocation of rights also determines the efficiency of the final allocation. This occurs because the outcome of trading differs with the
initial allocations. In the limit, if exchange of rights becomes pro-
hibitively costly, the highest feasible level of welfare will be
achieved only if property rights are initially assigned to the party
who places the highest value on them (Demsetz 1966). The resulting
equilibrium in which deadweight loss is minimized is constrained

efficient; an efficient equilibrium requires that deadweight losses be eliminated.[5]

Positive enforcement costs also reduce the value of property rights. Costly enforcement provides incentives for individuals to incur costs to appropriate property and for holders of rights to allocate resources to enforcement. One implication of positive enforcement costs is that some property becomes common property, as owners find it too costly to protect all margins of all property against appropriation. To limit the amount of property entering the common domain, holders of rights take actions to reduce costs of enforcement. Restricting the scope of property rights typically leads to lower enforcement costs; while restricted rights reduce gross benefits, holders of rights only act to restrict their own actions when the reduction in enforcement costs is sufficient to increase the net value of the property.

Expenditures on enforcement are related to the effectiveness of both public and private enforcement institutions as well as to the penalties that appropriators of rights pay after successful legal action. IPR legislation with insufficient penalties or inadequate mechanisms for public or private enforcement actions attenuates the property rights of IPR owners. Public enforcement institutions can only function efficiently if they receive sufficient funds, are allowed to impose sufficiently large penalties, and have incentives to enforce the law. Private systems are effective only if the IPR owner has the opportunity to pursue a possible violation of IPR laws without dissipating all of the rents associated with the IPR.

Intellectual property differs from most tangible property because it has a nonexclusive consumption technology: additional users can consume the good without incurring additional production costs. Following the theory of public goods, this implies that the optimal price for *using* intellectual property is zero. Given the set of production processes, *static* efficiency is then achieved. *Dynamic* efficiency is, however, violated at a zero price, as the rate of return on innovating activities falls below the competitive return, thereby reducing resources devoted to research and development (R&D). A reduction in R&D eventually leads to a reduced flow of new products and processes, thereby reducing the rate of economic growth in future years.

Assuming that lump sum taxes are infeasible, financing of this public good results either in deadweight losses from taxation or from charges on the users of the public good.[6] With positive transaction costs, it is impossible to find a nondiscriminating method for compensating inventors which reduces deadweight loss to zero. *The proposition that private rights in intellectual property must be limited to achieve constrained efficiency is independent of the type of property rights system established.* Systems of pure, private intellectual property are feasible, but inefficient. Rights are restricted to reduce both the costs of enforcement and the deadweight losses from charging a nonzero price for the use of the intellectual property.

Most OECD countries compensate inventors by awarding them limited monopoly rights in the products and processes utilizing their inventions. These limited rights serve to increase the production of creative works and innovations by allowing creators to charge a price above marginal cost for products utilizing the invention and thereby earn a quasi-rent on product production. While the added flow of new products benefits society, the monopoly price of those products produces a deadweight loss. The optimal life of the IPR is determined by comparing the deadweight loss generated by an additional year of monopoly pricing for existing inventions with the added gain from additional inventions.[7] Thus to achieve constrained efficiency, IPRs are restricted in their duration.

While the patent system allows firms to charge a positive price for the use of a public good, another dimension of the intellectual property which has properties of a public good retains a zero price. The state grants restricted property rights in the invention only when the inventor agrees to allow the idea behind the new product or process to be freely used. This feature of IPRs allows other inventors to use the ideas inherent in the invention, thereby reducing the cost of developing new products and inventions which improve on the new invention.[8]

This standard analysis of IPRs must be modified when we consider an open rather than a closed economy. This is because costs and benefits produced from IPRs in one country often spill over to other countries.[9] This means that while the overall world economy gains from properly specified IPRs, some countries lose. Conflicts between countries concerning the type and strength of IPRs should be expected. Countries have different supplies of and demands for inventions, enforcement costs, legal institutions, and transaction costs.[10] The optimal set of restricted rights protecting intellectual property varies across countries according to the factors listed above. Despite these differences, most developed and many developing countries are bound by a set of international agreements setting minimum standards for establishing and enforcing IPRs.

International agreements governing IPRs standards have been in existence since the late nineteenth century. The 1883 Paris Convention on Industrial Property covers inventions, trade names, trademarks, service marks, industrial designs, indications of source, and appellations of origin. The Convention is administered by the World Intellectual Property Organization (WIPO), an agency of the United Nations. The Convention's main accomplishment was to establish the principle of national treatment. Each signatory is obligated to offer citizens of other states belonging to the Convention the same rights and protections offered to its own citizens.[11] By giving up the possibility of discriminating against foreign patents at home, a signatory country gains equal treatment abroad. Yet the Convention does not standardize the level of protection; two early signatories to the Paris Convention, Switzerland and the Netherlands, did not even have patent systems.[12]

Three other articles of the Convention established important principles. First, a filing in one state would not preempt a filing in a second state within one year. This allows an individual or firm sufficient time to complete the many patent applications required to obtain protection in each signatory country and not lose the claim that the invention is "novel." Second, a state could not revoke a patent if goods manufactured with the assistance of the patent were imported from another signatory country.[13] Third, countries may not force compulsory licensing for nonworking of the patent until 4 years from the filing date or three years from the granting date.[14] While the Paris Convention has a dispute resolution mechanism (parties can appeal to the World Court), several nations have signed the convention only with the reservation that they will not adhere to the dispute resolution procedures (Gould 1987). The United States is a signatory to the Paris Convention.

The Berne Convention covers copyrights and is similar in its coverage to the Paris Convention.[15] Under WIPO's jurisdiction, the Berne Convention establishes national treatment; it allows for copyrights to be established without formal registration procedures; and it sets certain minimum standards for each signatory's copyright laws. The Berne Convention lacks any meaningful dispute resolution procedures. In 1988 the United States joined the Berne Convention. Proponents believe that signatory status will allow the U.S. to press piracy matters in the courts of countries that are Berne signatories (Miller 1987).

The United States is a signatory to the 1952 Universal Copyright Convention (UCC) which is administered by UNESCO -- an agency of the United Nations from which the United States has withdrawn. Revised in 1971, the treaty is important as it provides a simple mechanism for creators of literary works to obtain copyright protection. Article 3 states that to claim copyright, the letter "C" in a circle must be affixed to the book or film, along with the copyright owner's identity and the year of first publication. The UCC also makes it possible for governments to obtain preferred access to works protected by copyrights.

These multilateral agreements suffer from two main deficiencies. First, they are generally ineffective in resolving disputes between the parties, because they have failed to specify procedures that both parties have incentives to respect. Second, they specify only minimal standards of property rights protection. The equal treatment provisions allow foreigners to have access to a nation's courts, but this may not prove particularly valuable if the court system in the foreign country works poorly or if the nation's statutes provide only weak protection for intellectual property. While the procedures which reduce the transaction costs associated with filing patent and copyright applications in foreign countries are obviously beneficial, a producer gains little by obtaining access to an IPR system with only nominal protection. International agreements of this type are useful in coordinating relationships between well-functioning systems of intellectual property protection, but they do not provide incentives for small developing countries to strengthen their protection of IPRs.

Economic Factors Determining the Strength of IPRs

Small v. Large Economies

Small (i.e., low income) economies have fewer incentives than large economies to establish IPRs.[16] Most small economies run a deficit in technology transfers, importing more than they export. This often occurs because the small country participates in industries such as agriculture that generate few important patents or because there are external and/or internal economies of scale in R&D. Economies of scale lead to R&D activities being located in a large economy, as there are often complementarities between R&D and the number and variety of production facilities for the product and related products.

Countries that are net "importers" of technology may benefit from choosing to establish a very weak IPR system. This choice enables them to benefit by free-riding on foreign intellectual property if (1) the country has a low ratio of exports to output, thereby reducing the potential for retaliation; (2) the countries from which it appropriates intellectual property constitute a small part of its exports (thus reducing losses from retaliation); and (3) domestic R&D activity is small.

More generally, small economies that are net importers of technology will find it profitable to establish more restricted IPRs than those established in large economies. The term of protection which maximizes benefits to the country's citizens will be shorter than the term which maximizes benefits in the large economy.[17] The optimal rate for the world economy lies between the two rates: this is due to the reduced attention paid by the small economy to the world innovation rate (as it is a net importer of innovations) and to the reduced attention paid by the large economy to the effects imposed on consumers in the small economy from the longer protection period (as it is a net exporter of innovations).[18]

Patent System Standardization

The above analysis clearly illustrates why conflicts between nations over protection of IPRs held by foreigners are frequent and persistent. Nations that are net importers of technology have incentives to maintain short terms of protection for IPRs. Standardization of IPRs across nations must produce both winners and losers, as optimal patent standards for individual nations are scattered across a broad spectrum. Attempts to standardize IPRs across countries are unlikely to be fully successful because losing countries have incentives to adjust their IPR systems along margins which are difficult to measure or monitor. During the 1980s, the U.S. pressured many small economies to change their IPRs to resemble those in the U.S. As noted in the introduction, several small economies have agreed to longer terms of protection and other IPR features favored by the U.S. government. However, such agreements may only be marginally effective, as small economies have numerous policy tools at their disposal to ensure that enforcement costs are higher than in the U.S., and higher enforcement costs diminish the value of IPRs.

Several policies and conditions which increase enforcement costs for IPRs are worth discussing in more detail. First, if the primary enforcement mechanism is a *public* mechanism, the government can reduce effective enforcement of the law by allocating inadequate resources to the public enforcement agency. Given that the agency's resources are "stretched thin" and that it cannot pursue all alleged violations, there is a reduced probability that a patent or copyright infringer will be apprehended. Even well-funded public agencies usually have some discretion in deciding which cases to pursue and how many resources to devote to each case; bureaucrats in the enforcement agency may be prompted by their internal structure of incentives to spend more to protect a patent held by a domestic firm than by a foreign firm. Nor is the pace of investigation fixed; domestic infringement of IPRs held by foreigners may be investigated with "all deliberate speed."

Second, private enforcement of intellectual property rights may be an imperfect substitute for public enforcement. Civil suits brought by a patentholder could be stymied by a broad array of factors. The country's court system may not be adequately funded, and there may be long delays until a court case is heard and resolved. India's Supreme Court has a ten-year backlog of cases to be decided. Many patents and copyrights are obsolete by the time an action is finally resolved; more importantly, many defendant companies will have disappeared and others will be unable to pay. India's adoption of stronger IPRs surely would not affect the deeply rooted structural problems in its overall system of justice. In addition, temporary injunctions are often difficult to obtain in many developed and developing countries. As a result, violations of IPRs often persist until the civil suit is decided.

Third, domestic courts may be influenced by the infringing defendant, as nationalistic concerns are rarely absent even in a seemingly impartial court of law. Suppose we ignore the possibility of bias against foreign plaintiffs. Other circumstances are still present which increase the cost to a plaintiff of bringing private enforcement actions in a foreign country. Language barriers, different legal rules, and foreign travel surely add to the cost of bringing a foreign infringement action. In most developing countries the burden of proof is on the patentee to prove infringement, thereby increasing the cost of pursuing IPR violations. Foreign plaintiffs may also have a particularly difficult time hiring local experts to give testimony against a local company, for in a small economy local experts often have close ties to the defendant firm.

Fourth, judicial enforcement of IPRs can be "loose" or "strict." Determining the correct scope of patent enforcement is a difficult practical task for most courts. If patent laws are narrowly enforced, firms may be inhibited from engaging in innovating activity; if patent laws are enforced too loosely, they may not provide future inventors with returns sufficient to stimulate substantial research activities.[19] Determining whether a judicial decision constitutes a delicate balancing of complicated issues or is deliberately biased in favor of national interests will always be difficult.

In sum, standardization of written statutes and certain legal procedures is unlikely to standardize IPR protection across countries. Enforcement costs differ because (1) legal institutions vary in their procedures and efficiency across countries, and (2) the price of inputs to enforcement activities varies substantially across countries. Some degree of difference in *effective* IPR standards across countries appears to be inevitable.

The Mix of Manufacturing Firms

A third characteristic of developing countries which may affect the structure of intellectual property rights is their mix of manufacturing products. Most developing countries produce a different mix of products than industrialized countries. This may be due to differences in comparative advantage, differential resource and human capital endowments, or governmentally-induced distortions. Levin et al.'s recent studies have clearly demonstrated that the importance of patent protection varies across industries and with respect to firm size. This variation is due to a number of factors. First, competing firms vary in the time and cost required to *develop* closely related products not enjoined by the patent. Second, competing firms vary in their ability to *manufacture* the product within quality standards desired by consumers. By the time a firm reduces its cost of production and quality variation to profitable levels, the imitated product can be obsolete. Third, patents reveal additional information about how a product is produced and designed. Firms in industries where reverse engineering is very costly may choose not to patent their product or process to avoid revealing information vital to potential imitators. Fourth, sunk costs in production facilities by incumbent producers may be sufficient to deter entrance by imitating competitors. If the incumbent and entrant cannot simultaneously earn nonnegative profits, the sunk costs will provide protection for the product. Finally, firms with superior sales and service capabilities have advantages in capturing gains from innovation and may not require patent protection against imitators without these capabilities. In sum, there are many instances in which firms will eschew patent protection even if it is available.

If a country's manufacturing sector has a higher proportion of firms with the characteristics identified above than other countries, then the return to an effective patent system is reduced, and the country could gain by reducing the strength and length of its patent protection. A strong patent system would only provide foreign firms with monopoly protection for their products while exposing domestic firms to the same competition they would face in the absence of the patent system. Of course, this line of reasoning could explain not only some of the differences between IPRs in developing and developed countries, but also some of the differences between the property rights systems in developed countries.

If the mix of industries is a major determinant of the strength of a country's patent laws, then as the country develops and its comparative advantage changes, its IPRs will eventually change to fit the changing industry mix. Levin et al. identify industries in which patents provide high levels of protection: inorganic chemicals, organic chemicals, drugs, plastic materials, plastic products, steel mill products, pumps and pumping equipment, semiconductors, motor vehicle parts, and medical instruments.[20]

One problem with this explanation of IPRs is that it may be self-fulfilling. Suppose that property rights institutions are not efficiently specified and that too little protection is provided by existing institutions. Industries requiring strong patent protection choose to locate elsewhere while industries not requiring such protection thrive. Thus the pattern of industries in a developing economy does not necessarily provide us with evidence of the patent system's efficiency. It merely exhibits evidence of self-selection. We do not know whether institutions have efficiently evolved and have thereby established a stable environment for a particular mix of firms or whether the mix of firms has prompted the rise of inefficient intellectual property rights. The most likely result is that the property rights system and the industry mix have developed simultaneously in response to more fundamental forces and that change in the fundamental forces will change the firm mix and IPRs simultaneously.

The Political Economy of IPRs in Developing Economies

Demand for capital-saving process inventions will be greater in developing than in developed countries due to their relatively low capital-labor ratios.[21] Yet inventions from industrialized countries tend to be labor-saving rather than capital-saving and are often perceived as "too expensive" by the developing country. Why then don't foreign companies export capital-saving inventions? One reason may be that capital-saving inventions are best developed in firms using labor-intensive technologies and that these firms are located predominantly in developing countries. If, however, most developing countries protect property rights inadequately, then labor-intensive firms in developing countries will have few incentives to develop capital-saving inventions for they will be quickly imitated by competitors. Free-riding on labor-saving process innovations from foreign countries clearly yields some benefits for producers in developing countries, but it is unclear whether they outweigh the costs of having fewer capital-saving process inventions. If there are net benefits to imitating labor-saving technology, then a weak IPR system would be optimal.

Suppose, however, that an effective patent system would encourage the development and use of "more appropriate" technology which would generate net benefits for the country. Why then don't developing countries have stronger IPR systems? The answer may lie in the differential political power of various interest groups. Stigler (1971), Peltzman (1976), and Becker (1983) have developed theories of interest group interaction to show why some interest groups are successful in obtaining governmental policies that transfer income to them.[22] Balisacan & Roumasset (1986) and Gardner (1987)[23] have combined Becker's analysis with public choice theory to explain why only some agricultural commodities are subsidized in the U.S. and why agriculture is taxed in most developing countries. In this chapter we apply a variant of Balisacan and Roumasset's model to explain why relatively weak IPRs may constitute a political equilibrium although analysis indicates that stronger IPRs would maximize welfare.

In the model, IPRs are the endogenous products of investment in political influence by organized interest groups. Equilibrium group size is also an endogenous variable and is determined by the marginal benefits and marginal costs of group expansion. We ignore consumer groups due to free-riding problems with respect to group organization. We concentrate on three producer groups: foreign competitors, home producers importing technology, and home producers engaging in research and development. Foreign competitors (FC) and home producers engaged in R&D (HR) have incentives to spend resources (I) lobbying for stronger property rights while home producers imitating foreign technology (HI) have incentives to spend resources lobbying for weaker intellectual property rights. Each group maximizes the net benefits from its lobbying activities given the lobbying activities of other groups. This noncooperative game produces a Nash equilibrium in investment expenditures and an endogenous property rights specification:

(1) $PR = PR(I_{FP}, I_{HR}, I_{HI}, X)$; $\partial PR/\partial I_{FP} > 0$, $\partial PR/\partial I_{HR} > 0$, $\partial PR/\partial I_{HI} < 0$

where X is a vector of other variables affecting property rights, such as social norms. The benefits which each group derives from changes in property rights depends on a variety of firm characteristics:

(2) $B_i = B_i(PR, e_s, E/S, RD)$ i = HR, HI

where e_s is the elasticity of supply, E/S is the ratio of exports to sales, and RD is research and development expenditures. The elasticity of supply provides an indicator of the effect on market share from IPR changes. RD expenditures reflect the demand by domestic firms for stronger IPRs. The ratio of exports to sales represents the vulnerability of domestic firms to retaliatory measures by foreign governments. Similar variables affect benefits accruing to foreign competitors:

(3) $B_{FC} = B_{FC}(PR, e_s, ST)$

where ST is the value of the exclusive rights in the home market to the foreign firm's stock of intellectual property.

Collective action to achieve property rights is a costly endeavor. The cost is specified as:

(4) $C_i = V_i + G_i = V_i(i_i, N_i) + G_i(N_i, w_i)$

where V_i represents the opportunity costs of investment in political influence, G_i represents the organization costs (including information and enforcement costs) of political influence, and $I_i = i_i * N_i$ where i_i is investment in political influence per coalition member. N_i is the number of firms in the coalition, and w_i is a vector of other variables such as group heterogeneity with respect to R&D and exports and the capital intensity of production.

Given investments by one group, optimal investment and coalition sizes of other groups are determined by maximizing net benefits with respect to i_i and N_i. The first order conditions with respect to both choice variables are:

(5) $\dfrac{\partial B_i \partial R}{\partial R \partial I_i} - \dfrac{\partial V_i}{\partial I_i} = 0; \quad i = hi, hr$

(6) $\dfrac{\partial B_i \partial R}{\partial R \partial I} i_i - \dfrac{\partial V_i}{\partial I_i} i_i - \dfrac{\partial G_i}{\partial N_i} = 0$

Solution of the two first order conditions produces optimal N* and I* for each of the three interest groups. As the parameters in each group's cost and benefit functions change over time, they induce different levels of investment in political influence by each group, and thereby affect the strength of IPRs.

A country in the early stages of development is likely to have weak IPRs. A typical manufacturing firm is imitating technologies from developed countries, is unlikely to be undertaking much R&D, and is exporting only a small share of its output. Since there is a small number of firms, organization costs are low, and effective coalitions are likely to form. Moreover, foreign manufacturers are unlikely to be particularly concerned about the use of their technologies in such small markets. As development proceeds, the agricultural sector declines, and the manufacturing sector gains a larger share of GNP. With their increasing numbers, the political power of manufacturing firms grows; at some point increasing numbers of imitative firms lead to more free-riding by individual firms and a decline in political influence. Research and development activities by domestic manufacturing firms increase and more "original" products and production processes begin to be produced by the country's manufacturers. Moreover, foreign pressure on the developing country to respect international standards of IPRs grows as manufacturing exports of "imitation" goods increase. These changes in the model's parameters realign the political equilibrium and lead to the establishment of more rigorous IPRs.

The transition to a regime of stronger IPRs may, however, occur later than would be optimal in an income-maximizing model. Several factors contribute to this result. First, heterogeneity between home firms engaging in R&D increases organization costs for these firms and thereby reduces their political influence. Second, the political influence of home firms imitating foreign technologies somewhat off-sets the political influence of home and foreign firms favoring stronger IPRs. This opposition to stronger IPRs is only overcome when para-meters have reached higher levels; the net effect is to delay the adoption date for stronger IPRs. Finally, foreign threats to retaliate may not be credible until foreign countries have organized to prevent a "reshuffling" of international trade flows. Such organization is costly and may not occur until imitation of foreign technologies has reached critically high levels.

The model outlined above is based on the relative power of various groups of manufacturing firms. The incentives of agricultural firms should also be considered, as they dominate the economy during the early stages of development. Their large role in the economy may lead to weak intellectual property rights due to the low value of the patent system in this sector. *Many process innovations in agriculture are unpatentable, whereas a larger percentage of process inventions in industry are patentable.* A new pattern of plowing a field, an innovation in the manner in which a crop is harvested, a change in the timing of weeding, and a new method of irrigating fields are clearly unpatentable innovations which will quickly spread to some other farms. New plants can be stolen by rivals from the fields, farmhands skilled in new farming methods can be hired away, and observations by neighbors (in areas with small plots) are all techniques used by rivals to expropriate new innovations. Returns from capital-intensive in-ventions may be easier to appropriate, but are also less important for the labor-intensive agricultural sector. The agricultural economics literature has numerous articles arguing for the need for public research and development in agriculture given the difficulty of appropriating the returns from innovations.

Thus establishment of a patent system in a developing country would only affect a small proportion of the country's output, whereas in an industrialized country a larger percentage of total output would be affected by the imposition of the patent system. Cursory support for this notion is provided by the relatively late development of formal patent systems in industrialized countries. Thus another rationale for the lack of strong patent laws in developing countries may be that it does not pay to set up a patent system given the relatively small number of patents that would be generated by the small industrial sector. The free-riding by the industrial sector on foreign patents reinforces this tendency.

The relationship between the agricultural sector and patent law could be due to either rationale presented above or to other factors not investigated in this analysis. The source of the deficiency is of more than academic interest because depending on which scenario presented above is correct, *establishment of a strong patent system may harm or help the country.* If the efficiency rationale is correct, i.e., it does not pay to have a strong patent system until the agricultural sector becomes a smaller part of the economy, then international pressure on developing countries to establish strong patent systems may harm the country in both the long run and the short run. On the other hand, if political forces are determining the state of patent law, then international pressure on developing countries to establish strong patent systems may harm the manufacturing sector in the short run, yet help the overall economy in the short and long run. International pressure would then allow the country to overcome structural inefficiencies generated by interest group politics.

Judd and Evenson (1986) have emphasized the possibility for reforms in developing countries' patent systems to stimulate new innovations in agriculture.[24] Their data on private sector research spending indicate that firms in developing countries in Asia devote few resources to agricultural research. They conclude that "the private sector in South Korea, Malaysia, Taiwan, and surprisingly, Japan, is of minor importance" in developing new agricultural technology.[25] They note that private firms play a major role in developing new agricultural technology in industrialized countries, as expenditures on research by agricultural enterprises are approximately equal to expenditures made by the public sector.

Evenson and Judd further argue that the patent system in developing countries can be structured to encourage *adaptions* of foreign technology to local circumstances. They observe that "the technological opportunity for types of inventions is heavily biased toward biogenetic inventions and against mechanical/electrical inventions in developing countries; yet biogenetic inventions have not been afforded patent protection in developing countries."[26] In accordance with this observation, we note that ASEAN countries have relatively low levels of annual patents for agricultural inventions. From 1969-1972, Malaysia had 14.0 annual agricultural patents (AAP) and the Philippines 43.7 AAP. This compares unfavorably with the 417.5 AAP generated by Switzerland, Sweden's 185 AAP, Austria's 327 AAP or Australia's 133.5 AAP over the same period.

One way to stimulate domestic agricultural inventions without badly disrupting the international patent system is to develop a weaker patent covering adaptations of agricultural inventions. The Philippines issues just such a patent, often known as a "utility model patent." Predominantly granted to nationals, it provides protection to the first person discovering an invention; the requirement that the invention be novel is less rigorous than the standard patent requirement. Thus utility patents may be "quite successful in encouraging local adaptive invention."[27] Utility patents enable domestic firms to make minor modifications to farm machinery and capture some of the resulting rents. Without the utility patents, rents from the improvements on machinery produced with foreign patents would be captured by the foreign firm, thereby reducing domestic incentives to make modifications to "inappropriate technology." Such patents may stimulate R&D in developing countries without markedly affecting the capture of rents by foreign patent holders.

Conclusion

The basic problem with uniform standards for establishing and enforcing IPRs across international boundaries is easy to formulate. If the optimal standard of protection were to be adopted by all countries, world economic growth would increase in the long run, while in the short run some countries would gain and others would lose. Given the short time horizons of most governments, it is not surprising that short-run considerations often dominate policy considerations at the expense of long run economic growth.

In this case the dismal science's analysis of IPRs in developing countries does contain several rays of optimism. We observed that low levels of IPR protection may be due to low capital/labor ratios, to the importance of agriculture in the economy, to cumbersome and slow-acting legal systems, and, finally, to the mix of industries in developing countries. As developing nations accumulate capital, develop new manufacturing industries, reduce the proportion of the GNP derived from agriculture, and improve the efficiency of institutions governing law enforcement and dispute adjudication, IPRs should become stronger due to the decline of groups opposing stronger IPRs.

Pressuring developing governments into establishing stronger IPRs is a perilous game. It matters greatly how threatened sanctions affect interest groups supporting and opposing the government, as the government response to the external pressure depends on how the political equilibrium is affected. In addition, whether the stronger IPRs harm or help the economy in the short run and in the long run is a critical determinant of the government's response. Surely it is easier for a government to survive pressures from interest groups when the economy is expanding rather than contracting after increased property rights protection is imposed. A country reaching intermediate stages of development (such as South Korea) may experience welfare gains when it adopts stricter IPRs, while a country in the early stages of development (such as Indonesia) may experience welfare losses when it strengthens its IPRs. It is, therefore, important for the U.S. government to consider carefully the effects on the foreign economy before it pushes for increased protection. Stronger IPRs may not serve U.S. interests if they undermine otherwise stable, friendly governments.

Notes

*   Comments by Chung Lee, Michael Plummer, and the participants in the 1990 University of Hawaii Conference on Investment Coordination and the 1990 Western Economics Association Meetings were very useful. I am, of course, responsible for all remaining errors.

1   See *Foreign Protection of Intellectual Property Rights and the Effect on U.S. Industry and Trade, Report to the United States Trade Representative, Investigation No. 332-245, Under Section 332(g) of the Tariff Act of 1930,* January, 1988.

2   Mandated by Section 504 of the Trade Act of 1974, as amended in 1984 and 1988.

3   See Rozek (1987). Rozek, unlike most other commentators, argues that it is in the interest of developing countries to enact legislation providing strong protection for intellectual property rights.

4   See Coase (1960) and Cheung (1974).

5   See Arnott and Stiglitz (1986) for a discussion and application of the concept of "constrained efficiency."

6   Suppose the provider of the invention is compensated by a fixed a fixed fee and/or royalty paid by the state while users of the invention pay a zero price. The additional taxes imposed to compensate the inventor generate deadweight losses. Efficient taxes are set to maximize the gains from new product development minus the deadweight losses from the tax. This system restricts property rights in inventions by reducing payments to inventors to limit the deadweight loss from taxation. A user charge generates deadweight losses due to restricted use of the product. We assume no price discrimination in the user charges.

7   See Nordhaus (1969), Nordhaus (1972), and Scherer (1972). The traditional theory of optimal patent life has been challenged during the 1980s. Novos and Waldman (1984) and Johnson (1985) have identified a second cost resulting from strong protection. When protection is set at high levels and producers are able to charge monopoly prices, the consumer will spend up to the monopoly price to secretly copy the product. This means that illegal copies of the product or literary work may be produced at a higher cost than would be incurred by the patentholder. These additional costs should be considered in any normative discussion of optimal patent lives.

8   This feature of intellectual property rights systems is important, as one alternative to establishing publicly defined property rights is to maintain an innovative production process as a trade secret. Secret production processes provide de facto property rights to their inventors, but they provide fewer incentives to outside inventors to improve on the process. Since maintaining a process as a trade secret is often more costly than establishing intellectual property rights, firms can find it in their interest to patent new processes rather than to protect them as trade secrets. Of course, public knowledge concerning the particulars of the process may spur competition in the development of competing processes and reduce the useful lifespan of the process. An innovating firm takes this factor into account when it decides whether to maintain the process as a trade secret or apply for a patent. See Cheung (1982) for a good discussion of the economics of trade secrets. Cheung makes the important point that it is difficult to provide legal protection for trade secrets, as it is not known exactly what is being protected. He urges (p. 52) policymakers to concentrate on "refining of criteria for drafting and enforcing patent claims so that recourse to the trade secret option may be reduced."

9   See Berkowitz and Kotowitz (1982).

10   See Penrose (1951) for an early statement of this view.

11   International Convention for the Protection of Industrial Property (Paris Convention), March 20, 1883, 25 Stat.1372, T.S. No. 379, as revised, at Brussels on Dec. 14, 1900, 32 Stat. 1936, T.S. No. 411, at Washington on June 2, 1911, 38 Stat. 1645, T.S. No. 579 at the Hague on Nov. 6, 1925, 47

Stat. 1789, T.S. No. 834, 74 L.N.T.S. 289, at London on June 2, 1934, 53 Stat. 1748, T.S. No. 941, 192 L.N.T.S. 17, at Lisbon on Oct. 31, 1958, [1962], 13 U.S.T. 1, T.I.A.S. No. 4931, at Stockholm on July 14, 1967, [1970], 21 U.S.T. 1583 and 24 U.S.T. 2140, T.I.A.S. Nos. 6923 and 7727 [hereinafter Paris Convention].

12   See Cornish (1983) for a good discussion of the influence of the Paris Convention.
13   Paris Convention, article 5A(1). See also Cornish, pp. 174-5.
14   Paris Convention, article 5A.
15   Berne Convention for the Protection of Literary and Artistic Works of Sept. 9, 1886, completed at Paris on May 4, 1896, revised at Berlin on November 13, 1908, completed at Berne on March 20, 1914, and revised at Rome on June 2, 1928, at Brussels on June 26, 1948, at Stockholm on July 14, 1967, and at Paris on July 24, 1971, effective July 10, 1974.
16   See Berkowitz and Kotowitz (1982).
17   Berkowitz and Kotowitz (1982), p. 16.
18   Both parties will consider the effect on their own welfare rather than on the parties' joint welfare.
19   See Waterson (1990).
20   See Levin, et al. (1987) at Table 2, p. 797.
21   See Hicks (1932) pp 131ff for a classic discussion of technological change and capital/labor ratios. Other important articles include Hicks (1953), Findlay and Grubert (1959), and Kemp (1964). See Kawagoe, Otsuka, and Hayami (1986), for a modern application of Hicks' theories of technical change.
22   See Stigler (1971), Peltzman (1976), and Becker (1983).
23   Balisacan and Roumasset (1987) and Gardner (1985).
24   Judd and Evenson (1986).
25   Judd and Evenson (1986), p. 178.
26   Judd and Evenson (1986), p. 195.
27   Judd and Evenson (1986), p. 181.

References

Arnott, R., and J. E. Stiglitz. 1986. "Moral Hazard and Optimal Commodity Taxation." *Journal of Public Economics* 29: 1-24.
Balisacan, A. M., and J. A. Roumasset. 1987. "Public Choice of Economic Policy: The Growth of Agricultural Protection." *Weltwirtschaftliches Archives* 123: 232-48.
Becker, G. 1983. "A Theory of Competition Among Pressure Groups for Political Influence." *Quarterly Journal of Economics* 98: 371-400.
Berkowitz, M. K., and Y. Kotowitz. 1982. "Patent Policy in an Open Economy." *Canadian Journal of Economics* 15: 1-17.
Cheung, S. N. S. 1982. "Property Rights in Trade Secrets." *Economic Inquiry* 20: 40-53.

Coase, R. 1960. "The Problem of Social Cost." *Journal of Law & Economics* 1: 1-44.

Cooter, R., and T. Ulen. 1988. *Law and Economics.* Glenview, Illinois: Scott, Foresman & Co.

Cornish, W. 1983. "Patents and Innovation in the Commonwealth." *Adelaide Law Review* 9: 173-190.

Demsetz, H. 1966. "Some Aspects of Property Rights." *Journal of Law & Economics* 9: 61-70.

Findlay, R., and H. Grubert. 1959. "Factor Intensities, Technological Progress, and International Trade." *Oxford Economic Papers* 11: 111-121.

Gardner, B. 1985. "Causes of U.S. Farm Commodity Programs." *Journal of Political Economy* 95: 290-310.

Gould, J. M. 1987. "Protecting Owners of U.S. Process Patents from the Importation of Pharmaceuticals Made Abroad by Use of the Patented Process: Current Options, Proposed Legislation, and a GATT Solution." *Food Drug Cosmetic Law Journal* 42: 346-64.

Hicks, J. R. 1953. "An Inaugural Lecture." *Oxford Economic Papers* 5: 117-135.

_____. 1932. *The Theory of Wages.* London: Macmillan.

Johnson, W. R. 1985. "The Economics of Copying." *Journal of Political Economy* 93: 945-57.

Judd, M. A., and R. E. Evenson. 1986. "Resources for the Production of Agricultural Growth in Pacific Basin Region," in G. Edward Schuh and Jennifer L. McCoy, eds., *Food, Agriculture, and Development in the Pacific Basin.* Boulder: Westview Press.

Kawagoe, T., K. Otsuka, and Y. Hayami. 1986. "Induced Bias of Technical Change in Agriculture: The United State and Japan, 1880-1980." *Journal of Political Economy* 94: 523-44.

Kemp, M. C. 1964. *The Pure Theory of International Trade.* Englewood Cliffs: Prentice-Hall.

Levin, R. C., A. K. Klevorick, R. R. Nelson, and S. G. Winter. 1987. "Appropriating the Returns from Industrial Research and Development." *Brookings Papers on Economic Activity.* Pp. 783-831.

Miller, M. W. 1987. "Pressing Issue: Publishers Mobilize to Foil Revision of Copyright Law." *The Wall Street Journal* 3: 35.

Nagara, B. 1988. "Intellectual Property Legislation: Direction for the Pied Piper." Presented at the "US-ASEAN Trade: Current Issues & Future Strategies" sessions of the Malaysian Association for American Studies Regional Seminar.

Nordhaus, W. D. 1969. *Invention, Growth and Welfare: A Theoretical Treatment of Technological Change.* Cambridge, Mass.: MIT Press.

_____. 1972. "The Optimal Life of a Patent: Reply." *American Economic Review* 62: 428-31.

Novos, I. E., and M. Waldman. 1984. "The Effects of Increased Copyright Protection: An Analytic Approach." *Journal of Political Economy* 92: 236-46.

Peltzman, S. 1976. "Toward a More General Theory of Regulation." *Journal of Law & Economics* 19: 211-40.

Penrose, E. 1951. *The Economics of the International Patent System.* Baltimore: John Hopkins Press.

Rozek, R. P. 1987. "Protection of Intellectual Property Rights: Research and Development Decisions and Economic Growth." *Contemporary Policy Issues* 5: 54-65.

Scherer, F. M. 1972. "Nordhaus' Theory of Optimal Patent Life: A Geometric Reinterpretation." *American Economic Review* 62: 422-7.

Stigler, G. 1971. "The Economic Theory of Regulation." *Bell Journal of Economics* 2: 3-21.

Waterson, M. 1990. "The Economics of Product Patents." *American Economic Review* 80: 860-69.

6

The Role of Financial Institutions in Industrial Restructuring and Investment Coordination: The Implications for Certain ASEAN Developing Countries

*Ira W. Lieberman**

Industrial Restructuring: A Worldwide Phenomenon

Industrial restructuring has become a worldwide phenomenon, albeit with differing emphases across regions and countries. In the EEC countries, many industrial subsectors are preparing for the liberalization and union scheduled for 1992, at the same time that they are having to adapt to changes in technology and industry practices. Industrial restructuring and privatization are major themes in the Eastern bloc countries, which at the same time face the additional challenge of making the transition to more market-based economies. The United States is having to respond to the decline in its industrial competitiveness, one answer to which is industrial restructuring. Assailed by the oil crisis and then the related debt crisis, many Latin American countries are attempting to move from inward-looking, import-substitution strategies toward outward-looking development and sustained export growth. This process is necessitating massive restructuring, particularly of the large, state-owned enterprises (SOEs). As Peter Drucker (1989) notes, the trend of industrial restructuring is likely to continue throughout the 1990s: ". . . businesses will undergo more and more radical restructuring in the 1990s than at any time since the modern corporate organization first evolved in the 1920s."

In Asia, industrial restructuring has been taking place in two distinct groups of countries. First, Japan and the newly industrializing countries (NICs) -- Korea, Hong Kong, Taiwan and Singapore -- are actively "offshoring" their manufacturing operations to countries in ASEAN such as Malaysia, Thailand and Indonesia. Their aim is to offset their own rising labor costs, the scarcity of labor, the appreciation of their currencies and the trade barriers confronting traditional industries such as textiles.

The second group consists of the next-in-line NICs in ASEAN -- Malaysia, Thailand, Indonesia and the Philippines. (Singapore and Brunei are also members of ASEAN, but this chapter focuses on the four developing countries listed above.)   These next-in-line NICs are currently attempting to absorb the large inflow of direct foreign investment (DFI) from their successful neighbors without falling into their spheres of influence.

Several factors are critical to the success of the above group of ASEAN countries in restructuring their industry sectors. One is a world trade environment that is open and receptive to their exports. In its absence, efforts to promote regional trade liberalization in Southeast Asia, or, in a broader context, the Pacific Rim, will become particularly meaningful. Second is sound macroeconomic management, particularly in terms of controlling the inflationary pressure that will emerge as their economies grow rapidly and of maintaining a realistic exchange rate regime that permits an increase in manufacturing exports.   Third is liberalization of their financial sectors and a deepening of their capital markets.

The next section provides some background on industrial restructuring, specifically, why it has emerged as an important trend worldwide, how it is defined and the economic arguments pro and con restructuring.   Section III looks at investments in industrial restructuring in the last decade, while the following section discusses the importance of the financial sector to the success of industrial restructuring.   Investment coordination in the next-in-line NICs in ASEAN is addressed in the last section, along with the edge that these countries have over other developing nations.

An Overview of Recent Industrial Restructuring

Why Has Industrial Restructuring Become So Important?

The common answer to why industrial restructuring has become so important is that the oil crises and resulting debt crises triggered a need for it. In the case of Latin American and certain Asian states that adjusted too slowly to the debt crisis, this explanation may hold true (Lee 1983). It is the author's view, however, that restructuring would have emerged even without these crises, although perhaps more slowly, because of several factors. A key one is the successful economic performance of Japan, Korea and the Asian Tigers in the 1980s. Despite significant differences in their domestic economies, all followed a non-traditional economic model for growth characterized by an outward orientation that emphasized exports and international competitiveness (World Bank 1987), a model that differed fundamentally from prior ones. In the light of their success and the failure of the traditional economic models, much of the rest of the world is seeking to emulate their success, a process that requires significant industrial restructuring.

A second factor is the emergence in the 1980s of what some analysts are calling the fourth industrial revolution. Driven by information technology, this industrial revolution involves non-smokestack industries such as telecommunications, robotics, computers, fiber optics and micro-electronics. With the emergence of these industries and their widespread effect on all other industrial sectors, managerial practices have emerged that are having a profound impact on how business is done. Examples are "total quality control," "just on time" distribution and inventory management systems, and integrated manufacturing systems (Hoffman 1989). While a number of these technological advances first appeared in the United States, it has been Japan, followed quickly by the Asian NICs, that have advanced the state of the art in how best to apply these practices to industry to increase efficiency and competitiveness.

Finally, at the same time that the model for growth of Japan and the Asian Tigers was proving so successful, there was a recognition that other economic models have been failures. Most dramatic has been the collapse of central planning or command economies. Similarly, there has been a general failure of the import substitution-oriented, protectionist model widely pursued by most developing countries in Latin America and Africa and even some Asian ones. (Examples in East Asia are the Philippines, Indonesia and Malaysia, while India provides a very clear example of the failure of such policies in Asia overall.)

A particular weakness of the inward-oriented model is that it incorporates a perversion of the infant industry argument. Developing countries, once having established "strategic" basic industries such as steel, cement, fertilizers and petrochemicals, often through state monopolies and virtually always with state subsidies, concluded that they then had to protect them because they were too fragile and uncompetitive to expose to world markets or import competition. In contrast, competitiveness, and therefore the presence of competition, are basic premises of industrial restructuring. As C. R. Frischtak, a Brazilian economist, explains (1989),

> Developing countries should use competition as a powerful tool of industrial policy. . . competition is required if countries are to move beyond the initial stages of industrialization. As Japan and other successful East Asian countries have shown, stimulating domestic producers to compete at home and in international markets is the key to helping firms mature technologically and managerially.

These various models have failed in part because they have been too slow to respond to the debt crisis, to the competitive challenge of Japan and the other Asian NICs, and to the new technological and managerial thrusts in the world economy.

What Is Industrial Restructuring?

As used here, industrial restructuring refers to actions by enterprises to bridge the gaps between their current performance and what is required to become or remain internationally competitive. These gaps have emerged as a result of global changes in technology, organization, marketing, factor prices, competition, etc. Changes in policy, regulation and institutions also prompt firms to restructure so as to improve their competitiveness. Restructuring is said to have occurred when a firm, subsector or industry has shifted to a product mix and cost structure that are currently competitive and have positioned themselves dynamically to remain competitive in the foreseeable future. Restructuring can involve a shift of resources within enterprises as well as between enterprises, subsectors, sectors and countries. In market-based economies, restructuring at the enterprise level normally occurs naturally in the form of corporate Darwinism. That is, only the strongest, most competitive firms survive; the others are acquired or merged or go bankrupt and are liquidated. In these economies, which have clear processes for exit, this evolutionary process is ongoing. However, at times the social and political ramifications of large-scale industrial failure can be such that even in these economies government supports the restructuring. Examples at the enterprise level are numerous -- Chrysler Corporation (United States), British Steel (United Kingdom), AEG (Federal Republic of Germany) and Dome Petroleum (Canada) -- as well as at the subsector level -- the ship-building industry in Japan and numerous other countries, the steel, petrochemical and synthetic fiber industries in the EEC, and the steel and automobile industries in the United States.

In developing countries, restructuring at the enterprise level may not take place automatically in response to changes in macroeconomic policy or rapid shifts in global conditions. The primary reason is policy distortions. In such cases, an active program at the subsector level to promote industrial restructuring may be necessary. To be successful, however, these programs need to be pursued within a framework of sound macroeconomic policy and an environment that fosters competition (Lieberman 1989b).

In Asia, those countries whose governments have intervened excessively in their economies -- specifically, the Philippines, Malaysia and Indonesia -- have had to implement restructuring programs. In Malaysia, for example, industrial restructuring is proceeding under the auspices of an Industrial Master Plan (IMP), consisting of a set of indicative plans for various subsectors of the economy within the context of the country's overall industrial development policy. The restructuring program focuses on three subsectors -- textiles, industrial machinery and equipment, and wood-based industries. The government has established an Industrial Adjustment Fund[1] to support the restructuring of these industries, once the government and the private sector reach consensus on such matters as required changes in policy, investments, training and institutional support. Other industries are to be included in the program as it proceeds.

The restructuring program is also linked to government efforts to restructure, privatize and "corporatize" various SOEs such as Perwaja Steel. In addition, the government has adopted an Industrial Technology Development Action Plan for its Sixth Plan that is meant to improve Malaysia's competitive position in emerging technologies, many of which cut across traditional industry boundaries.

These three tracks -- subsector restructuring, SOE restructuring and privatization, and technology development -- all of which stress increased reliance on private sector initiatives, are designed to modernize an industrial sector developed around the traditional model of excessive protection, import substitution and reliance on SOEs to develop basic industries such as steel.

Two other next-in-line NICs, the Philippines and Indonesia, are in the process of developing similar but unique programs. In other countries in Asia, restructuring is occurring naturally. In Korea, for example, the major conglomerates, or *chaebol*, have for the most part been responsible for the country's rapid economic growth. In the process, however, they have become dangerously overextended as Korea's currency has appreciated, labor costs have risen and debt has come to exceed their equity by four to five times. According to *The Economist* (Dec. 9, 1989), "These groups know that the great days of unhindered expansion are behind them. To survive in world markets, they must restructure fast."

The Economic Arguments Pro and Con Restructuring

There are strong economic arguments for and against industrial restructuring. The main point made by those opposing restructuring (bolstered recently by the failure of the interventionist, centrally planned and import-substitution/inward-directed economic models) is that restructuring involves targeting, or the picking of winners and losers. It is seen as a form of intervention, which is unacceptable to the free market school of economists. Instead, they call for getting the prices right, liberalizing trade and allowing free market competition. Perhaps the outstanding example of a country outside of Asia that has pursued this type of reform is Chile, which now has a blossoming market-based economy, achieved, however, only after a wrenching adjustment. Poland is attempting a similar "cold shower" approach, but it intends, unlike Chile, to provide restructuring support for industry.

The classical argument in favor of restructuring is to redress widespread market failure. A second argument, an extension of the first, is to alleviate the negative political and social consequences of that failure. This rationale is applied in particular where restructuring might result in regionally concentrated layoffs in a dominant industry such as mining or steel.

A third argument involves the large-scale SOEs that dominate basic sectors of developing countries. Often these SOEs are so important that their performance adversely affects downstream industries dependent on their inputs as a source of supply (Lieberman 1989b). The preferred route in dealing with this situation is privatization, although there are also strong arguments against private monopolies. SOE restructuring may be used to prepare for privatization or to provide a transitional period in which the enterprise is operated under a program of corporatization, i.e., autonomously, without ministerial intervention, with its future to be determined based on its efficiency. Malaysia illustrates one such approach: it established a restructuring unit in the Treasury that is trying to turn the major loss-making enterprises owned by the state around. The goal is eventually to privatize these enterprises either entirely or partially through market flotations. As an interim step, a number of these enterprises are currently being corporatized.

A fourth case where government-sponsored restructuring is deemed appropriate involves "strategic" or "priority" subsectors in developing countries that are consuming scarce government budgetary resources in the form of subsidies and unilateral transfers and that have added substantially to government deficits. It is here where the infant industry argument has been turned on its head, with governments protecting ossified industry structures. A prime example is automotive assembly operations, historically viewed as a driver of economic development. These industries generally need to be down-sized to liberate scarce economic resources.

A case in point is the Malaysian automotive assembly industry, established based on the importation of knock-down kits (CKD units). In 1985, 11 independent assemblers were serving the small domestic market. The National Car Program, which initiated production of the Proton Saga under a joint venture between the Malaysian government and Mitsubishi, has since forced a number out of business. It is clear, however, that the industry must be further rationalized.

A fifth case for government support for restructuring is as a transitional strategy. This strategy is particularly appropriate in centrally planned economies to prevent backsliding in the adjustment effort and to counter the political and social forces that might try to derail the process. Key issues here are the tricky tasks of managing inflation and unemployment while making progress on industrial reform (World Bank 1989). On the other hand, in the case of the East European countries, there is a strong argument for doing as little restructuring as possible under government auspices. Several of these countries (Poland, Czechoslovakia and Romania) have programs for large-scale privatization to accelerate the conversion to more market-based private economies.

Investment in Restructuring

Early projects (1982-1985) involving industrial restructuring in developing countries focused on plant rehabilitation in response to the poor operating performance of manufacturing firms. These projects were a natural extension of the traditional "greenfield" project. If the projects addressed policy issues at all, typically the emphasis was on raising prices to some economic or shadow price that would permit the enterprises to earn a financial profit and avoid decapitalizing. It is generally recognized that for the most part these projects failed because they focused almost exclusively on physical rehabilitation (Lieberman 1989).

By 1985-86 it had become clear that effective restructuring involved all aspects of a firm's operations and that, to succeed, restructuring projects had to be broader in scope. First and foremost, the policy environment needed to provide sound, stable macroeconomic management, while trade and industrial policy had to be liberalized to allow competition (Frischtak 1989).

Second, eligible investments needed to be more diversified. For convenience, the types of investments can be categorized as: (i) hardware; (ii) software, or managerial change; and (iii) financial engineering. In the case of the World Bank, hardware investments were its traditional focus because of its historical support for greenfield projects. Plant rehabilitation or engineering assistance are examples of hardware investments in restructuring projects.

Increasingly important are management-related investments, such as export promotion and marketing; applied research and development; upgrading of distribution and just on time delivery systems; process controls; CAD/CAM and integrated manufacturing systems; and total quality control. (These are just a few of the managerial initiatives that have emerged over the last 10 years [Hoffman 1989].) As product differentiation, movement up the value-added chain, quality and service, and timely delivery to world markets become the most important considerations in competitiveness, related investments are being emphasized. The competitive gap between best practices in the OECD and developing countries is the greatest in these areas.

Also important is support for financial restructuring, or financial engineering. Here the thrust has been to reduce the burden of overleveraged firms through a variety of financial instruments and engineering techniques, such as: debt/equity conversions; maturity extensions; debt consolidations; constant amortization; quasi-equity instruments such as convertibles, or debentures with warrants; and debt/equity swaps. At the subsector level, mergers, acquisitions, divestitures, liquidations and privatizations have been required to change the structure and characteristics of industries.

Restructuring and the Financial Sector

Until recently, there has been an implicit assumption in industrial lending for development that the industrial sector could be strengthened despite the weak financial intermediaries and thin or non-existent capital markets. It is now known that restructuring requires a strong and diverse financial sector -- investment banks, commercial banks, venture capital firms and capital markets -- because of the heterogeneous and extensive financing requirements.

Unfortunately, strengthening of the financial sector has lagged terribly in most developing countries. In many of them, the industrial development banks are insolvent, following years of loans and investments that were politically motivated. These banks have typically held a quasi-monopoly on intermediate and long-term financing. Further, they have offered directed credits at subsidized rates of interest to specific target groups. Their portfolios often hold an abundance of credits to or investments in SOEs, many of which will never be able to repay them.

Restructuring, privatizing or liquidating these SOEs is an important step in reducing the distortions created by government-supported or directed lending to industry. One such program is underway at the Development Bank of the Philippines (Vuylsteke 1988) and another at the Instituto de Fomento Industrial (IFI) in Colombia. At the same time, commercial banks in developing countries have tended to make only short-term loans with very stiff collateral requirements. Because the commercial banks have been protected from entry by transnational banks into the domestic market, they are behind in terms of modern banking practices. In essence, they are the mirror image of their industrial counterparts in developing countries.

Similarly, until recently these countries have placed relatively little emphasis on strengthening their capital markets. Over the last decade, the International Finance Corporation (IFC), the arm of the World Bank that lends to the private sector, has had a program aimed at emerging capital markets.

A recent World Bank report has brought this issue into the open, claiming that under present economic conditions industrial development cannot succeed without strong financial intermediaries, financial sector reform and robust capital markets (World Bank 1989b). For the foreseeable future, World Bank restructuring projects will be inextricably linked to financial sector reform and liberalization. In this area, some of the next-in-line NICs in ASEAN appear to have an advantage over their counterparts, for example, in Latin America (Cho and Khatkhate 1989).

Implications for Next-In-Line ASEAN NICs: Industrial Restructuring and Investment Cooperation

The Trade Environment

As noted, an open world trade environment is crucial to restructuring. Moreover, trade liberalization is potentially an important component of policy reform for developing countries seeking to modernize their industrial sector (Thomas, et al. 1990; Papageorgiou, et al. 1990) and promote exports. Many analysts believe, however, that trade will be subject to increasing protectionism in the United States and Europe. They have, for example, described the result of the economic unification or liberalization of the EEC as "fortress" Europe. The protectionism in both the United States and Europe is a reaction to their loss of competitiveness vis-à-vis Asia, particularly Japan, but also the Tigers and Korea.

Another strong trend has been the setting up of trading blocs and spheres of influence. This trend is also true for monetary activities and capital markets. One emerging bloc centers around North America and the U.S. dollar, as evidenced by, for example, the U.S. -- Canadian Free Trade Agreement and the U.S. -- Mexico trade agreement. It has recently been agreed that Canada and Mexico will also negotiate around trade liberalization to create a North American free trade zone. In addition, Miami has become the informal capital market for flight capital from the region.

The European bloc will center around the EEC, the European Monetary Union and the ECU. The EEC already has extensive reciprocal trade agreements with its neighbors in EFTA; countries such as Turkey are pressing for full membership. Europe's dilemma now is how to assist East Europe while moving ahead with its own integration. At the same time, East Europe is a natural trade and investment market for Western Europe, and more formal economic ties are only a question of time and a matter of how best to proceed. Although a vague concept now, there is already talk within Europe of creating an economic and political unit known as the "European Space."

A third bloc is found in Asia, with Japan at its center, Korea and the Tigers posing economic competition and the ASEAN group seeking to attract their investments, technology and economic support without being swallowed up. (The large South Asian nations -- India, Pakistan and Bangladesh -- are not dealt with here, as their developmental problems are of a different magnitude.) While China will likely develop in autarky for the moment, its impact on Hong Kong and possibly on Taiwan and its potentially destabilizing role in the region are of critical importance. Moreover, China's potential for attracting large-scale investments from Japan and the Tigers while serving as a center of comparative labor advantage is an important consideration related to future development in the region.

Drucker (1989) has commented on this phenomenon of trading blocs:

> Economic relations will increasingly be between trading blocks rather than between countries. Indeed an East Asian Block loosely organized around Japan and paralleling the EC and North America may emerge during the decade. Relationships will therefore increasingly be conducted through bilateral and trilateral deals in respect both of investment and trade.

Drucker warns, however, that reciprocity can easily degenerate into protectionism of the worst kind. This situation arose in the interwar years when, following the start of the Depression and the failure of the World Economic Conference, trade and monetary relationships formed into blocs -- the Sterling Bloc, the Gold Bloc and the Dollar Bloc -- while economic and military powers such as Germany, Russia and Japan functioned autarkicly, outside the world economy (Kindleberger 1973; Arndt 1944). In fact, managed trade or non-tariff trade barriers have become important obstacles to continued export penetration by the Asian countries, particularly the developing ones of ASEAN (World Bank 1987; Naya, et al. 1989a; Naya, et al. 1989b).

One current trade pattern is clearly problematic: the triangular relationship in which the United States is the taker of last resort of the world's goods and services, with serious consequences for its balance of payments and external debt, and Japan is America's banker. This relationship is inherently unstable, given its strong susceptibility to a downturn in the U.S. or world economies.

The Edge of the ASEAN NICs

Within this shifting and difficult economic environment, the Asian and next-in-line ASEAN NICs have some real advantages over other developing countries:

- Relatively good macroeconomic management has allowed them to develop within a reasonably stable economic framework.
- Their export promotion strategies have been based on the maintenance of a competitive exchange rate.
- Domestic resource mobilization and a relatively high savings rate have permitted them to sustain relatively high levels of investment and to develop their capacity to supply a diversified bundle of export goods.
- For the most part, they have maintained a favorable climate toward DFI and technology transfer.
- These countries have minimized trade and industrial policy distortions and thus have been able to achieve more efficient investment and production, less "rent-seeking" behavior and a low level of export bias, conditions that are rarely found under protectionist trade regimes. Countries that suffer from such policy distortions, such as Indonesia and the Philippines, have performed poorly relative to their neighbors.
- The export success of these countries has created a high degree of openness and exposure to world markets that in turn has led to a more flexible response to changing economic circumstances.
- Exports have been encouraged with successful incentive structures and export promotion programs.
- Finally, there has been a noteworthy lack of bias against agriculture.[2]

Based on a variety of objective measurements -- GNP growth, shares in world exports, shares in world gross domestic product and manufacturing valued added -- it is clear the Asian NICs, including the next-in-line ones (except the Philippines), have benefited greatly from their economic policies. They have outperformed the NICs in Latin America and Europe and the large South Asian economies. The exception is the Philippines, whose economy, which resembles that of the Latin American NICs, has clearly lagged (Dahlman 1989).

The Financial Sector

Financial Liberalization -- The Banking Sector. A recent World Bank study compares the experience with financial liberalization of five Asian countries -- Korea, Malaysia, Sri Lanka, the Philippines and Indonesia -- and the major Latin American countries. It concludes that the Asian countries that have undertaken liberalization measures have clearly outperformed those that have not. Korea, Malaysia and Sri Lanka are cited as successful performers, the Philippines as largely a failure and Indonesia as a mixed case (Cho and Khatkhate 1989).[3]

The World Bank's 1989 *World Development Report*, which focuses on the financial sectors in developing countries, directly correlates economic growth and investment productivity with the maintenance of positive real interest rates, i.e., interest rates above expected rates of inflation. The Asian developing countries that have maintained positive real interest rates -- Thailand, Malaysia, Korea, Singapore and Sri Lanka -- clearly outperformed those that did not -- Indonesia and the Philippines (World Bank 1989c). Although many other variables can also explain these differences in performance, important lessons derived from the linkage between financial liberalization and the maintenance of positive real interest rates (see Cho and Khatkhate 1989) are discussed below.

Interest rates. An upward adjustment to positive, market-level interest rates, which was an expected outcome of deregulation, occurred, although each country evaluated experienced a unique adjustment.

Financial sector growth. The faster growth of the financial sector was evidence of the beneficial consequences of deregulation. Its expansion has been most rapid when the level of real interest rates has been high and stable. This pattern points to the importance of stable rates of inflation: there is evidence that relative price stability may be as important, or even more important, than liberalization of the banking system. Taiwan and Japan both experienced very rapid growth of their financial sectors while maintaining control over their banking systems.

Competition in the financial sector. Competition increased perceptibly following liberalization.

Term credit. The availability of long-term credit increased in Korea but not in Indonesia and the Philippines. In Indonesia the reason was the volatility of interest rates, in the Philippines the fragility of the banking sector and the political instability. In Malaysia, maturities on deposits and loans increased but only marginally. The conclusion is that development of the capital markets and new financial instruments to attract and provide long-term capital has to take place parallel with financial sector reform.

Intermediation costs. Financial liberalization did not result in lower intermediation costs in the Asian countries. The reason is that a substantial portion of the spread was attributable to high government taxes, reserve requirements (the Philippines) and the burden of selected and directed credit programs (Malaysia, Philippines and Indonesia). The lesson is that liberalization of interest rates and deregulation are insufficient measures if governments maintain selective or directed credit programs, which often lead to highly politicized investment decisions.[4]

Integration of the domestic and foreign financial markets. The consequences of financial reform on the integration of domestic and world market interest rates differed across the countries studied, and not in accord with expectations. Full integration of the rates did not take place even when capital movement was basically free. It appears that access to international sources of funds is a more critical determinant.

Corporate financial structures. Again, the experience was quite diverse. In the Philippines and Indonesia, distress borrowing caused the already high gearing ratios (debt/equity ratio) of corporations to rise even further in the face of deregulation. In Korea, however, the gearing ratio declined following the privatization of the banks and phase-out of selective credit schemes and as a result of the high real interest rates. The government's participation as a risk partner simply declined. In Malaysia, the corporate debt/equity ratio was relatively low and declined somewhat following liberalization.

In conclusion, liberalization of the financial sector in some Asian countries, for example, Korea, has taken place in parallel with the adoption of macroeconomic and industrial policies conducive to dynamic growth and development. Those countries that have failed to eliminate industrial policy barriers, Indonesia and the Philippines being examples, have also failed to liberalize their financial sectors.

Capital Market Development. The formation of capital markets in Asia that are able to meet the heterogeneous demands for investment and trade finance of Asian developing countries is a critical factor in the long-term economic growth of the region. In many ways, the present situation in Asia parallels the nineteenth century experience in Europe. In 1815, London became the world's primary capital market because of its position as the foremost industrial nation. However, as industrialization spread, cities in other countries emerged to compete with London in the export of capital. In those cities, the prominent merchant banks, *hautes banques* and other banks provided long-term industrial financing through the sale of bonds, often working as syndicates. The European capital markets became the primary source for long-term industrial capital both for building infrastructure such as railways and ports and for establishing basic industries. In the case of trade finance, the world drew bills on London. Today, these same capital centers are the heart of the Eurocurrency and Eurobond markets, along with the offshore convenience centers (Lieberman 1989a).

An important trend in the last decade has been the development and deepening of capital markets in Asia, with Tokyo at the center, Hong Kong and Singapore as secondary but well-established markets, and emerging ones in Taiwan, Korea and Malaysia. In the next decade, the continued development and deepening of these markets and the ability of other Asian countries and their enterprises to tap long-term, low-cost capital will provide these nations with a major competitive edge. A critical issue will be the continued liberalization of the Tokyo markets (*The Economist*, Sept. 16, 1989). Given that, historically, relatively few capital markets have emerged during the long process of industrial development (Kindleberger 1978), the formation of capital markets in Asia is a very important, perhaps critical, factor for future economic development in the region. By comparison, at present Latin America has no capital market, with the possible exception of Chile's and Mexico's, that merits serious consideration (I.F.C. 1989).[5]

As Drucker (1989) notes, "Financially, only the Japanese can still afford to go multinational. Their capital costs them around 5% or so. In contrast, European or American companies now pay up to 20% for money." He goes on to say that foreign investments, with their attendant risks, will be particularly affected by these disparities in the cost of capital. In the first half of 1989, for example, Japanese companies raised $65 billion on the Tokyo stock market versus $20 billion for American companies on stock markets in the United States (*The Economist*, Nov. 11, 1989).

Investment Coordination. Given the rapid changes in the global economy, the increasing competition for world markets, the rise in protectionism and the growing reliance of all industrial subsectors on new technologies, a fundamental question is whether it is reasonable to expect the next-in-line NICs to grow and develop similarly to the Tigers and Korea. If so, what opportunities are there for the investment coordination needed to allow this process to happen? As Purcell (1989) observes,

> The traditional product cycle would postulate that the Koreas and the Taiwans of the world will move into the more sophisticated manufacturing pursuits that the industrial countries have

abandoned on their path to services and higher technology, and that second tier NICs will thus have the opportunity to seek comparative advantage in the manufacture and export of the more prosaic products from which NIC success has sprung.

Possible areas of investment coordination include a shift by investors in Japan, Korea or the Asian Tigers to manufacturing operations in the next-in-line NICs in order to remain competitive in the more traditional industry subsectors such as garments and textiles, toys, leather goods and shoes and to reduce the push in the United States for further trade barriers (Purcell 1989). Although in recent years investors in Hong Kong have invested heavily in China, there is evidence of a rapid shift to the next-in-line NICs by Japan, Korea and the Tigers (*The Economist*, June 24, 1989).

Another possibility involves expansion by U.S. investors of their in-bond (807) assembly and processing operations into the next-in-line NICs in order to compete with Japan, Korea and the Tigers. Some analysts are calling this shift the new international division of labor. In principle, it is also possible that the new technologies such as CAD/CAM, (computer-aided design/manufacturing), CIM (computer inventory management) and advanced robotics will produce a relocation of industry back to the United States. This possibility may be accelerated as time-based strategies increasingly take root in U.S. retail and manufacturing operations. However, Castells and D'Andrea Tyson reject the notion that relocation to the "North" will occur. They cite the trend well underway for Japanese firms in more advanced technology industries such as electronics to follow the U.S. lead in redeploying or moving assembly operations offshore (Castells and Tyson 1989).

The most important opportunity for investment coordination is the growing movement toward strategic alliances. It appears that it will be increasingly difficult for developing countries to purchase advance technology as they have in the past (Castells and Tyson 1989). Alliances are one mechanism for doing so. Up to now, most alliances have been between enterprises in the OECD countries, entered into for four basic reasons: (i) sharing of existing technologies; (ii) cost of developing new technologies; (iii) pre-competitive alliances; and (iv) the potential for market access.

Mody (1989) is one who sees alliances in the future:

> . . . strategic alliances among major international firms will influence both the volume and composition of technology flows to developing nations. A significant effort on the part of the next-in-line Newly Industrializing Countries (NICs) and other Less

Developed Countries (LDCs) will be needed if they wish to remain in the technology transfer loops in those industry groups being characterized by rapid technological change.

Rapid adoption of new technologies will, it appears, marginalize the labor cost advantage of many developing countries. The next-in-line NICs that will emerge as economic forces will be those that have a capacity to adapt to new technological conditions. In addition, countries that offer market access have potential for negotiating alliances.

Positive restructuring is oriented toward moving the next-in-line NICs into areas of potential comparative advantage. It is, however, a risky business. Given the time required to effect change in industry, restructuring projects require intermediate-term commitments by government, industry and the financial sector. The World Bank's experience indicates that the most successful approach is a series of restructuring projects over an intermediate time frame (5-8 years), supported by a coherent set of industrial and financial sector policy changes. The various forms of investment coordination discussed above are likely to serve as catalysts for change and will enhance the possibility for successful industrial restructuring.

Notes

* Much of the material is derived from work and research done by the author for the World Bank.

1 The Industrial Adjustment Fund will consist of M$500 million (ringett). It is being offered through the country's industrial development banks under the supervision of the Central Bank, Bank Negara, at interest rates below market levels, specifically, at a fixed 4.5 percent for up to eight years' maturity. A major problem with the fund is its potential distortionary effects as a result of the interest rate subsidy.

2 These points are elaborated on in World Bank (1987:17-19).

3 The authors defined the financial sector as the banking system. Liberalization meant a substantial reduction in government intervention in setting interest rates and allocating credits.

4 Malaysia's Industrial Adjustment Fund, discussed earlier, perpetuates the tendency toward providing highly directed credits, in this case at below market interest rates.

5 During the course of 1991, capital markets in Latin America, particularly Mexico and lately Argentina, have boomed. However, most of these markets are extremely thin and are having trouble supporting the privatization programs underway in these countries. For a discussion of

Latin American capital market development, see *Latin Finance* (1991: 17-19).

References

Arndt, H. W. 1944. *The Economic Lessons of the Nineteen Thirties*. Oxford: Oxford University Press.

Ayub, M. A., and S. O. Hegstad. 1986. *Public Industrial Enterprises -- Determinants of Performance*. Washington, D.C.: The World Bank.

Castells, M., and L. D'Andrea Tyson. 1989. "Changes: Implications for the U.S. Economy," in R.B. Purcell, *The Newly Industrializing Countries in the World Economy*. Boulder: Lynne Reinner.

Cho, Yoon-Je, and Deena Khatkhate. 1989. *Lessons of Financial Liberalization in Asia*. Washington, D.C.: The World Bank.

Dahlman, K. 1989. "Structural Change and Trade in East Asian Newly Industrial Economies and Emerging Industrial Economies," in R. B. Purcell, *The Newly Industrializing Countries in the World Economy*. Boulder: Lynne Reinner.

Drucker, P. 1989. "The Futures That Have Already Happened." *The Economist* . October 21-27, 1989.

The Economist. June 24, 1989; September 16, 1989; November 11, 1989; December 9, 1989.

Frischtak, C. R. 1989. *Competition Policies for Industrializing Countries*. Washington, D.C.: The World Bank.

Hoffman, K. 1989. *Technological Advance and Organizational Innovation in the Engineering Industry*. Washington, D.C.: The World Bank.

International Finance Corporation (I.F.C.). 1989. *Quarterly Review of Emerging Stock Markets* (third quarter).

Kindleberger, C. P. 1978. *Economic Response -- Comparative Studies in Trade, Finance and Growth*. Cambridge, Mass.: Harvard University Press.

_____. 1984. *A Financial History of Western Europe*. London: George Allen and Unwin.

_____. 1973. *The World in Depression, 1929-1939*. London: Allen Lane.

Latin Finance. 1991. "Latin Equities the Bulls are Running" 20 (July-August): 17-19.

Lee, J. 1983. "The External-Debt Servicing Capacity of the Asian Developing Countries."

Lieberman, I. W. 1989a. "The History of External Sovereign Debt: The Reaction of Creditors and Debtors to Disruption of Debt Service." Ph.d thesis, Oxford University.

_____. 1989b. *Industrial Restructuring Policy and Practice*. Washington, D.C.: The World Bank.

Massachusetts Institute of Technology (MIT) Commission on Industrial Productivity. 1989. *Made in America*. Cambridge, Mass.: MIT Press.

Malaysian Industrial Development Agency (MIDA). 1989. *Malaysian Foreign Investment Statistics 1988-89*. Kuala Lumpur: MIDA.

Mody, A. 1989. "Changing Firm Boundaries: Analysis of Technology-Sharing Alliances." Washington, D.C.: The World Bank.

Naya, S., W. E. James, and M. Plummer. 1989a. "Pacific Economic Cooperation in the Global Context." East-West Center, Honolulu, Hawaii.

Naya, S., K. S. Sandhu, M. Plummer, and N. Akransanee. 1989b. "ASEAN-U.S. Initiative." East-West Center, Honolulu, Hawaii.

Papageorgiou, D., A. M. Choksi, and M. Michaely. 1990. *Liberalizing Foreign Trade in Developing Countries*. Washington, D.C.: The World Bank.

Purcell, R. B. 1989. *The Newly Industrializing Countries in the World Economy*. Boulder: Lynne Reinner.

Rhee, Y. W. 1989. "The Role of Catalytic Agents in Entering International Markets." Washington, D.C.: The World Bank.

Stalk, G. 1989. "Time -- The Next Source of Competitive Advantage." *Harvard Business Review*.

Thomas, V., K. Matin, and J. Nash. 1990. *Lessons in Trade Policy Reform*. Washington, D.C.: The World Bank.

Vuylsteke, C. 1988. *Techniques of Privatization*. Washington, D.C.: The World Bank.

World Bank. 1987. *East Asia and Pacific: Regional Study on Trade, Export and Industry Policies*. Washington, D.C.: The World Bank.

_____. 1989a. "Poland: Improving the Efficiency of Polish Industry." Washington, D.C.: The World Bank,

_____. 1989b. *Report of the Task Force on Financial Sector Operations*. Washington, D.C.: The World Bank.

_____. 1989c. *World Development Report*. Washington, D.C.: The World Bank.

PART TWO

The East Asian Experience and Pro-Market Planning for Economic Development

7

Industrial and Agricultural Investment Coordination Under "Plan" and "Market" in China

Louis Putterman

Introduction

A persistent theme in the literature on the comparison of economic systems is that there are two basic methods for coordinating economic decisions in a large economy composed of specialized, interdependent production and consumption units. Coordination can be the "unintended" result of individualized pursuit of profit, income, and leisure -- that is, it can be achieved by the "invisible hand" of the market system. Or it can be brought about by the intentional action of administrative agents overseeing economic behavior hierarchically -- in other words, by "central planning."

Like all simplifying frameworks, the "market" or "plan" dichotomy has its limitations. No known "market economy" operates without a considerable range of public regulatory interventions and governmental economic functions; no "planned economy" has ever achieved correspondence with the ideal of complete centralized dictation of all microeconomic decisions. The scope for discretionary filling-in of incomplete details in state plans has been substantial in even the most centralized systems, such as that of the Soviet Union.

One reason why the abstraction of the market-or-plan dichotomy breaks down in practice is that both markets and planning as methods of coordinating economic activity have their practical limitations. Examples of economically successful systems utilizing voluntary, self-interested production and exchange as basic elements are universally observed to be predicated upon institutional infrastructures of laws, property rights, and behavioral norms that do not themselves spring from the competitive process, and that, in their emphasis upon trust and honesty, may even appear to be at odds with aspects of the behavioral logic of the marketplace. Markets do not respond to social demand for public goods, and they generate externalities that call for collective or public administrative responses. Even within the sphere of competitive activity itself, exchange relations entailing idiosyncratic investments by the parties involved may be too costly to undertake without setting up long-term governance structures, such as vertically integrated corporations or what Victor Goldberg and Oliver Williamson call "relational contracts." The welfare and distributive outcomes of markets regularly lead to public interventions, in the industrial democracies, because the unadjusted results of the market process seem to be unacceptable to major segments of the population.

Replacing market systems with comprehensive state control, which is one possible response to the market's deficiencies, leads to a different set of problems. The substitution of planning for markets, which at first appeared to some to be a simple administrative problem, helped to clarify the role that markets performed as implicit processors of information. In a large and complex economy, administrative directors at the center would require an overwhelming amount and variety of information, means of eliciting that information from the agents-on-the-spot to whom it is known (and to motivate those agents to continually seek out such information), means of processing the information into economically appropriate directives, and means of motivating the agents-on-the-spot to energetically fulfill those directives. In an idealized market system, and in a real one to the extent that theoretical models hold, a great deal of the relevant information about scarcities, technical possibilities, and tastes, comes to be summarized to agents throughout the economy in the compact form of prices, which to a considerable degree automatically adjust in the face of changes in underlying conditions.

Agents-on-the-spot are induced to reveal the necessary aspects of their local circumstances and opportunities as an unintended by-product of profit-seeking, no central information processing is required (to the extent that markets fulfill their functions), and agents-on-the-spot do their part in the unwritten plan of economic life in the normal course of profit-seeking. In a nonmarket economy, it turns out to be exceedingly difficult to solve the same problems through visible and explicit methods. Managers have reason to distort their circumstances to planners, it is impossible in any case to summarize all of the information that influences choice in a market system into reports travelling up the hierarchy, planners prove incapable of manipulating the provided information so as to derive economically rational plans, plans are inevitably incomplete, and it is impossible to design incentives to fulfill them which do not turn out to have unwanted consequences.

All of this is part of the familiar critique of the planned economy. The fact that it is shared not only by Western specialists who receive consulting fees and research grants from governmental bodies of dubious objectivity, but also by a large number of analysts in the socialist countries, leads to confidence that there is something more to the critique than simple propaganda. Yet, it is also true that discussions of the limitations of planning often idealize the market alternative. Moreover, the achievements of state-managed economies such as that of the Soviet Union and China, with respect to industrialization, structural transformation, and the provision of basic necessities to their populations, are real and need to be acknowledged.

In this chapter, I wish to discuss the virtues and deficiencies of the two methods of economic coordination, plan and market, in the context of the economy of mainland China over the past quarter century. The time frame allows me to consider both periods of heightened central direction, or at least of maximum suppression of market allocation, and periods in which decentralized decision-making was given greater sway. I will focus first on industry, then on agriculture.

Coordination and the Growth of Chinese Industry

Building largely upon a base of pre-standing and generally foreign-owned light industrial factories and a few dozen large heavy industrial enterprises constructed with Soviet assistance in the 1950s, China established a comprehensive industrial sector during the first 30 years of Communist Party rule (Cheng 1982). By the mid-1980s, China's industrial labor force numbered 63 million workers, equal to the sum of the industrial labor forces of all of Western Europe and North America (Tidrick and Chen 1987). Unlike most underdeveloped countries, China is largely self-sufficient in the production of producer goods, manufactures a vast number of refrigerators, washing machines, television and radio sets, and other appliances and consumer goods to meet the needs of its own population, produces space-worthy rockets and satellites, and, with its greater opening to international trade at the

124 Louis Putterman

end of the 1970s, became a vigorous competitor in world markets for light industrial manufactures, such as textiles.

Whether such a transformation could have taken place with equal speed under a system of private ownership and market competition is an open question. The historical reality is that from the inception of its contacts with the technologically and institutionally more dynamic nations of Western Europe in the 17th and 18th centuries, the once powerful Chinese empire responded too slowly to new conditions, and fell into a state of internal decay, dissolution, and subordination to foreign interests. Although some economic historians contend that China had a developed market system centuries before the West, modern industry as such developed slowly, and mostly in a few foreign-dominated enclaves, and capitalism in its modern form came to be perceived in China, as in much of the colonized world, as an immoral, destructive system inextricably linked to exploitation by foreigners. The Chinese imperial system, under which the nation's decline began, was overthrown by would-be modernizers in 1911, but political unity proved elusive. As a result, when Japanese aggression against China reached its peak in the 1930s, China still lacked both economic strength and a strong and effective government. The accession to power by the Chinese Communist Party in 1949 is widely viewed as the beginning of China's reunification under such a government. It is unclear whether a non-Communist government, had one remained in power in the post-War period, could have succeeded in ushering in an era of growth comparable to that experienced by China after 1949.

A number of general arguments have been made in favor of government planning as a means of breaking the bottleneck of underdevelopment. The establishment of an industrial economy, it is argued, depends upon the simultaneous growth of numerous interdependent enterprises. For example, modern textile manufacturing requires the availability of certain kinds of machinery, raw materials, and skilled labor, and it may not be profitable to invest in a textile plant unless these can be readily acquired. Yet the incentives to produce the machines, supply the raw materials, or acquire the skills may be absent without the demand of textile manufacturers. The potential machine producer may be as reluctant to invest without existing demand from the textile producer, as the textile producer is to get started without an existing machine supplier. Moreover, both may be dependent upon the availability of railroads and other forms of infrastructure, which it may not pay either a private or a governmental agent to supply unless there is a definite prospect that they will be used, generating tolls or taxable revenues. Accordingly, it is argued, interdependence of investments in a nonindustrialized economy may prevent any of the investments from taking place, since those with investable funds may prefer the more certain returns of land ownership or foreign bank accounts.

One way of looking at this coordination problem of investment is to say that each investor creates positive externalities for the others, but that since those benefits are not privately captured by them, they will under-invest from the viewpoint of the society. The logjam can be broken -- so the argument for "balanced growth" goes -- by collective action. Either the investors can get together and draw up a plan for mutually beneficial and coordinated investment, or some public body can draw up such a plan for them. In either case, it is necessary that all believe that the others will fulfill their part. If the plan is privately beneficial to all parties, provided that all adhere to it, the problem is simply one of "assurance" (Sen 1967). However, if some agents could be tempted to defect from their roles even when the others adhere to the plan, then the collective action problem has the character of a "prisoners' dilemma" and a mechanism to police or enforce the cooperative solution is required.

Some economists, notably Albert Hirschman (1958), have argued against this case for coordinated or balanced industrialization. In Hirschman's view, bottlenecks or the manifestations of imbalance are the sources of economic dynamism. The textile industry pushes ahead, perhaps using imported machinery, and this creates a new profit opportunity which stirs the potential domestic machine producer to action. Hirschman also argues that the positive externalities of investment are often outweighed by negative ones -- harsh working conditions, air pollution, socially traumatic destruction of traditional ways of life -- and that if the government is in charge of coordinating the industrialization process, it may come under pressure to moderate these negative effects through the kinds of intervention that may prove too costly to the poor country at an early stage of industrialization.

If the argument for "balanced growth" is accepted, this does not necessarily imply that the state will take over the industrialization function in its entirety. That is one possible approach to the problem of enforcing the plan (as well as a way of responding to other ideological and political concerns). But there are others. Of particular note is the fact that while the contrast between the market-oriented and high-growth East Asian success stories (Japan, Taiwan, S. Korea, Hong Kong and Singapore) and the slower-growth industrialization experience of mainland China is often drawn along the lines of the market versus plan dichotomy, most experts agree that the state played a strong coordinating role in several of these cases.[1] The difference between the two approaches is accordingly to be found in the area of the property system, on the one hand, and in whether planners coordinated and intervened in the economy in a market-exploiting or in a market-destroying fashion, on the other; it is not a contrast between planning and *laissez faire*.

The planners of Taiwan and South Korea, exercising control over their nations' banks, worked closely with private business leaders to stake out strategies for industrialization, exploiting local resources and world market opportunities not by adhering to proven comparative advantage, but by betting on their vision of what was possible. One might say, too, that since development emphasized national power and business profitability objectives, Hirschman's concern about excessive attention to negative externalities did not materialize. In this last connection, it may be noted that while China's Communist leaders attempted to place a consumption floor beneath both the peasantry and the more privileged urban workers, their priorities lay with national growth and capital accumulation, and attention to negative externalities was again minimal. In all three cases, it may be fair to say that strong governments prevented the short-run interests of the ordinary citizens from receiving more than a minimum of attention.

Industrialization in China was certainly not immune to the typical problems plaguing socialist planned economies. As in the Soviet Union, pride of place went to heavy industry, and the state paid more attention to output indicators than to the utility of what was produced, or to its mutual consistency from an inter-industry standpoint. Investment was pushed up, and consumption down, to proportions unimaginable elsewhere, with poor results. Using a simple Harrod-Domar growth equation, $g = s/k$, where g is the rate of growth of output, s is the share of national income saved, and k is the capital-output ratio, China's average growth rate of about 6% and savings rate of around 35% implies a capital-output ratio of about 5.8, which compares unfavorably with rates of 3.3, 2.6, 2.8, 4.2, and 4.0 calculated for South Korea, Indonesia, Brazil, the Ivory Coast, and Kenya by the World Bank.[2] The general lack of improvement in levels of consumption between the mid-1950s and the late 1970s is said to have undermined worker morale; moreover, it was associated with a weakening of individual material incentives and, what might be worse for morale, increasing indefensibility of some pay differentials that persisted.

The truism about the notion of a "planned economy" being a misleading conceit is especially true of China, where central planning was limited to a small number of strategic commodities, where the organs of such planning were virtually emptied of personnel during the final decade of Maoist dominance, and where most industrial enterprises were directed more by provincial, municipal, or county governments, than by the government in Beijing. This means not only that such plans as were implemented must have failed the rigorous tests of either consistency or full economic rationality (Pareto optimality), for lack of sophisticated planning tools (such as input-output and mathematical programming models), but also that much of the industrial activity that took place occurred, as it were, on "automatic pilot" -- that is, by way of maximum attainable growth along pre-established paths. There was also a great tendency towards the autarchic reproduction of the same production structure in each province, each county, and each municipality, causing the nation as a whole to forfeit potential benefits of internal trade and specialization. And the standard problems of enterprises lacking incentives to economize on inputs, providing distorted information to superior organs, producing substandard output, engaging in unauthorized horizontal contacts, etc., most likely prevailed.

How can China's industrial performance to 1978 be explained in view of these problems? To be sure, some economists (such as Malenbaum 1982 and Sen 1985) have questioned the growth statistics, such as those published by the World Bank, which show China growing at least as rapidly as, and possibly more rapidly than, the average less developed economy, and at a rate comparable to that of typical industrialized economies in the post-War period. But such statistics continue to be viewed as the best available by most Western specialists (for example, Dernberger, forthcoming). One element in a plausible explanation should probably be the imbalance, as of 1949, between China's low per capita stock of modern industrial technology, on the one hand, and its much higher level of development of human capital and social infrastructure. While China's existing industry and income levels at that starting point were close to those of the poorest nations of Africa or Oceania, for example, centuries of hierarchical social and political organization, intensive cultivation practices, dense irrigation, canal, and internal trade networks, a large literate elite, etc., could be said to have positioned China for relatively rapid recovery of the advanced status it boasted in earlier times, under any regime capable of establishing a modicum of social and economic stability and national sovereignty.

Another attractive explanatory framework, and the last that I will offer here, is the economic-historical model of Soviet-style central planning, wherein that system is held to be capable of achieving rapid growth and structural transformation at an early stage of industrial development via the marshalling of previously underutilized resources. Such extensive growth -- i.e., growth of output based upon growth of inputs, rather than improvements in technical efficiency -- is facilitated by the state's ability to allocate labor, to squeeze output from agriculture at semi-confiscatory prices, and to enforce high savings rates through direct control over personal incomes. It does not require a high degree of efficiency or perfect consistency of plans, nor that maximum output be squeezed from the resources utilized.

This same explanatory model implies that the possibility of extensive growth exists only during a limited transition period, and that its very success spells the end of that possibility. Surplus reources are exhausted as industrialization proceeds, and future growth requires economizing on scarce inputs. With an industrial foundation in place, further progress depends upon the development of consumer goods industries, requiring more attention to quality and assortment. Especially pertinent to China would appear to be the socio-political fact that the original mobilizational regimes, such as those of Stalin and Mao Zedong, lose steam or simply die with their founders, and motivation for economic activity becomes less a matter of coercion or ideological indoctrination, and more one of material reward. In China's case and more belatedly, that of the Soviet Union, the pressure of world economic trends in the late 20th century plays its own particular part: industrial and organizational milieus in which planning performed reasonably well, viz the mechanical world of the early and middle of this century, are replaced by a world of sophisticated consumer goods and high technology, intensified international competition, and the powerful demonstration effects of neighboring high growth economies. There is pressure to change the economic mechanism, and the introduction of more market forces is the only visible candidate. Turning Marx on his head, the knell of socialist accumulation is sounded, the bureaucratic expropriators are under siege, and state socialism begins to appear as if destined to play the role of a transitional stage between pre-capitalism and capitalism, rather than that of the post-capitalist bridge to communism that the "teacher of the proletariat" had predicted.

Industrial Coordination in an Era of Reform

Post-Mao China has seen efforts both to strengthen the mechanisms of planning, much weakened during the Cultural Revolution, and to move towards a system in which enterprises made more independent decisions in the decentralized pursuit of profits. While in part these two trends were consistent in that the vision of the reformers included macroeconomic and indicative planning functions, as well as planning of strategic sectors during a certain transitional period, in part they were inconsistent and reflected the absence of unity in a leadership that lacked Maoists but included the two other competing trends of Chinese Communist leadership, "pragmatists" epitomized by the late Liu Shaoqi and by Deng Xiaoping, and orthodox Stalinists such as Chen Yun, other octogenerian survivors of Mao, and their younger proteges. In what follows, I treat the reform trend, which was dominant from late 1978 to mid-1989, with periods of greater and lesser strength, as the basic policy approach of the People's Republic.

Reformism in China, as in Hungary before it and much of the Soviet bloc today, began with the premise that centralized direction of economic life saps the nation of economic vitality. It is accordingly agreed that enterprises are to be given greater autonomy in decision-making. But in an economy of state ownership, in which the enterprises are merely branch offices of the "nation as business concern," what are to be the objectives of the enterprises, whose managers were previously asked simply to follow administrative directives without formulating goals of their own? A long tradition of criticism of the Soviet-type system argues that managerial incentives are dysfunctional, because the criteria established for evaluating enterprise performance, such as quantity, weight, or value of output, are inevitably incomplete representations of socially desired objectives, whereas a reward function based on a large set of these criteria is complicated to administer, and it is difficult to determine what weight should be attached to each component. Profitability is then proposed as the ideal alternative, since it ideally captures all factors influencing revenue and costs, including technical efficiency and saving on inputs, quality, quantity, and suitability to the market of output, and appropriate technological change. Let enterprise managers pursue profits, conclude the reformers, and let them be motivated to do so by being permitted to retain at least part of those profits, rather than remit them to the government, and by being permitted to distribute part of the profits as bonuses, and to finance expansion from the remainder.

Chinese industry has followed this prescription since the early 1980s, its reform leaders hoping to begin gaining, thereby, the advantages of market economic coordination and market incentives. The results have included growth of industrial output at about 12.4% per annum between 1979 and 1987, which is somewhat above the 11.2% average for 1952-1979, and reverses a declining trend over the latter period.[3] A few recent studies (e.g., Chen, Jefferson, Rawski, Wang and Zheng 1988) have also suggested an improvement in the rate of increase of technical efficiency, which is thought previously to have been either negative or negligible. But several other studies (see Tidrick and Chen, eds. 1987; Reynolds, ed. 1987; and Walder 1989) have suggested substantial problems with the reform.

As with the critique of central planning, there is already a rather widely accepted body of analysis regarding the problems of economic reform in countries such as Hungary and China. Although this analysis has been expounded in different ways with different points of emphasis, two basic obstacles to reform are identified by most observers: the problem of price reform, and the problem of financial discipline, dubbed by Hungarian economist Janos Kornai the "soft budget constraint." It is easy enough to grasp the problem of an unreformed price system: having enterprises independently make their production and investment decisions in pursuit of profits could just as easily lead to results inferior to as to results superior to those of an imperfect planning system, if prices remain administratively determined and unreflective of scarcities and product values.[4] Why not "get prices right," then? In the first place, control of prices may continued to be guarded by the authorities as a last bastion of power. But more importantly, decontrol has generally been followed by inflation, in part because latent inflationary tendencies were repressed for decades due to the regime's desire to deliver on a political promise of stable prices. A sudden rush of inflation is feared.

The "soft budget constraint" problem can be explained to Americans by suggesting that they think of the would be reforming socialist economy as a nation of Chrysler corporations (circa 1982), that is of unprofitable providers of employment, generators of tax revenue, and holders of domestic market share whose demise is viewed as politically unacceptable to the government, and which are accordingly delivered from bankruptcy by public funds, tax relief, or other favors. If a state-owned enterprise is not ultimately accountable for its losses, the financial discipline to which it is subject is accordingly weakened, and the more so as the funds with which "losers" are subsidized must inevitably come from the profits of "winners," so that there is effective redistribution of profits (a welfare regime for firms, rather than people). There is a link between the "soft budget constraint" problem and that of price reform: if "losing" and "winning" is as much a function of the configuration of administratively determined prices as of efficiency in transforming scarce resources into socially desired outputs, "losers" can with some rights argue for special dispensation. There is also a similarity in the political respect that the state's failure to effectively address the "soft budget constraint" problem is in large part a function of the fact that its resolution requires abandoning a claimed superiority of socialism, that of stable employment.

Reforming the price system entails forfeiting another such claimed superiority, that of stable prices.

Just as it is unreasonable to assume as realistic either a pure market or a pure planning system, or to presume the superiority of either one over the other in all respects, so it is unrealistic, even if one grants the superiority of competitive markets over central planning under certain conditions, to suppose that a system with more scope for competition, profit-seeking, and decentralized choice, always performs better than one with less. Some illustrations will be drawn from China's experience with industrial reform here, and from that with agricultural reform later in the chapter. I have already suggested that letting enterprises seek profits holds no guarantee of increasing efficiency so long as prices do not reflect scarcities. The situation has been more complex in China of recent years in that, while the government was unwilling to abandon physical output planning and allocation of some inputs and products at controlled prices, it attempted to move towards a market system on the margin by keeping planned output and sales well within the productive capacity of most enterprises -- in contrast to the "tautness" marking the traditional Soviet system -- and allowing them to purchase inputs and sell products outside of planned quantities at negotiated or market prices. The idea was that as enterprises made their decisions on additional inputs and outputs on the basis of market prices, their behavior would become more and more efficient, with the differences between controlled and market prices merely acting as lump sum input subsidies and output taxes.

The double track price system had several inherent problems. For one thing, the system was seen as permitting smaller collective firms, such as factories run by rural township and village governments, to compete "unfairly" with state factories, inasmuch as the former could sell all of their output at the higher market prices, while the latter might have to sell the major part at low state prices. It was argued that in some industries in which efficient scale was achieved only by the larger state factories, inefficient small-scale factories thrived due to this price advantage. (This advantage was offset insofar as the state factories received some inputs at low state prices while nonstate competitors purchased theirs at higher market prices.) A second problem was that the degree to which outputs had to be sold and that to which inputs could be obtained at low state prices became one more factor over which bargaining took place between state enterprises and their administrative superiors, thus contributing to the arbitrariness of profits and the "softness of budget constraints." A third problem, although one rarely mentioned in this context, is that the "market prices" obtaining in such a system are imperfect measures of scarcities, because, like prices in black markets, they deviate from prices in a free market when a substantial percentage of transactions continue to take place at controlled prices. Finally, when market prices deviated very substantially from controlled prices, there were strong temptations to circumvent controls, diverting goods from state to market channels for private profit. This practice, labelled *guandao* ("official profiteering") in popular Chinese parlance, was perceived by the public as a major form of corruption, and became a major focus of the protest movement suppression of which brought down the reformist leadership of Zhao Ziyang in June, 1989.

Another key problem in China's industrial reform was that while the reform had the character of an economic decentralization of decision-making power to enterprises, in some respects, it also had the tendency to decentralize power administratively, to local governments which were the ultimate decision-makers in many other respects. Although I am prepared to believe that these governments, especially at the level of townships and villages, often acted in genuinely entrepreneurial fashions, creating new production opportunities which increased the prosperity of their communities, it also seems clear that (as argued in Tidrick and Chen 1987, and by Naughton 1988, among others) administrative decentralization exacerbated the tendency towards "cellularity" in the Chinese economy, because regions were able to make their residents a captive market for home-produced products by restricting entry of outside products, thus allowing factories of inefficient scale to thrive at the expense of residents' purchasing power and access to products of higher quality.[5]

A half-reformed economy may be subject to many problems and not clearly superior to a more centralized one. But rather than blaming marketization, should not the failure to move further in the direction of a market economy be judged the culprit? Perhaps so, but this leaves open the question of why China has been unable to move more speedily in that direction. It is possible, to be sure, to seek explanations in the political domain plain and simple: China's reformers have not had a free hand, but rather have had to compromise with a more conventional socialist faction in implementing policy. Despite containing an element of truth, this approach strikes me as inadequate, however. Although Chinese politics has remained complex and factionalized, reformers were able to push through the virtually complete decollectivization of agriculture, over the opposition of top political conservatives. I would argue that that "breakthrough" was possible because the results of early experiments with decollectivization were dramatically positive from the standpoint of productivity, without readily visible or dramatic drawbacks. With industrial reform, on the other hand, results from the beginning have been economically and socially mixed, and reform opponents have been given plenty of ammunition with which to fight continuation of the process.

The fundamental problem with industrial reform in China, in my view (for a more extended discussion, see Putterman, forthcoming), is that the two necessary preconditions -- the transition from administered to competitive prices, and the hardening of enterprise budget constraints -- threaten the living standards of incumbent state employees, since in a market economy wages would be determined by labor's opportunity cost to the economy, which is the lower wage at which nonstate workers would be willing to move to state enterprises. Since the state remains committed to protecting the living standard of these employees, it has to put off indefinitely steps necessary to achieve the preconditions of full marketization. The consequences of the half-reformed situation which results include, paradoxically, upward pressure on state sector wages, resulting from the conjunction of retention of disequilibrium profits by state enterprises with the influence of workers upon the enterprises in which they have *de facto* life-time tenure (Naughton 1988, Tidrick and Chen 1987, Walder 1989).

Coordination and the Management of Chinese Agriculture

Between 1949 and 1978, China remained a predominantly rural country, with 89% of its population classified as rural in the earlier and 82% in the later year. In between, overall population grew by 421 million, and 73% of the increment occurred in rural areas.[6] Although China was densely populated and the productivity of its rural population was low, its leaders found themselves unable to transfer much of the population from the countryside to the city, despite the priority placed on industrialization. The basic reason was that, in view of its commitment to providing industrial workers with housing, education, medicine, and other services, a growing urban population came to be viewed as an excessive burden on the state's resources.

While the growing rural population could be more cheaply fed and housed in the countryside, at almost no direct cost to the state, and could be busied providing the country with food, the extra hands alone were not enough for that task, for the marginal product of labor on a declining cultivable area was small and falling. Yet achieving rapid industrialization using capital intensive methods implied keeping state investment in agriculture low. The state's answer to this problem was centered on the idea of utilizing seasonally underemployed rural labor to create *capital de novo*. This was done through farm capital construction projects that employed as many as 140 million workers a year and, between 1957 and 1979, helped to expand China's irrigated area by 65%, or 17.7 million hectares.[7]

The key to the mobilization of all of this labor without monetary compensation by the state was the three-tier system of rural collective organization consisting of the people's communes, at the top, the production brigades, in the middle, and the agricultural production teams, at the bottom. The communes were formed after the completion of agricultural collectivization, in 1958, precisely with the aim of mobilizing labor for capital construction. Although management of crop production at too high a level proved disastrous during the initial years of this innovation (which coincided with the Great Leap Forward, 1958-1961), the system was stabilized and made viable by decentralizing cultivation to the teams (20 to 30 households), while maintaining the brigade and commune levels for the management of capital construction, rural industry, and services such as education and health care.

Commune organization facilitated the mobilizing of off-season labor for farm capital construction in two ways. The first has to do with the payment system for collective labor. Commune members received most of their income in the form of distributions in cash and kind based on number of points earned for collective labor (called "workpoints") and on household size. Although capital construction work did not enlarge the size of the income pool available for distribution, in the short term, teams nevertheless awarded workpoints to compensate members for time spent on such work. Thus, teams financed this work by diluting the value of payment for directly productive work, without direct cost to the state, but perhaps with the hidden cost of reduced incentive for rural work in general.

The second way in which the commune system helped in mobilizing capital-construction labor was organizational. The communes and their constituent brigades (as well as the immediate superior government organs, the counties), helped to identify projects which might benefit from labor mobilization, and to manage those projects, while the organizational hierarchy running from the commune center to the brigades, from the brigades to the production teams, and from the teams to the individual members or households, was used to deliver workers to the work sites. This leaves open the question of the degree to which labor was contributed voluntarily, either on the basis of exhortation or of the expected value of the workpoints to be earned, or was involuntarily secured by means of the monopoly on economic and political power exercised by the commune hierarchy.

An idealization of the commune system might suggest that labor was mobilized readily because projects palpably benefited the local population, with all benefiting more or less equally due to the egalitarian nature of the income distribution and of collective access to land. While there might still remain a free rider problem of motivating individuals to contribute, since the completion of projects could be viewed as a public good, that problem might be solved through mutual monitoring and social pressure, which should have been facilitated by the face-to-face relations in the bottom layer of the system, the neighborhood-sized production teams. An even more ideal variant of this viewpoint would see the free rider problem as having been neutralized by the internalization of collectivist motivation by members, a process that might have been made easier by the ideological indoctrination mechanisms of the commune system.

It seems reasonable to suppose that such ideal factors operated some percentage of the time, at least in the best organized and most effectively led communes. On the other hand, following the reform of the commune system which began in 1978, Chinese spokesmen have argued that that system had allowed the authorities to order the population about and to treat their labor as a free good. While there was apparently a significant degree of democracy involved in the election of team leaders in many communes, commune- and often brigade-level leaders were chosen by higher level Party and government officials, and these organizations were cooperative and democratic in name only. Such organizational parameters as the collectivization of land, and the size of the private plots left to households, were not freely chosen by the peasants, and officials in each of the three tiers controlled critical resources, and could make life very difficult for team members who failed to do their part in politically-initiated construction campaigns.

Rural Change After Mao

Whatever the true mix of factors that allowed rural labor to be mobilized for farm capital construction during the era of the people's communes, these factors ceased to be operative once the communes and brigades had been replaced by township and village governments, once these had been ordered to desist from arbitrarily conscripting local labor, and once the production teams had been disbanded and farming operations returned to the individual households, a transformation concluded by 1983 or 1984. Since households' agricultural earnings in cash and kind came directly from their own production activities, there were no workpoints with which to compensate those who participated in collective capital construction efforts. Villages were permitted to make contributions of labor to local public works one of the terms of the contracts by which land use rights were transferred to their households, but this system was slow to be institutionalized, and more difficult to enforce given the somewhat reduced control of resources by cadres and the greater number of resources in the hands of individual farmers. Moreover, the opportunity cost of labor rose for many households with the rapid growth of nonagricultural employment and self-employment, so the incentive to resist demands for uncompensated labor contributions was strengthened.

It has been difficult to document the effects of these changes in more than an anecdotal fashion. The previously reported rise in China's irrigated area, to about 45 million hectares, was largely achieved by 1968; the figure remained roughly constant thereafter, with a small decline after 1978. Qualitatively, there are many reports of deterioration in irrigation and drainage systems, and major concern has been expressed by officials in the last few years.[8] Some reduction in farm capital construction activities might be socially as well as individually rational, because such work may have been pushed to extremes in the past by cadres placing too much weight on quantitative indicators like the number of meters of earth moved, and too little on either the social cost of the labor mobilized, or the qualitative effects -- i.e., the benefits for rural productivity -- of the projects sponsored. On the other hand, there are grounds for believing that the failure to develop an effective alternative mechanism for organizing collective action in the area of rural farm capital construction is a net cost of China's decollectivization.

Although few observers doubt the advantages of decollectivization in the sphere of crop production as such, here too decentralization has not been without its problems. As in industry, those problems can be chalked up to obstacles in the way of completing the transition to a market economy. Also as in industry, effective ways to eliminate these obstacles has stubbornly eluded China's leaders, and in the meantime, China's agricultural system is plagued by internal contradictions.

The spectacular growth of grain and other crop products between 1978 and 1984 is well known. Grain production rose by nearly 34% in those six years, while output of cotton, oil-bearing crops, sugarcane and sugar beets, fruits, and pork, beef and mutton grew by 189%, 128%, 101%, 50% and 80%, respectively. The output value of rural industry simultaneously increased by 223%, the value of construction, transport and communications, and commercial services rose by 475%, while the share of the rural labor force employed in these nonagricultural activities grew from 11% in 1980 to 16.4% in 1984.[9] However, agricultural growth since 1984 has been more modest. Grain production has failed to grow at all, causing the 1978-1988 growth rate for grain output (2.6%) to be nearly identical to that for 1952-1978 (2.5%), and the growth rate of total crop output value declined from 12.7% during 1978-1984 to 9.1% during 1984-1987, with the decline perhaps much steeper in real terms.[10] The main reason for the slowdown is that while the prices paid by farmers for agricultural inputs, and the returns to investment and labor in noncrop sectors of the rural economy, continued to rise, the prices paid by the state for grain, cotton, and other products produced under contract to it, stagnated in absolute and declined in relative terms. [11]

While the liberalization of Chinese agriculture has been much trumpeted, the fact remains that nearly 80% of land is still cultivated in grain and other crops subject to state purchase, and that sharply lower per acre and per man-day returns to these crops are a strong indication that planting decisions are powerfully influenced by administrative interventions. Why do state prices for these crops continue to lag, and why are farmers not free to sell all of their output on the market and to make production decisions according to profitability considerations? The basic answer is that despite the return of direct farm management from collectives to households, China remains wedded to the classical Soviet-style pattern of promoting industrialization by extracting cheap staple output to feed urban workers at low cost, and cheap industrial inputs from the farm sector to support production of textiles and other products, to maintain high rates of industrial profit and hence of industrial capital accumulation. The sharp increases in grain prices which spurred the output boom of 1978-1984 produced a large drain on the treasury, since prices charged to urban residents were not raised correspondingly. With the state unable to proceed further in raising grain prices or liberalizing grain marketing, returns to the farmer declined even while the profitability of growing uncontrolled crops and engaging in nonfarm activities continued to grow. The result has been flat agricultural performance, alongside a continued boom in the rural nonfarm sectors. The latter, in turn, have experienced pressures of late as the government's inflation-fighting program has given preference to state over rural collective industry in the allocation of inputs and credit.

Chinese agriculture is thus seen to be plagued by a coordination problem of a special character. Collectivization was adopted as the Soviet and Chinese strategy for transferring resources from agriculture to industry not only because of the ideological appeal of such a proto-socialist micro-organizational structure, but also because it facilitated administrative control over the peasantry, and the involuntary transfer of output to the state at prices below those required to elicit a comparable volume of sales. China decollectivized to eliminate the incentive-blunting features of group production,[12] but was unable to eliminate the need for output extraction and administrative control. To some extent, China's ability to control peasant behavior had by the late 1970s become so great, due to the pervasive presence of party and government organizations at all levels, that collective control over production had become less essential to the procurement effort. However, this situation has not been impervious to the forces of institutional change. As China's peasants were given vastly more opportunity to pursue self-interest in a wide variety of spheres, as the disbanding of teams as production units caused local administrators to lose direct powers of control over household labor time, and as the returns to the production of state-purchased crops lagged, the administrative apparatus found it increasingly difficult to enforce the production and transfer of these products from the countryside. One result has been the resort to interference in planting decisions as a method for influencing farm output. Since administrative influence over labor time and over the use of inputs once disbursed to farmers is smaller, this type of intervention can influence the output mix only at the cost of overall economic inefficiency, since grain and similar crops will be grown using more land and less nonland inputs, and uncontrolled crops with less land and more nonland inputs, than in an unconstrained situation. In principle, more of both types of crops could be produced if more appropriate input mixes were employed. So the combination of household control over labor time with part market, part administrative coordination of production activities, generates some inefficiencies that may not have been present in a fully collective system.

The problems of agricultural pricing also impact upon agricultural investment. As mentioned earlier, the Chinese state since 1949 has focused its investment efforts upon industry, leaving agriculture to finance most of its investment needs from its own resources. The use of labor to directly create capital, and the impact of system reform upon this particular investment method, has also been discussed above. With regard to the use of households' and collective units' surplus funds for investment, the point to be made here is that while the availability of such funds has grown phenomenally in the reform period, the share being directed to agriculture has sharply declined. In part, this is a function of the relaxation of administrative controls that forced communes, brigades, and production teams, under the old system, to plow large parts of their revenue, including that from small-scale industry, into agricultural investments promising relatively low rates of return; in part it may be due to an increase in the divergence in rates of return as such; and in part it is probably due to an increase in the share of funds under the control of households, now that they rather than the collective teams are the direct units of farm production, and also carry on a variety of private sideline businesses. Under the reforms, with rates of return disfavoring crop production perhaps more than ever due to the expansion of nonagricultural investment opportunities, and with reduced control over investment (including those decisions taken by the reconstituted collective units, village and township governments) by higher levels, agricultural investment has become a major problem area. Both village and township governments and individual households and business partnerships favor noncrop endeavors; households have also shown a high propensity to invest in housing, rather than means of production. Early in the reform period, the state announced plans to drastically increase the share of state investment funds going to agriculture, but when agriculture responded so well to improved prices, liberalized markets, crop diversification, and decollectivization, the government decided to keep the money for industry. Now, with the early reform gains over and voluntary investment in agriculture so obviously lagging, the idea of such a shift in state investment has again gained prominence in official pronouncements.

Conclusions

In this chapter, I have applied to China's post-1949 experience some rather familiar themes of the economic systems literature. First, that there are two basic methods of economic coordination -- markets and plans. Second, that each has its strengths and liabilities. Third, that while there appears to be a developing consensus in both East and West that the market method is superior in many contexts, that method is not sufficient for all purposes (e.g., it does not solve collective action problems such as those related to the provision of public goods). Fourth, markets, or market-like institutions (such as decentralizing decisions to individual profit-seekers) may work badly when prices give wrong signals, as they do under a half-reformed socialist economy like that of China in the 1980s.

In the first part of the chapter, I discussed the Soviet-type forced draft industrialization approach as a solution to the coordination problem of developing an industrial sector from a limited base. I related this approach to discussions in the economics of development literature about balanced versus unbalanced growth, and about comparative advantage versus planned structural transformation. I suggested that the distinction between China and other, more successful cases of industrialization in East Asia, is not really a matter of plan or state versus market or private coordination. Japan, South Korea, and Taiwan all employed state intervention and coordination of their industrialization programs. Perhaps the main difference was that in their cases, the state used the market in its development strategy, while in China, at least until 1978, the state more often tried to substitute itself for the market, and to minimize contacts with other economies.

I then illustrated the idea that the introduction of some market forces does not lead to uniform improvements, by referring to some problems in China's semi-reformed economy of the mid- to late-1980s. These include the difficulty of making enterprises financially accountable (the "soft budget constraint" problem), and the problem of each locality trying to expand its revenue sources by backing many new investments, even as enterprises, empowered to retain profits and distribute them as bonuses, support an expansion of consumer demand, leading to inflation. I also discussed the idea that in view of the political necessity of maintaining the relatively high wages of labor in the state industrial sector, it is difficult to move to market resource allocation, because in a market system, industrial wages would fall due to the availability of cheap rural labor.

Turning to agriculture, I discussed the manner in which China before the 1980s managed to feed nearly a half billion additional people without much state investment in agriculture, by organizing its rural population into a hierarchy of "collective" units. I raised the question of whether the partial success of this approach should be attributed to the facilitation of local cooperation in a voluntary sense, or rather to the facilitation of coercive control. Whichever is the case, the process of rural capital formation, coupled with improvements in the availability of improved seeds and manufactured inputs, laid the basis for further growth after better price and payment system incentives were put in place after 1978.

The deficiencies of the collective system included its excessive focus on the production of grain, leading to very slow growth or declines in output of most other crops; unreliable work incentives; and unnecessary restrictions on ancillary activities such as transportation, construction, and small scale industry. The post-1978 reform regime partially corrected these deficiencies through improved producer prices, liberalization of production planning and marketing, and returning farming to the household level. However, it recreated the basic collective action problem of investment in the irrigation system, and the problem of incentive provision to agriculture remained resistant to complete resolution because of structural problems in the emerging three-sector system.

Notes

1   See, for example, Johnson, Tyson and Zysman, eds. (1989), and Amsden (1989).

2   See Gillis et al. (1987:48). Note that the Chinese figure is comparable to ICORs of 6.0 and 6.8 computed for India and Venezuela.

3   State Statistical Bureau (hereafter SSB) (1988:28).

4   As Barry Naughton (1988) puts it, "accounting profits" may bear no relationship to true economic profits, and some firms earning negative accounting profits may be socially efficient while some of those earning positive accounting profits may be socially inefficient and candidates for shut down under a competitive regime. Note, however, that prices in a market economy reflect the value of commodities as conditioned on a particular distribution of income and purchasing power, only. If one prefers that production respond to some socially sanctioned alternative sense of value, being that conditioned on a more "just" distribution of income, then either the market mechanism must be abandoned, or income must be appropriately redistributed prior to the market's operation.

5   See also Lyons (1987).

6   Based on data reported in SSB (1988:75).

7   The estimated number of participants is drawn from Nickum (1978). Irrigation data are from SSB (1988:197). If 1952 is taken as the base year, irrigated area expanded by 125%, or 25 million hectares. This was by no means the only source of growth in inputs to Chinese agriculture. Both the pre- and post-reform periods saw massive growth in the supply of chemical fertilizers and electricity to the countryside, and the pre-reform period especially saw an equally massive increase in the supply of farm machinery and power-driven irrigation pumps.

8   See Kojima (1988).

9   All data from SSB (1988), except those on rural labor allocation, which are based on Zhongguo Nongye Nianjian and Zhongguo Nongcun Tongji Nianjian, as reported in Putterman and Wiemer (1989).

10 Average state purchasing prices of farm and sideline products rose by an average of 7.6% in 1978-1984 and 9.0 in 1984-87, according to SSB (1988: 691). This implies a real growth rate of 5.1% in the first period and of 0.1% in the second; however, the indices may be unreliable and do not in any case reflect changes in market prices, at which a considerable part of output was sold.

11   A more detailed treatment would require discussion of the transition
     from the two-tiered price system, with a state guarantee to purchase
     additional crops at an "above quota" premium price, to a system with a
     uniform state price, and no promise to purchase surpluses. See Sicular
     (1988, 1990).
12   These incentive problems are the focus of several papers by the author,
     including Putterman (1987) and (1988).

References

Amsden, A. 1989. *Asia's Next Giant: South Korea and Late Industrialization.*
   New York: Oxford University Press.
Chen, K., G. Jefferson, T. Rawski, H. C. Wang, and Y. X. Zheng. 1988.
   "Productivity Change in Chinese Industry: 1953-1985." *Journal of
   Comparative Economics* 12: 570-591.
Cheng, C. 1982. *China's Economic Development: Growth and Structural
   Change.* Boulder: Westview Press.
Dernberger, R. forthcoming. "The Drive for Economic Modernization and
   Growth: Performance and Trends," paper delivered at the International
   Conference on A Decade of Reform under Deng Xiaoping, Brown
   University, November 4-7, 1987; to appear in a conference volume.
Gillis, M., D. Perkins, M. Roemer, and D. Snodgrass. 1987. *Economics of
   Development,* Second Edition. New York: W. W. Norton.
Hirschman, A. 1958. *The Strategy of Economic Development.* New Haven:
   Yale University Press.
Johnson, C. 1982. *MITI and the Japanese Miracle: The Growth of Industrial
   Policy, 1925-1975.* Stanford: Stanford University Press.
Johnson, C., L. D'Andrea Tyson, and J. Zysman, eds. 1989. *Politics and
   Productivity: The Real Story of Why Japan Works.* Cambridge, Mass.:
   Ballinger.
Kojima, R. 1988. "Agricultural Organization: New Forms, New Contra-
   dictions." *China Quarterly* 116: 706-735.
Lyons, T. 1987. *Economic Integration and Planning in Maoist China.* New
   York: Columbia University Press.
Malenbaum, W. 1982. "Modern Economic Growth in India and China: The
   Comparison Revisited, 1950-1980." *Economic Development and Cultural
   Change* 31: 45-84.
Naughton, B. 1988. "Industrial Decision-Making in China." Background
   paper prepared for the World Bank, May.
Nickum, J. E. 1978. "Labor Accumulation in Rural China and its Role Since
   the Cultural Revolution." *Cambridge Journal of Economics* 2: 273-286.
Putterman, L. 1987. "The Incentive Problem and the Demise of Team
   Farming in China." *Journal of Development Economics* 26: 103-127.
_____. 1988. "Group Farming and Work Incentives in Collective-Era
   China." *Modern China* 14: 419-450.

_____. Forthcoming. "Dualism and Reform in China." *Economic Development and Cultural Change.*
Putterman, L., and C. Wiemer. 1989. "China's Structural Transformation: An Empirical and Analytical View of Labor Re-allocation from Agriculture." Paper prepared for a joint session of the American Economic Association and the Chinese Economic Association of North America, Atlanta, December 29.
Reynolds, B., ed. 1987. *Reform in China: Challenges and Choices.* (A Summary and Analysis of the CESRRI Survey. Prepared by the Staff of the Chinese Economic System Reform Research Institute.) New York: M. E. Sharpe.
Sen, A. 1967. "Isolation, Assurance, and the Social Discount Rate." *Quarterly Journal of Economics* 81: 112-124.
_____. 1985. *Commodities and Capabilities.* Amsterdam: North-Holland.
Sicular, T. 1988. "Agricultural Planning and Pricing in the Post-Mao Period." *China Quarterly* 116: 671-705.
_____. 1990. "Ten Years of Reform: Progress and Setbacks in Agricultural Planning and Pricing." Harvard Institute of Economic Research Discussion Paper Number 1474, March.
State Statistical Bureau of the People's Republic of China. 1988. *China Statistical Yearbook 1988.* Beijing: China Statistical Information & Consultancy Service Center.
Tidrick, G., and C. Jiyuan, eds. 1987. *China's Industrial Reform.* New York: Published for The World Bank by Oxford University Press.
Walder, A. 1989. "Factory and Manager in an Era of Reform." *China Quarterly* 118: 242-264.

8

Industrial Policy in Japan and South Korea: Some Causes of Success

Mukesh Eswaran and Ashok Kotwal

Introduction

The performance of the Japanese economy since 1949 and that of the South Korean economy since 1962 are impressive by any historical standards. Both of these economies quickly attained international competitiveness in their industrial sectors, exported industrial goods, absorbed labor from agriculture, lowered the burden on land and thus brought about an increase in real wages. The structural transformation and hence an improvement in living standards of the masses has been remarkably swift in these countries. It is not surprising, therefore, that there is a growing interest among development economists in understanding the processes at work there. Moreover, these remarkable successes have been guided as much by the visible hand of the state as by the invisible hand of the market. To which aspects of the state policies, if any, can we attribute credit for such impressive results? The present chapter analyses two relatively under-appreciated aspects of Japanese and South Korean industrial policy: (a) the promotion of industrial conglomerates, and (b) industrial targeting or conferment of a special status ("strategically important") on a sector (or a small group of sectors). We argue that there are sound theoretical reasons to believe that both these policies are conducive to productivity growth in a closed economy. This suggests that these policies may have played an important role in fulfilling the avowed goal of these late industrializers to become internationally competitive, and thus in enabling the adoption of an outward-oriented strategy.

It is fruitful to review at this point some relevant features of industrial policy, first in the post WW-II Japan and then in South Korea.

Industrial Policy in Japan

The orientation of Japanese economic policy has always been nationalistic; economic independence has been the supreme goal. During the Tokugawa regime, this goal was sought through isolationism. Since the Meiji Restoration, however, the same goal has been pursued through the development of modern industry that could compete internationally. In the post-war era, after a brief reconstruction period, the government created institutions such as MITI which guided the Japanese economy to international prominence. Although the Japanese strategy of development has been characterized in the literature as "export-led-growth," it is important to note that trade liberalization in Japan was implemented with a great deal of caution; no industrial sector was exposed to international competition prematurely. The emphasis was on raising the productivity of select industrial sectors so that within a few years these sectors could compete internationally. The criteria for selection were two: technological possibilities for rapid productivity growth and high income elasticity of demand (Komiya 1988). The select sectors were favored through preferential allotment of foreign exchange, tax breaks and subsidies.

An aspect of industrial policy relevant to this chapter is the promotion of conglomerates. Industries were organized in bank groups *(Keiretsu)*. A typical *Keiretsu* included a big bank, several industrial firms, and a general trading company. The six big conglomerates that came into being during the 1950s were those based on the Fuji, Sanwa, Dai Ichi, Mitsui, Mitsubishi and Sumitomo banks (Johnson 1982:205). Under American occupation the old *Zaibatsu* trading companies were broken up but MITI rebuilt them in new form. Johnson (1982:206) elaborates:

> MITI helped the trading companies by issuing laws that authorized tax write-offs for the costs of opening foreign branches and for contingency funds against bad debt trade contracts, and as early as 1953 the ministry's powerful Industrial Rationalization Council (discussed below) called for the "keiretsuization" of trading companies and manufacturers. This meant, in practice, that MITI would assign an enterprise to a trading company if it did not already

have an affiliation. Through its licensing powers and ability to supply preferential financing, MITI ultimately winnowed about 2,800 trading companies that existed after the occupation down to around 20 big ones, each serving a bank keiretsu or a cartel of smaller producers. The bank groups were the successors to the old zaibatsu, and they came into being for the same reason that the old zaibatsu had been fostered in the Meiji era -- to concentrate scarce capital on key developmental projects. However, they differed from the old zaibatsu in that their internal organization was much more businesslike than the old family-centered empires, and they competed with each other much more vigorously.

The nature of competition among the different bank groups is, however, not very clear. These bank groups competed with each other for the acquisition of industries designated by MITI as strategically important. Thus, each conglomerate acquired a large number of complementary industries. But throughout the high growth period (after 1955) MITI was following a set of policies designed to "rationalize" the industrial structure. Along with an effort to increase the scale of production, there was an attempt to coordinate investment and form cartels to prevent recessions and excess capacity. All such policies created tensions with the anti-trust policy but eventually it became clear that anti-trust policy would take a backseat. Even small and medium enterprises were organized into cartels. The evolution of industrial policy in the critical period of 1949-1970 has been meticulously described by Chalmers Johnson in his book *MITI and the Japanese Miracle*. The overall picture that emerges is that MITI forged an industrial structure in Japan that was characterized by concentration of decision-making. A decision to undertake investment that would lower the production costs of, say, steel, by the management of the parent conglomerate meant that it would have a beneficial impact on the aggregate income and hence on the demand of other products of the conglomerate. This, in turn, was bound to create incentives for management to invest in these other sectors. It is this sort of interaction made possible by concentration of decision making power that we propose to analyze in this chapter.

Industrial Policy in South Korea

In 1962, the Government of South Korea launched an economic policy under the guidance of Economic Planning Board (EPB) that was similar in many ways to the successful strategy employed earlier by Japan. Like their Japanese counterparts, the South Korean policymakers were well aware that for a land-short (labor surplus) economy there was no alternative to the expansion of modern industry and that the demand for its products would have to be found abroad. But the prerequisite for a successful export drive was a rapid productivity growth in the export sector. Thus, productivity growth or cost-reduction became an explicit objective of the development policy. Just as in Japan, the Economic Planning Board in Korea designated certain industries as strategically important and their selection was carried out on the basis of income elasticity and the scope for productivity improvement. This enabled South Korea to mount export offensives in these sectors.

Having come even later than Japan on the industrialization scene, the Korean policy-makers were acutely aware that low cost production implied very large scale production. Moreover, in order to be able to market internationally, large conglomerates *(Chaebol)* were promoted along the lines of the Japanese *Zaibatsu*. Three leading *Chaebol* are Samsung (twenty-seven companies) which produced primarily consumer goods, Hyundai (eleven companies) which concentrates on producer goods and automobiles, Daewoo (seventeen companies) which is spread among trade, finance, machinery, electronics and engineering and Lucky which includes Bando Trading Company, Honam oil refinery, petrochemicals, electronics, nonferrous metals, insurance and securities. There are two differences between the Korean *Chaebol* and the Japanese *Zaibatsu*. Firstly, a *Zaibatsu* was typically built around its own bank. A *Chaebol*, on the other hand, relied on government controlled credit institutions. Secondly, the *Chaebol* were more specialized in their productive activities than were the *Zaibatsu*. Thus, a sector is much more under the control of a single management in Korea than in Japan.

Conglomeration and Strategic Sector Selection

The foregoing review of the development strategies followed by Japan and South Korea highlights two common features.

First, the promotion of conglomeration across many industrial sectors concentrated the decision making powers across many sectors into the hand of a single management.

Johnson (1987:160) argues:

> Today, with several more decades of global experience and knowledge of intentional development programs, ranging from Stalinism to the Alliance for Progress, it seems that the *Zaibatsu* may have been underappreciated. They function as powerful institutions for concentrating scarce capital for developmental

projects in underdeveloped countries, and they constitute a compromise between the inefficiencies of purely state enterprise and the indifference to developmental goals of purely private enterprise.

As stated by Johnson (1987:161):

> Vertical and horizontal integration allow an enterprise to alleviate risks and the uncertainties of market instability and rapid structural change. Vertical integration eliminates the need to depend on monopolistic suppliers of input materials or assures steady flows of needed inputs in adequate amounts. . . . Horizontal integration (participation in many different activities not related to input linkages) increases information flows and consequently reduces the uncertainty surrounding investment and production decisions. . . . These are some of the important reasons for the birth of the so-called general trading companies and enterprise groups, started in Japan and recently copied in Korea. . . . Such groups internalize uncertainty, information, and factor-market flows, and substitute for a perfect market as a way of coping with market imperfections in less developed countries.

Second, a few sectors were designated by the planning agency as strategically important ones. They were favored overtly by the government through special help in terms of credit, foreign exchange, industrial land allotment, etc.

We have chosen to focus on these two features of the Japanese type of development because they are central to the process of productivity growth that we want to analyze in this chapter. The model has implicitly in the background a country which is keen on improving the productivity of its industrial sectors to international standards so that exports become a possibility. Moreover, industrial sectors are characterized by market power. We would then like to ask whether either conglomeration or preferential treatment to a few sectors would, in any way, aid productivity growth.

Rosenstein-Rodan's Idea of "the Big Push"

Conglomeration implies that a single body of management makes investment decisions across many industrial sectors simultaneously. Rosenstein-Rodan (1943) was the first to argue for the coordination of investment decisions of individual producers; this idea become well known as the "Theory of the Big Push." It is essential at this point to understand Rosenstein-Rodan's idea since it provides the inspiration for this chapter.

Consider a subsistence economy in which a single entrepreneur contemplates starting a modern shoe factory for which he would have to hire some workers. To the extent that the modern technique of producing shoes is more productive than the traditional technique, the real income of the society must increase as a result of his decision to invest. As long as his action will yield positive profits, he will undertake such an investment. But whether or not he realizes positive profits will depend on whether he finds a market for the shoes he produces. If his workers and he are the only members of the society who expect to experience an increase in their incomes, they are the only ones who would be willing to buy these shoes. We can hardly expect them to spend the entire increment in their incomes on shoes alone; they would want to buy other goods. Under the circumstances, a single entrepreneur contemplating an investment decision in a single sector is likely to conclude that the investment would not be profitable. All entrepreneurs deciding on their own would think similarly and decide not to invest. As a result, the backward economy would remain trapped in a low-level equilibrium.

This, Rosenstein-Rodan asserted, called for "investment coordination" by the government. If each entrepreneur is assured that others will invest, he would expect his own investment to yield positive profits, and thus the economy would escape the low-level trap. What is needed, therefore, is indicative planning. Another way to think about this is that, depending on the prevalent belief (whether or not others will invest), a different Nash equilibrium in investment decisions is possible. And coordination by the government can be instrumental in creating the right belief (that all will invest) to guide the economy to the socially more desirable equilibrium. Basu (1984), and more recently Murphy, Shleifer and Vishny (1989), have offered formal models that capture this idea quite elegantly. The model by Murphy, Shleifer and Vishny (1989) is more elaborate and helps to clarify many issues that remain obscure in Rosenstein-Rodan's verbal presentation. For example, it brings out the conditions under which investment coordination matters. The investment decision here is a binary decision -- "invest or don't," and as such the "good" Nash equilibrium obtained through coordination is also the first-best outcome.

This is the point of departure for the model in this chapter. The model is formally analyzed in our paper "Demand Externality as an Impediment to Productivity Growth" (1990), and the entire discussion that follows is based on that paper. First of all, we model the investment or entrepreneurial effort explicitly as instrumental in reducing production costs (or, alternatively, as causing productivity growth). Secondly, we model entrepreneurial effort more realistically as a continuous variable. We then show that even the "good" equilibrium arrived at through government coordination is suboptimal. If the decisions are centralized through conglomeration across many sectors, even the "good" equilibrium can be improved upon. This, we believe, is one way that conglomeration may have spurred productivity growth in postwar Japan and South Korea. We also show how the decentralized outcome can also be improved upon if one sector can play a leading role (that of Stackelberg leader), which we relate to the industrial targeting or strategic sector selection.

Model and Summary of Results

We now present a simple general equilibrium model and discuss the implications that follow from it. The model and results are drawn from Eswaran and Kotwal (1990). We envisage an economy comprised of n entrepreneurs and one worker. Each entrepreneur produces a distinct good as a monopolist. All individuals have identical utility functions, $U(x,E)$, given by

(1) $U(x,E) = \prod_{i=1}^{n} x_i^{\alpha_i} - \beta E^{\gamma}$; $\beta > 0$, $\gamma > 1$, with $0 < \alpha_i < 1$ for all i and

$\sum_{i=1}^{n} \alpha_i = 1$, where x_i denotes amount of good i consumed by the individual and E is the effort applied. As consumers, all agents are assumed to be price takers. If p_i is the price of good i, the demand for the good from an individual with income y and the above preferences is then given by

(2) $x_i = y\alpha_i / p_i$ i = 1,..., n.

Each entrepreneur can produce his good at constant per unit labor requirement. However, this labor requirement can be reduced if the entrepreneur applies his effort towards cost-reducing innovations. We assume that if E_i is the amount of R&D effort applied by entrepreneur i for this purpose, the labor requirement per unit of output for good i is given by

(3) $C_i(E_i) = c_i E_i^{-\theta_i}$; $c_i > 0$, $\theta_i > 0$.

Each entrepreneur determines his R&D effort and the price of his product so that his effort level and the income generated (i.e., his profits) maximize his utility. The worker chooses to supply as much labor as is necessary to maximize his utility with the wage income he generates. (We take the wage as the numeraire.) The demand curve facing entrepreneur i is obtained by aggregating (2) across all agents. In their choices of R&D efforts and prices, we assume the entrepreneurs entertain Nash conjectures regarding the choices of other entrepreneurs. In the general equilibrium the markets for the n goods and that for labor clear.

There is a unique non-trivial general equilibrium in the model presented. (There is also a trivial, Pareto-inferior equilibrium, in which the entrepreneurs engage in no R&D and there is no production; we ignore this equilibrium.) Let us define the first best R&D effort levels and product prices as those that maximize the sum of the utilities of the worker and the n entrepreneurs. Then, relative to the first best, there are two sources of inefficiency in the decentralized Nash equilibrium: (1) For a given cost of production, the equilibrium price of a product exceeds its marginal cost. This is the standard inefficiency arising from the existence of monopoly power in each product market. (2) The R&D effort of each entrepreneur is suboptimal and, hence, the marginal cost of production is too high for each product.

Inefficiency (2) is the one of interest to us here. It would seem that while it is in the interest of a monopolist to underproduce, it would not be in his interest to allow his unit production cost to be higher than the first-best level. After all, cost minimization is a necessary condition for profit maximization. This inefficiency arises from demand spillovers in our general equilibrium model. The intuition for this is as follows. Suppose an entrepreneur considers increasing his R&D effort marginally. This would lower the marginal cost of production and this, in turn, would translate into a lower price for his product. As a result, all consumers would experience an increase in their real incomes. Since, for Cobb-Douglas preferences, all goods are normal, the increase in real incomes would push out the demand curves of *all* goods -- not just of the good the price of which was reduced. Thus the entrepreneur who marginally increased his R&D effort does not capture the full benefits of the cost reduction he brings about. This dilutes his incentives to lower costs.

It is natural to inquire if, in our framework, conglomeration would improve matters relative to the decentralized Nash outcome. By conglomeration we mean that the n entrepreneurs form a single firm, producing the same n products. As long as no sector commands on expenditure share in excess of a critical value, α_c , the outcome in the conglomerate equilibrium Pareto dominates the decentralized Nash outcome. To begin with, the R&D effort of each entrepreneur is higher in the conglomeration equilibrium, because the demand spillover effects discussed above are largely internalized by conglomeration. Roughly speaking, instead of $(n-1)/n$ of the benefits generated by a marginal increase to an entrepreneur's effort accruing to outsiders (as it did in the decentralized case), only $1/n$ accrues to outsiders (i.e., the worker) in the case of conglomeration. The higher marginal returns to R&D effort results in a higher effort and, hence, lower production costs in the conglomerate equilibrium. The price of each product is correspondingly lower compared to that in the decentralized Nash equilibrium. The entrepreneurs earn higher aggregate profits and achieve higher utility levels under conglomeration. The lower product prices increase the worker's real income and thus make him better off, too. The higher real wage of the worker induces him to increase his labor supply. This, together with the lower per unit labor requirement for each product, results in the GNP being higher in the conglomerate equilibrium, relative to the decentralized Nash equilibrium.

The need for the qualifier that no sector command an expenditure share in excess of a critical value, α_c, arises from the fact that conglomeration also leads to an increase in market power, which tends to raise, not lower, prices. However, as long as $\alpha_i < \alpha_c$ for all i, each sector is small enough that the demand externality that is internalized upon conglomeration has the dominant effect. (The smaller the sector, the greater the proportion of benefits accruing to other sectors of a lowering of costs in this sector.)

The above results provide one reason why conglomeration may have been an useful developmental industrial strategy in Japan and South Korea. As noted in the Introduction, the stated reasons for the fostering of conglomeration in these countries was quite different. Our results indicate that there is yet another reason why conglomeration may have encouraged productivity growth in industry.

Apart from conglomeration, we have also seen in the Introduction that an explicit strategy followed by Japan and South Korea has been the targeting of specific sectors for special, favored treatment. Standard policies in such treatment have involved, for example, the provision of capital at subsidized interest rates. A favored sector which is developing under the aegis of the government may be construed as having Stackelberg advantages vis-á-vis other sectors. So we might ask how a Stackelberg equilibrium that obtains when an arbitrary sector is given a leadership role compares in performance with the fully decentralized Nash equilibrium. Paradoxically, every entrepreneur's effort is higher, all product prices are lower, and every agent is strictly better off in the Stackelberg equilibrium.

The intuition for the above results is as follows. Each entrepreneur's Nash best response effort is an increasing function of the

efforts of all other entrepreneurs. This is because the marginal return
to an entrepreneur's effort is increased, through demand spillover
effects, by an increase in the effort of another entrepreneur. Consequently, if others increase their efforts, it is to an entrepreneur's
advantage to increase his own. Now suppose we begin at the decentralized Nash equilibrium and make one entrepreneur the Stackelberg
leader. What incentives are there for the effort levels to change? As a
Nash player, an entrepreneur takes the effort levels of all other
entrepreneurs as parametric in the computation of the marginal return
to an increase in his effort. As a Stackelberg leader, however, this
entrepreneur incorporates the best responses of his followers into his
decision making. He recognizes that an increase in his effort will elicit
higher effort levels from the other entrepreneurs. An entrepreneur's
marginal return to increase effort, evaluated at the Nash equilibrium,
is thus strictly greater when he behaves as a Stackelberg leader than
when he behaves as a Nash player. Therefore, the entrepreneur who
becomes the Stackelberg leader has the incentive to increase his R&D
effort beyond his Nash equilibrium level. This, in turn, provides the
followers with the incentive to increase their R&D efforts beyond
their Nash equilibrium levels. This lowers the unit costs and prices of
all products. All entrepreneurs are better off at the Stackelberg
equilibrium than at the Nash equilibrium. The lower prices ensure
that this is true also of the worker.

Conclusions

In the 1950s and 60s, it was argued that the existence of demand
externalities could justify "planning" that would ensure a "balanced
growth." Implicit in this prescription was the view of the economy as
a closed economy. If you follow an open economy policy instead, the
critics argued, the whole notion of balanced growth becomes
meaningless and the value of Rosenstein-Rodan's insight about the
existence of demand externalities becomes dubious. What we have
shown is that the measures to internalize demand externalities in
Japan and South Korea may have, in fact, helped their policy-makers
in following a successful outward-oriented strategy. We believe that
the failed experiment of central planning in many developing countries
may have resulted in an undervaluation of Rosenstein-Rodan's
theoretical insight.

Many industrializing countries are advised these days to follow
the examples of Japan and South Korea and pursue an export-led-
growth path. It is important to note, however, that neither Japan nor

South Korea followed a trade strategy that was dictated by their initial comparative advantage. On the contrary, they purposefully developed comparative advantage in those sectors which had high income elasticities and which allowed greater scope for technical progress. The main lesson to be drawn from these successful late industrializers is not simply that they followed an outward oriented strategy but that they undertook measures that rapidly brought about productivity growth in "the right" sectors so that they could compete internationally. We have shown in this chapter how the measures that could only have increased the concentration of market power domestically may have helped the industrial sectors in these economies to attain international competitiveness.

During the industrial revolution in Great Britain, technological innovation occurred in a competitive environment. One way to view the competitive process at work then is that of multiple experimentation. Different entrepreneurs performed different experiments and the most successful ones became the dominant technologies. At the inception of new technologies such process of trial and error was indispensable. For the late industrializing nations the problem was different because the early industrializers had developed technologies that the late industrializers could adopt. Trial and error through multiple experiments became less important than creating adequate incentives for entrepreneurs to supply effort directed toward adoption of modern technologies and increasing productivity. The process of internalizing the demand externality that we have discussed is one way to enhance entrepreneurs' incentives.

Many countries that are now industrializing face the same problem that Japan and South Korea faced. For sustained growth they have to gain comparative advantage in sectors characterized by high income elasticities -- typically modern manufacturing sectors. If the economy is opened before the productivity of the domestic industrial sector has been brought up to the international standard, the economy stands the risk of being deindustrialized. The prerequisite for an outward oriented strategy is therefore a campaign to increase industrial productivity. We have argued in this chapter that the industrial policy that Japan and South Korea followed had an additional merit of enhancing productivity growth. We could suggest on the basis of the analysis so far that newly industrializing countries would be justified in examining the wisdom of anti-trust policies. We would, however, hesitate at suggesting any concrete policies based on this highly stylized model. An industrial policy that promotes conglomeration and favors specific industries is likely to lead to rent-seeking. We have completely ignored the efficiency loss through rent-seeking in our discussion so far, and have thus biased the case against the decentralized outcome. Perhaps, the most intangible and yet important aspect of Japanese and Korean policies is how the policy-makers managed to keep the losses through rent-seeking activities low enough to make the net gains from such policies so substantial.

References

Basu, K. 1984. *The Less Developed Economy*. Delhi: Oxford University Press.
Eswaran, M., and A. Kotwal. (1989). "Demand Externality as an Impediment to Productivity Growth." Economics Department, University of British Columbia.
Johnson, C. 1982. *MITI and the Japanese Miracle*. Stanford: Stanford University Press.
_____. 1987. "Political Institutions and Economic Performance: the Government-Business Relationship in Japan, South Korea, and Taiwan," in Frederic C. Deyo, ed., *The Political Economy of the New Asian Industrialism*. Pp 136-164. Ithaca and London: Cornell University Press.
Komiya, R. 1988. "Introduction," in R. Komiya, M. Okuno, and K., Suzumura, eds., *Industrial Policy of Japan*. San Diego: Academic Press.
Lim, Y. 1981. *Government Policy and Private Enterprise: Korean Experience in Industrialization* (Korea Research Monograph No. 6). Berkeley: Institute of East Asian Studies, Univ. of California.
Murphy, K. M., A. Shleifer, and R. W. Vishny. 1989. "Industrialization and the Big Push." *Journal of Political Economy* 97 (5): 1003-1026.
Rosenberg, N., and L. E. Birdzell, Jr. 1986. *How the West Grew Rich: the Economic Transformation of the Industrial World*. New York: Basic Books.
Rosenstein-Rodan, P. N. 1943. "Problems of Industrialization in Eastern and South-Eastern Europe." *Economic Journal* 53: 202-211.

9

The Visible Hand and Economic Development: The Case of South Korea

Chung H. Lee

Introduction

The conventional wisdom has it that the rapid industrialization of South Korea (henceforth Korea) in the past three decades is a consequence of an outward-oriented development strategy that the country adopted in the early 1960s (e.g., Balassa 1980 and 1981). The strategy has presumably brought about efficient allocation of resources by establishing neutral and stable incentive structures and by limiting the role of government to that of providing social infrastructure and a stable political environment. Thus, implicit in this view are the assumptions that price distortions in the economy are basically a result of government intervention, and that but for the intervention, resources would be allocated efficiently and the economy would be developing at a rapid rate.

In recent years, however, this interpretation of the role of the Korean government has been challenged, as accumulating evidence seems to indicate that the government has played a much more active role in promoting economic development (e.g., Alam 1989; Amsden 1989; Hong 1990; Johnson 1985; Lee and Naya 1988; Roh 1990; and Whang 1987). An example of such a role is the visible hand of the government in allocating credit. For instance, during 1960-1969, when the objective of the government was export expansion and when there were not much of manufacturing industries to speak of, an increasing share of bank loans were channeled to the manufacturing sector in general. In the 1970s, however, when the government began its push for heavy and chemical industries the share of banks loans received by these industries increased from less than 20 percent in 1970-1974 to over 29 percent by 1980. Furthermore, during this period a majority of foreign loans were also allocated to these industries (Park 1991:59-60). Thus by controlling the allocation of credit, the government has directed the pace as well as the pattern of industrialization and the course of economic development in Korea.

The fact that the government has directed credit allocation does not necessarily mean that its intervention has contributed to economic development. In fact, such intervention by the government, which has been extensively analyzed under the rubric of "financial repression," is supposed to be an impediment to economic development. One could even argue, as many with the neoclassical bent are wont to do, that without such intervention the Korean economy would have done better (e.g., Fry 1988). Thus, in the absence of a satisfactory explanation of why and how the government may interfere with credit allocation for the purpose of promoting economic development, many of the challenges to the conventional wisdom would go unheeded.

Standard neoclassical economics, however, provides no explanation for the type of government intervention observed in Korea. Even when government intervention is admittedly warranted, it is believed that direct subsidies are better than direct government intervention (e.g., Park 1991). In fact, a general presumption in standard neoclassical economics is that government intervention is worse than the problem it is supposed to correct. For example, Deepak Lal (1985:16) has argued that:

> . . . no general rule of second-best welfare economics permits the deduction that, in a necessarily imperfect market economy, particular *dirigiste* policies will increase welfare. They may not; and they may even be worse than *laissez-faire*.

The issue is not whether government intervention carried out for purposes other than economic development can bring about an efficient allocation of resources. Instead, what is at issue is whether a government *committed to achieving economic development* can interfere with markets with positive results. The neoclassical presumption that it may not, as expressed above by Lal, is based on the view of an economy in which every transaction takes place across a market and is thus price-mediated. It then follows that government intervention which is not price-mediated cannot bring about an efficient allocation of resources. Thus it would be difficult for economists of the neoclassical bent to accept the dual fact that the Korean economy has grown rapidly during the past three decades, but that during that period the government has actively intervened in resource allocation. Their way out of this dilemma is either to deny that such intervention has existed or to argue that the economy would have grown faster without the intervention.

The purpose of this chapter is to present an alternative view of the role of the Korean government in economic development during the period preceding the recent liberalization. This historical demarcation is imposed because the role of government has changed as a result of the economic and political liberation undertaken in the 1980s and as it therefore needs a different explanation.

The view of the government presented here differs from the view of the government in either a *laissez-faire* or *dirigiste* economy, and admits the possibility that government can play a positive role in economic development. In this view, government is not seen as an institution existing outside the market system but instead as constituting, in combination with large private enterprises, an internal organization imbedded in the system. Government intervention with these enterprises is then a transaction internal to the organization and therefore need not be presumed inefficient simply because it is not price-mediated. In other words, by regarding the government and large private enterprises as constituting together an internal organization, we can regard government intervention not as intervention with markets, but as an internal transaction within the organization. It then follows that an action taken by the government, which is necessarily inefficient in the framework of the standard neoclassical economics, may not be inefficient.

Section II describes the structure of an organization consisting of the government and large private enterprises, which is called a quasi-internal organization to differentiate it from private internal organization. Section III then provides reasons why the quasi-internal organization could have played a positive role in accelerating the pace of economic development in Korea. Section IV points out the importance of competition for the efficient operation of the quasi-internal organization and thus the importance of an outward-oriented development strategy. Section V evaluates standard arguments against financial repression in light of the theoretical points raised in this chapter regarding the efficiency of the quasi-internal organization. Section VI concludes the chapter.

Structure of the Quasi-Internal Organization in Korea

One salient feature of Korea's manufacturing sector is its dual structure: it has a small number of large enterprises which dominate it in terms of value added, and a large number of small and medium-sized enterprises which account for the remainder of its value added. In 1982, for instance, there were 35,971 firms in the manufacturing sector but the largest 271 firms (0.75 percent of the total number) accounted for 33.2 percent of value added in that sector (40.7 percent of the value of shipment, 18.6 percent of employment, and 37.2 percent of capital stock of that sector) (table 9.1). In terms of control, the Korean manufacturing sector was actually more highly concentrated than the above figures indicate as these 271 firms all belonged to the top 30 business groups or conglomerates called *Chaebol*. Even among these large business groups the top five, which controlled 89 companies, accounted for a disproportionate share of shipment and value added in the manufacturing sector, 22.6 percent and 17.4 percent, respectively (table 9.1).

These business groups, which numbered 40 at the end of 1977, include such giant firms as Daewoo, Hyundai, Lucky-Gold Star and Samsung, and have become an increasingly dominant feature of the Korean economy. For instance, in terms of the value of shipment, the share of the top five increased continually from 15.7 percent in 1977 to 22.6 percent in 1982. The same upward trend was also experienced by the top

TABLE 9.1 Large Business Groups' Share of Shipment, Employment, and Capital of the Manufacturing Sector,[a] 1982

	Shipment (%)	Employment (5)	Value added (5)	Capital (5)	Number of companies
Top 5	22.6	8.4	17.4	16.3	89
Top 10	30.2	12.2	23.1	23.8	153
Top 15	33.9	14.5	26.6	27.8	187
Top 20	36.6	16.0	29.4	31.5	223
Top 25	38.8	17.1	31.2	34.3	241
Top 30	40.7	18.6	33.2	37.2	271

[a] Total number of firms in the manufacturing sector = 35,971 in 1982.

Source: Lee and Lee. 1985. "Business Integration and the Concentration of Economic Power." Research Report 85-02, Korea Development Institute.

TABLE 9.2 Share of Shipment by Top 30 Business Groups in the
Manufacturing Sector (percentage)

	1977	1978	1979	1980	1981	1982
Top 5	15.7	15.9	16.3	16.9	21.5	22.6
Top 10	21.2	22.0	22.7	23.8	28.4	30.2
Top 15	25.6	26.2	27.1	28.1	32.6	33.9
Top 20	29.3	29.4	30.3	31.4	35.3	36.6
Top 25	31.9	31.9	33.0	33.9	37.7	38.8
Top 30	34.1	34.1	35.2	36.0	39.7	40.7

Source: Lee and Lee. 1985. "Business Integration and the Concentration of Economic Power." Research Report 85-02, Korea Development Institute.

30 business groups (table 9.2). This trend clearly indicates that the growth of these large business groups has paralleled that of the Korean economy during the past three decades, and they have in fact played a leading role in its growth.

From this dual structure of Korea's manufacturing sector it follows that the relationship between the government and the private sector had a dual characteristic. The relationship between the government and large business groups was more direct and intimate than that between the government and a large number of small and medium-sized enterprises. In fact, for the former the government was like a senior member in a partnership, and as in a partnership, communication was maintained through direct contact established at meetings such as "deliberation councils" and "discussion groups" where government officials and business leaders met regularly (Jones and Sakong 1980). At such meetings information was exchanged and government directives were handed down.

The relationship between the government and large private enterprises was, however, more than the meetings of deliberation councils and discussion groups. There were other measures, such as the auditing of balance sheets, through which the government could monitor the conduct of private enterprises. But probably the most important instrument for the government was its control over the formal financial system, and thus its control over credit allocation. By controlling the allocation of credit, it controlled the availability of credit to large private enterprises and thus their business decisions. Given the fact that they were highly leveraged, their access to bank credit was a critical factor for survival, and they could ill afford to ignore directives from the government.

The relationship between the government and small and medium-sized firms resembled, in contrast, an arm's-length relationship. Their sheer number made it impossible for the government to maintain direct contact with these enterprises. Furthermore, they were not the targets for preferential credit allocation which was designed for the purpose of promoting certain large-scale industries. Thus, they were by and large left alone, but when government did intervene, the intervention took the form of price-mediated transactions. As far as small and medium-sized firms were concerned, the government's role very much resembled the role prescribed in standard neoclassical economics. Consequently there is very little that is puzzling about the relationship between the government and these enterprises. What remains to be explained however, is the relationship between the government and large private enterprises, because although it was direct and intimate, it does not seem to have brought about deleterious effects on the economy. In fact, one could even argue that this unique relationship accelerated the pace of export expansion and economic growth in Korea in the 1960s and 1970s.

Quasi-Internal Organization in a Market Economy

It is proposed here that the government and large private enterprises in Korea be viewed as constituting an internal organization. This internal organization is to be regarded as possessing the M-form (multi-divisional) structure, where the government is its general office and large private enterprises its subunits. This quasi-internal organization differs from a centrally planned economy in that it is a part of and imbedded in a market economy. It also differs from the "Anglo-American 'free-enterprise'" economy in that the government is directly involved in managing a subset of the economy, and the quasi-internal organization constitutes a significant part of the economy.

The structure and advantage of the M-form structure for a private enterprise are clearly spelled out in the following (Williamson 1985: 283-284):

> The M-form structure removes the general office executives from partisan involvement in the functional parts and assigns operating responsibilities to the divisions. The general office, moreover, is supported by an elite staff that has the capacity to evaluate divisional performance. Not only, therefore, is the goal structure

altered in favor of enterprise-wide considerations, but an improved information base permits rewards and penalties to be assigned to division on a more discriminating basis, and resources can be reallocated within the firm from less to more productive uses. A concept of the firm as an internal capital market thus emerges.

Effective multidivisionalization thus involves the general office in the following set of activities: (1) the identification of separable economic activities within the firm; (2) according quasi-autonomous standing (usually of a profit center nature) to each; (3) monitoring the efficiency performance of each division; (4) awarding incentives; (5) allocating cash flows to high-yield uses; and (6) performing strategic planning (diversification, acquisition, divestiture, and related activities) in other respects. The M-form structure is thus one that *combines* the divisionalization concept with an internal control and strategic decision-making capability.

In other words, the M-form structure allows the firm to carry out enterprise-wide strategic planning and efficiently allocate resources among its subunits. It also allows the firm to effectively monitor and control the efficient use of resources by its subunits.

Similarity between the M-form structure and the quasi-internal organization seems clear. The activities of their subunits and transactions between them are internalized, and these units are monitored and coordinated by salaried employees (i.e., bureaucrats) rather than market mechanisms. Given this similarity, and given that the modern multiunit enterprise is an efficient institution (Chandler, Jr. 1977), it follows that the quasi-internal organization *can* be efficient in achieving its objectives.

A parallel between the quasi-internal organization and the M-form structure can be clearly seen in Korea. For example, the Economic Planning Board (EPB) was established on July 22, 1961, as an organization for drafting and organizing economic plans. Its functions included planning, budgeting, and statistical functions, and it was placed on a level higher than a ministry in the government hierarchy. Thus, combined with the authority to control related agencies in economic planning and management, EPB became a central agency in the government for planning and implementing economic plans.

One of the stated objectives of the Korean government was export expansion. An annual export goal was set by the President in consultation of the Ministry of Commerce and EPB, and then export subgoals were assigned to general trading as well as major exporting companies, which themselves were subunits of large business groups. The President monitored their export performance at the Monthly Economic Review meetings and at the Export Promotion Joint Meeting which took place every three months. In addition, the government undertook various supportive measures such as tax reductions or exemptions, favorable bank loans, favorable access to foreign exchange, foreign currency loans, and trading privileges to promote exports (Choi 1988).

It is proposed that the quasi-internal organization parallels the M-form structure, and is thus efficient for the same reasons the M-form structure is efficient in achieving the objectives of a private enterprise. It follows that government can achieve its objectives (export expansion and economic growth in the case of Korea) more efficiently in this way than through price-mediated policies. This argument is supported by the observation that capital markets in developing countries are imperfect, and that effective policy implementation is a costly transaction.

Quasi-Internal Organization as an Internal Capital Market

Recent research on capital markets has raised serious questions regarding the efficiency of free capital markets in developing countries. These markets are underdeveloped and cannot be assumed to operate as "textbook models" of perfect competition. The problems of adverse selection, moral hazard, and costly contract enforcement are inherent to capital markets even in developed countries, and consequently they do not operate like a market for a common commodity (Stiglitz 1989a and 1989b). Instead, "credit rationing" and "equity rationing" are pervasive features of capital markets.

Due to asymmetry of information and their risk-averseness, banks do not necessarily allocate credit to those willing to pay the highest interest rate, but instead ration credit at a below-market-clearing rate (Stiglitz and Weiss 1981). A consequence of this practice is the underfinancing by banks of risky but potentially rewarding projects which could be financed in a well-functioning equity market. Thus a financial system without such an equity market will not bring about an inefficient allocation of resources (Cho 1986).

Even with well-functioning equity markets, equity rationing is practiced by the firm since it is afraid that issuing new shares will lead to a large decrease in the market valuation of its equity (Stiglitz 1989a). Asymmetry of information causes the market to heavily discount the equity value of a firm when new shares are issued. Unwilling to see its net worth decrease, the firm is thus reluctant to rely on equity markets for capital, but unable to divest itself of risks. For capacity expansion it may instead rely on internal financing, but unless the firm is large and has the M-form structure, such financing may result in a less than efficient allocation of resources.

The problems of imperfect capital markets are more serious for developing countries because their markets are less developed and their economies are subject to greater changes and uncertainty (Diaz-Alejandro 1985). These countries are not likely to have developed private institutions capable of coping with the problems of imperfect capital markets. They are more likely to have small-scale firms with inefficient internal capital markets and to lack private institutions capable of collecting, evaluating and disseminating information.

How to solve these problems of imperfect capital markets is certainly a challenge faced by the developing countries, and the quasi-internal organization can be regarded as Korea's response to this challenge. It is an internal capital market where the government has allocated credit among a number of large enterprises. Although such a practice is commonly called financial repression, it differs little from the way an internal capital market operates within the M-form structure enterprise.

Informational imperfections which lead to credit and equity rationing are more serious for developing countries, because the developmental process itself leads to greater informational problems. Again, the quasi-internal organization can be viewed as an institutional response designed to overcome these problems.

In discussing the efficiency of internal transactions relative to that of market transactions, Williamson (1975) has pointed out two characteristics of the internal organization that enable it to better handle informational imperfections. First, because of its hierarchical structure which allows specialization of decision making and lowers communication costs, an internal organization is able to extend the bounds of rationality. Second, an internal organization is able to reduce uncertainty by coordinating the decisions of interdependent units to adapt to unforeseen contingencies.

The quasi-internal organization in Korea had the advantages of both of these characteristics. Because of the direct contact maintained through channels such as deliberation councils and discussion groups, the government and large private enterprises were able to share information which would otherwise have had to be conveyed indirectly through prices. Thus, decisions as to the allocation of credit could be made before price changes could signal the direction of credit allocation and private agents could respond to these signals. Also, by coordinating these enterprises the quasi-internal organization could adapt to unforeseen contingencies. For example, the Korea Trade Promotion Corporation (KOTRA) was established in the early 1960s to collect economic and trade information virtually all over the world. The information collected by KOTRA, commercial attaches stationed abroad, and general trading companies was then shared by all members of the quasi-internal organization and used for establishing annual export goals.

Quasi-Internal Organization for Efficient Policy Implementation

Another reason why the quasi-internal organization could have contributed to Korea's economic development is that it made possible the efficient implementation of policies. In neoclassical economics government intervention, if it is warranted, should be indirect and parametric through policy instruments such as taxes and subsidies and through arm's-length regulations. Here the cost of policy implementation (ignoring the cost of policy formulation) is the cost of collecting taxes on appropriate activities, ensuring that subsidies are used for targeted activities, and seeing that regulations are enforced. This method of policy implementation works by controlling market parameters and thus modifying the behavior of market agents.

In Korea, policies were implemented through alteration of market parameters, especially when the government was dealing with small and medium-sized enterprises, In addition, however, policies were implemented within the quasi-internal organization as a direct transaction between the government and large private enterprises. This kind of policy implementation is an internal transaction and does not rely solely on changes in market parameters. Since such a transaction parallels that within a private internal organization, it is efficient for the same reasons that internal organization is more transactions-efficient than markets (Williamson 1975). That is, because of extended bounded rationality, reduced opportunism and uncertainty, reduced small-number indeterminacies, better information, and a group-oriented atmosphere, internal organization can be superior to market in achieving transaction efficiency.

Direct and continuous contact between the government and the large private enterprises that existed within the structure of the quasi-internal organization permitted the sharing of information which would have otherwise occurred indirectly through prices. The government possessed nonprice as well as price incentives and control techniques to be brought to bear upon the enterprises in a selective manner, it could coordinate interdependent enterprises to adapt to unforeseen contingencies, and it could resolve by fiat small-number bargaining indeterminacies among enterprises. The government also had the authority to audit the balance sheets of enterprises. Thus with better information and with various incentives and control techniques, the government could see to it that its policies were effectively carried out by the enterprises.

Quasi-Internal Organization and Competition

Stiglitz's argument that the internal capital market of a large enterprise can substitute for imperfect capital markets, and such substitution will improve allocative efficiency, presupposes that the firm operates in a competitive market environment. Otherwise, as to be expected from the theory of second best, such substitution may not improve allocative efficiency. For example, if a firm with the M-form structure has monopoly power in one market but is competitive in other markets, its internal allocation of funds may not be welfare-improving even though imperfect capital markets are now bypassed. In other words, to correct capital market imperfections so as to be welfare-improving, the markets for the firm's products must be competitive. Likewise, whether the quasi-internal organization will efficiently allocate funds among its subunits will depend on the external environment in which it operates.

It goes without saying that the quasi-internal organization must be committed to developmental goals for it to allocate resources toward achieving these goals. Efficiency in allocation does not necessarily mean efficient allocation toward achieving developmental goals. It is in fact possible that the quasi-internal organization is efficient in achieving objectives which diverge from those of the country, and thus may expand at the expense of the entire economy.

In the case of a private enterprise with the M-form structure and with its own internal capital market, the choice of the wrong product or technique may lead to bankruptcy and thus to its dissolution. Furthermore, market competition ensures the survival of only those firms which on average choose the right products and production techniques and thus achieve an efficient structure of internal organization. It follows that paradoxically, market competition is essential for internal organization to be more transactions-efficient than markets.

Within a given economy, the quasi-internal organization does not face the kind of competition that private enterprises generally face, since it is the only such organization. But in the context of the world economy it may face competition, if it chooses to do so, because it is then only one among many competitors for a share of world markets. It is in part for this reason that a country's adoption of an outward- or inward-oriented development strategy affects to its economic success.

For a small developing country committed to an outward-oriented development strategy, prices are parameters determined in the rest of the world. For its quasi-internal organization, prices are not then something that can be arbitrarily changed to cover the consequences of an inefficient allocation of credit. Because of this constraint, an inefficient internal allocation of credit to support unsuccessful wrong projects will result in financial losses for the subunits undertaking the projects. They may be able to survive with subsidies from the government, but their losses are internal losses for the quasi-internal organization. Thus whether subsidized or not, the quasi-internal organization will suffer financial losses and will be eventually forced to correct its pattern of internal credit allocation.

In contrast, a small developing country which has adopted an inward-oriented development strategy can alter prices to cover the adverse financial consequences of an ill-advised internal credit allocation. Potential losses of the private enterprises can be made to disappear by changing prices, with little noticeable effect on the nation's treasury. The quasi-internal organization can thus avoid losses caused by an inefficient allocation of credit, and there would be (at least in the short run) little or no incentive or compulsion to correct the existing pattern of internal credit allocation.

The foregoing discussion provides an additional reason why a developing country should adopt an outward-oriented development strategy. The standard neoclassical argument in favor of this strategy is that the neutrality of incentives between exports and import-substitutes brings about allocative efficiency in resource allocation. This argument fails to recognize that even with the neutrality of incentives, a developing country may not achieve allocative efficiency because of capital market imperfections and the limited size of firms. The quasi-internal organization can overcome the problems of market imperfections, but only when it is subject to international competition.

Quasi-Internal Organization and Financial Repression

A financial system such as the one that existed in Korea until its recent liberalization is called financial repression, and its theoretical consequences are well known. It reduces saving because the actual rate of return on deposits at financial institutions is low or even negative. In addition, it brings about an inefficient allocation of resources because credit in short supply is allocated by bureaucrats rather than by markets (Fry 1988).

In spite of the theoretical strength of the argument against financial repression, much of the empirical work attempting to show its adverse effect on saving has not been successful. At most it has been able to show that low or negative real rates of return on financial assets have only a marginally significant effect on national and household savings (Dowling, Jr. 1984; Giovannini 1983; van Wijnbergen 1982).

One of the allocative inefficiencies resulting from financial repression is supposed to be overly capital-intensive and large-scale production techniques as credit is allocated by the government at an artificially low rate. This inefficiency will result, however, only if the receivers of credit in fact use the credit for the projects targeted by the government. They may instead divert the funds to the informal credit market, capturing the rent arising from the difference between high rates in that market and artificially low rates on preferential credit.

Cole and Park (1983) and Hong and Park (1986) argue that there probably was a high degree of credit diversion in Korea, in as much as firms receiving preferential credit could capture large rents by diverting it to other more profitable projects. If this were true, the actual pattern of credit use would differ from the pattern of allocation directed by the government. In the extreme case of perfect credit diversion, the pattern of credit use would be the same as that which would prevail in a free-market financial system, and the receivers of preferential credit would be acting only as financial intermediaries.

Due to lack of data it is difficult to estimate the extent of credit diversion in Korea. But given that preferential credit was given primarily to the large private enterprises, and given that these enterprises were subunits of the quasi-internal organization, government monitoring of the use of rationed credit would have been close and effective. In other words, because the relationship between the government and the recipients of preferential credit was an internal and not a market transaction, it would have been easier for the government to monitor and thus reduce opportunistic behavior by the recipients.

The extent of credit diversion depends on the expected gains from credit diversion (the difference between the expected rate of return from a designated project and that from the best alternative chosen freely by the borrower) and the expected cost of credit diversion. The expected cost includes the penalties the borrower must pay if credit diversion is discovered by the government and the future loss resulting from losing the preferred status accorded by it. The cost would in turn depend on the monitoring ability of the government and the severity of the penalty it would impose. Thus the ability of the government to direct resource allocation through credit rationing cannot be analyzed without first addressing the government's ability to monitor the actual use of funds and the penalties it is ready to impose on infractors.

In Korea of the 1960s and 70s, the expected cost of credit diversion may have been extremely large because of effective monitoring within the quasi-internal organization, and because of the severity of penalty that the authoritarian government was willing and capable of imposing on infractions. The high cost may have offset many of the potential gains from credit diversion, thus reducing the extent of credit diversion.

As previously noted, the M-form structure is an internal capital market which is able to efficiently allocate financial resources among its subunits for the purpose of achieving high rates of return. It is proposed that the quasi-internal organization is also an internal capital market which can efficiently allocate financial resources to achieve developmental objectives. What is commonly called financial repression is in fact this internal allocation of credit, and from the discussion of the quasi-internal organization, it emerges that financial repression can be alternatively viewed as an efficient internal capital market. The theoretical conclusion that financial repression results in an inefficient allocation of resources follows from a market paradigm where markets are perfect and government intervention necessarily results in an inefficient allocation of resources. This no longer holds, however, once it is admitted that markets are not always perfect, and in those instances internal organization can be an efficient alternative to markets.

Conclusion

This chapter has examined the role of government in Korea's economic development and especially its relationship with large private enterprises. The standard neoclassical explanation of the role of government in economic development is inadequate in the case of Korea, as the government has played a much more direct and active role in allocating resources. The institutionalist view (Johnson 1985), on the other hand, falls short of explaining the role because it lacks a coherent theory of why government intervention has resulted in rapid economic growth in Korea. The point of this chapter is that the government and large private enterprises in Korea should be viewed as a quasi-internal organization with the efficiency attributable to internal organization. Government intervention in financial markets is thus analogous to an allocation of funds in the internal capital market of a modern enterprise with the M-form structure, without any presumption that it will result in an inefficient allocation of resources. There is no reason why the institution of the quasi-internal organization cannot be applied to other developing countries. For such an institution to succeed in these countries, however, there would need to be a commitment to an outward-oriented development strategy and a bureaucracy as competent as that in a large private enterprise. Unfortunately, these many developing countries may lack precisely these conditions. Nevertheless, the experience of Korea demonstrates that government can play an important role in accelerating the pace of economic development if its policies are basically complementary to markets.

In the case of Korea, the role of the quasi-internal organization will diminish as the economy develops further. Organizational failures will result if it is to expand to deal with an increasingly complex economy. To avoid organizational failures, the quasi-internal organization will diminish relative to the rest of the growing economy, and its influence will abate. But more fundamentally, the rationale for the quasi-internal organization will disappear because with further economic development, the problems of imperfect capital markets can be better handled by private market institutions.

References

Alam, S. M. 1989. *Governments and Markets in Economic Development Strategies: Lessons from Korea, Taiwan, and Japan.* New York: Praeger.

Amsden, A. H. 1989. *Asia's Next Giant: South Korea and Late Industrialization.* New York: Oxford University Press.

Balassa, B. 1980. *The Process of Industrial Development and Alternative Development Strategies.* Princeton Essays in International Finance, No. 141. Princeton: Princeton University Press.

_____. 1981. *The Newly Industrializing Countries in the World Economy.* New York: Pergammon Press.

Chandler, Jr., A. D. 1977. *The Visible Hand.* Cambridge, Mass.: Harvard University Press.

Cho, Y. J. 1986. "Inefficiencies from Financial Liberalization in the Absence of Well Functioning Equities Markets." *Journal of Money, Credit and Banking* 18 (2).

Choi, D. K. 1988. "Evolution of Administrative Organization to Promote Economic Development in Korea." East Asia Economic Policy Studies, No. 2, East-West Center, Honolulu.

Cole, D. C., and Y. C. Park. 1983. . *Financial Development in Korea, 1945-1978.* Cambridge, Mass.: Harvard University Press.

172																																																																																				Chung H. Lee

Diaz-Alejandro, C. 1985. "Good-Bye Financial Repression, Hello Financial Crash." *Journal of Development Economics* 19 (1/2): 1-24.
Dowling, J. M., Jr. 1984. *Domestic Resource Mobilization through Financial Development,.* Manila: Asian Development Bank.
Fry, M. J. 1988. *Money, Interest, and Banking in Economic Development.* Baltimore: Johns Hopkins University Press.
Giovannini, A. 1983. "The Interest Elasticity of Savings in Developing Countries: The Existing Evidence." *World Development* 11 (7): 601-607.
Hong, W. 1990. "Export-Oriented Growth of Korea: A Possible Path to Advanced Economy." *International Economic Journal* 4 (2): 97-118.
_____ and Y. C. Park. 1986. "The Financing of Export-Oriented Growth in Korea," in Augustine H. H. Tan and Basant Kapur, eds., *Pacific Growth and Financial Interdependence.* Sydney: Allen & Unwin.
Johnson, C. 1985. "Political Institutions and Economic Performance: The Government-Business Relationship in Japan, South Korea, and Taiwan," in R. Scalapino, S. Sato, and J. Wanadi, eds., *Asian Economic Development -- Present and Future.* Berkeley: Institute of East Asian Studies, University of California.
Jones, L. P., and I. Sakong. 1980. *Government, Business, and Entrepreneurship in Economic Development: The Korean Case.* Cambridge, Mass.: Harvard University Press.
Lal, D. 1985. *The Poverty of "Development Economics."* Cambridge, Mass.: Harvard University Press.
Lee, C. H., and S. Naya. 1988. "Trade in East Asian Development with Comparative Reference to Southeast Asian Experience." *Economic Development and Cultural Change* 36 (3): S123-152.
Lee, K. U., and S. S. Lee. 1985. "Business Integration and the Concentration of Economic Power." Research Report 85-02, Korea Development Institute. (in Korean).
Park, Y. C. 1991. "The Development of Financial Institutions and the Role of Government in Credit Allocation," in Lee-Jay Cho and Y. H. Kim, eds., *Economic Development in the Republic of Korea: A Policy Perspective.* Honolulu: East-West Center.
Roh, S. J. 1990. "Government Market Distortions and Multinationals: Expansion of Japanese and Korean Business Groups Abroad." A paper presented at the international symposium on "MNEs and 21st Century Scenarios," Tokyo, Japan, July 4-6, 1990.
Stiglitz, J. E. 1989a. "Markets, Market Failures, and Development." *American Economic Review, Papers and Proceedings* 197-203.
_____. 1989b. "Financial Markets and Development." *Oxford Review of Economic Policy* 5 (4): 55-68.
_____., and A. Weiss. 1987. "Credit Rationing in Markets with Imperfect Information." *American Economic Review* 71: 393-410.

van Wijnbergen, S. 1982. "Stagflation Effects of Monetary Stabilization Policies: A Quantitative Analysis of South Korea." *Journal of Development Economics* 10 (2): 133-169.

Whang, In-Joung. 1987. "The Role of Government in Economic Development: The Korean Experience." *Asian Development Review* 5 (2): 70-88.

Williamson, O. E. 1975. *Markets and Hierarchies: Analysis and Antitrust Implications.* New York: The Free Press.

_____. 1985. *The Economic Institutions of Capitalism.* New York: The Free Press.

10

Japanese Economics:
The Theory and Practice of
Investment Coordination

Keizo Nagatani

Introduction

Throughout the 120-year history of modern Japan, the United States of America has been her single most important trading partner in the entire world. See Table 10.1 below.

TABLE 10.1 U.S.'s Share in Japan's External Trade

Year	Export Share	Import Share
1900	28.5%	22.5%
1920	29.0	37.5
1940	15.6	35.9
1960	26.7	34.4
1975	20.0	20.0
1985	37.1	20.0

Source: *Nihon No Hyaku Nen* (One Hundred Years of Japanese Statistics). Tokyo: Kokusei-sha (1986), pp. 305-306.

The importance of the U.S. to Japan has not been limited to the trading of goods; Japan imported many social institutions from the U.S. in the early stage of modernization including the banking and public school system; the cultural influence of the U.S. through music, movies and sports has also been great; and in return the Japanese have always had a special affinity for the U.S. and her people.

Today, the U.S.-Japan relation is quite tense, however. The chief reason for this tension is economic. For two decades, the U.S. economy has experienced low levels of investment and productivity growth. While the policy-makers pursued monomaniac goals such as combating inflation and defending the dollar, and while the business managers preoccupied themselves increasingly with the new corporate money games for quick profits, the long-term health and strength of the U.S. economy gave away. Table 10.2 shows the profound changes that took place in the U.S. economy during the last quarter century relative to the Japanese economy.

What the U.S. has lost to Japan she has not gained from the others. As a result, the U.S.'s trade deficits have stayed high, and her external debt has been snowballing, with all the sectors, government,

TABLE 10.2 U.S.-Japan Trade: 1960 and 1985

U.S. Exports 1960		Japanese Exports 1960	
1. Raw cotton	13.9%	1. Clothing	10.8%
2. Machinery	12.0	2. Steel	6.6
3. Scrap iron	10.1	3. Radios	6.4
4. Soy beans	6.7	4. Metal products	6.3
5. Coal	5.9	5. Marine products	5.3
U.S. Exports 1985 ($25.8 billion)		Japanese Exports 1985 ($65.3 billion)	
1. Machinery	20.3%	1. Machinery	38.6%
2. Corn	5.7	2. Automobiles	29.5
3. Aircraft	5.6	3. Prec. machines	5.0
4. Lumber	4.4	4. Steel	4.3
5. Soy beans	4.1	5. Motorbikes	2.8

Source: Nihon No Hyaku Nen (One Hundred Years of Japanese Statistics). Tokyo: Kokusei-sha (1986), p. 309.

business and households, contributing to the cause. America's frustration and anger have found expression in increasing attacks on some of her trading partners, and especially on Japan.

In 1989 "Japan bashing" broke out of the conference rooms of academics and bureaucrats and was taken over by journalists all over the world. The American journalist James Fallows wrote two articles for the Atlantic Monthly (1989a, 1989b); in the first article Fallows argued that the Japanese lacked principles such as justice and charity and hence that their "destructive expansion" must be "contained" by external forces; Fallows continued his appeal in the second, arguing that preaching principles to the Japanese to change their behavior was pointless and therefore that the U.S. too had better forget principles and adopt whatever countermeasures would produce "results." Karel van Wolferen (1989a, 1989b), the Dutch journalist and long-time resident of Japan, took issue with Japan's "enigmatic" power structure and decision-making process and argued how the failure of the Japanese intellectuals to stand on principles and offer rational guidance and counsel to those in power contributed to the growth of a might-is-right political culture. Later in the year the British journalist Bill Emmott (1989) took the labor of demonstrating that "the sun also sets," due largely to such internal factors as the greying of the population and the deteriorating work ethic and discipline among the Japanese youths.

In the face of these very serious charges the Japanese have been rather silent. True, Akio Morita and Shintaro Ishihara kicked off the year with their booklet entitled *The Japan That Can Say "No"* (1989) which has been gaining popularity on this side of the Pacific. It argued that Japan's superiority over the U.S. in technology and organization was clear and that Japan should use this superiority to her advantage and stop being a pushover in dealing with the U.S.; it is a book on power politics and not intended to seek a better communication and understanding of the U.S.-Japan economic conflict by both sides.

I find this lack of communication and persistence of a deep "perception gap" between the U.S. and Japan deplorable. Although much of this "gap" may be attributable to the differences in Weltanschauung and culture at large between the two nations, I also believe that today's U.S.-Japan economic conflict and the perception gap related thereto derive from the differences in the economic doctrines they act on.

The main goal of this chapter is to bring out the essence of "Japanese Economics" that has shaped Japan's economic policies over the past 120 years. Contrary to the claim by Western critics, it is my belief that Japanese economic policies and strategies are based firmly on principles and quite consistent within the framework of their doctrines and therefore that knowing Japanese Economics is useful for the Westerners not only to better understand Japan but to cope more effectively with her. The chapter begins with Japan's reactions to the charges laid by Fallows and van Wolferen (Section II). They are based on interviews I had with several prominent economists and government officials of Japan in the summer of 1989 and are intended to convey to the reader an idea of the perception gap between the two nations mentioned earlier. Section III presents an overview of Japan's investment policy and coordination which epitomizes the spirit of Japanese economics. From my own experience first as a Japanese bureaucrat and later as an academic in North America, I have long been keenly aware of the vast differences between Western (neo-classical) and Japanese Economics. Whereas Western Economics is natural -- scientific, impersonal, non-historical, static and universal, Japanese Economics is social -- scientific, game-theoretic, historical, dynamic and relative. These doctrinal differences naturally lead to different policy formulas and different styles of policy making, the most notable difference having been in the area of investment policy. Whereas Westerners believe that people's free choice over assets in the market place will produce an efficient and socially desirable pattern and pace of capital accumulation and that governmental intervention in this process will necessarily entail distortions and waste, the Japanese believe that economic growth and development do not come naturally, that different forms of capital have different effects on economic growth and development (equal private rates of return notwithstanding), and that a proper sequence of investments must be designed and implemented by a "visible hand" in order to succeed. Section IV provides the basic tenets of what we may say Japanese Economics by way of recapitulation of the discussion. Finally, Section V concludes the chapter with a summary.

A Characterization of the Japanese Economy:
Popular Impressions and Commentary

This section summarizes my interviewees' comments and opinions on Fallows (1989a) and, by implication, van Wolferen. Because the comments and opinions received from the interviewees varied in focus and scope, I have taken the liberty of rephrasing, rearranging and amplifying them so they may match Fallows' statements. The reader will notice in Japan's reactions to the charges a deep "perception gap" much of which originates in the differences between the basic philosophy of the two economies.

Conflict of Interests and Trade Imbalance

The continued trade imbalance between Japan and the U.S. dominates any discussion on the relationship between the two nations. Fallows (1989a) pointed that Japan's inability or unwillingness to restrain the one sided destructive expansion of its economic power and unfair trade practices. With Japan's industrialization, the trading pattern changed dramatically from an exporter of tea and silk to manufactured products. The Japanese do not think anything wrong with this change, but Americans perceive an increased competition from Japan. The doctrinal differences between the two economies are prevalent in ideas put forward by Fallows (1989a) and the U.S. Advisory Committee for Trade Policy and Negotiation (ACPTN) on the one hand and the Japanese official view on the other hand.

Fallows (1989a) pointed out that conflict arises from Japan's inability or unwillingness to restrain the one-sided destructive expansion of its economic power and unfair trade practices. The Japanese find this argument strongly disagreeable for a number of reasons. First and foremost, Japan is not at all interested in the economic conquest of the world, let alone the world hegemony in politics. "[F]or much of the past four decades Japan seems to have done everything in its power to avoid being a leader" is Emmott's testimony. Until the mid-1950s, for example, the MITI was pessimistic about the future of the Japanese automobile industry. Ten years later, it held a similarly negative view of the computer industry. What these industries have accomplished to date was not by design. Indeed, much of Japan's postwar economic "success" came as a surprise to her government officials and even to industrialists themselves. The current superior performance of the Japanese economy is largely the fruit of its efforts at reorganization since the 1970s in anticipation of the age of more variety and shorter production run. Its pace is bound to slow down as its population is expected to stabilize at 130 million around the year 2020 (and the grayest one at that) and as the neighboring NIEs claim a growing share of its production and exports (Japan's imports from them have accelerated dramatically since 1986, with the annual growth rate of over 30% in 1987 and 1988). As far as the Japanese are concerned, their current prosperity is hard-earned but temporary in nature.

Second, Japan already has fewer import restrictions and lower tariff rates than any other country in the world. Even in agriculture, the pace of liberalization has been remarkable in the recent past. (The Japanese are aware that nearly three-quarters of U.S. farm crops including wheat, rice, cotton, corn, grain sorghum and barley are receiving income and price support from the government and that the federal government spent $25 billion in 1987 for these purposes as against $2.8 million in 1980. The Japanese also resent the fact that the U.S. demands the opening of Japanese markets for only those items in which she has an overwhelming advantage, while protecting as many as 14 items on waiver from GATT negotiations.) In the field of finance, where Japan has been receiving a great deal of heat lately, the Japanese market again has opened up significantly in the last several years. As a result, 83 foreign banks with 120 branches, 9 local establishments and 127 representative offices are operating in Japan as of June 30, 1989. By comparison, 42 Japanese banks are operating abroad with 267 branches, 246 local establishments and 426 representative offices as of the same date. While more foreign banks could and perhaps should be doing business in Japan, the experience after the opening up of the Japanese financial markets shows a decline in the market share of foreign banks both in Japan and in the offshore markets; the creation of unsecured call loans market designed to help foreign banks has merely resulted in the domination by Japanese banks; indeed, as many as 12 foreign banks have withdrawn from Japan since 1985.

Third, the technology gap between Japan and the U.S. remains wide and growing even wider. A recent estimate of the total factor productivity increase over the 16-year period 1967-1982 puts Japan's average annual growth rate at 3.7% against the U.S.'s 0.0% (Morrison and Diewert 1988). In March, 1989, Ford decided to replace domestic steel with Japanese-made steel for auto bodies because of the latter's greater malleability at the press stage. The Japanese automobile producers stick to Japanese-made semiconductors because of their superior reliability. On the other hand, Schick's razor blades and Rockwell's semiconductors for fax machines are examples of great success in the Japanese markets. Some foreign cars such as Audis, Benzes and BMWs are enjoying a similar, though less spectacular, success in Japan. These examples indicate that the Japanese markets are more open than they are made out to be but that the technology gap is a significant factor behind the Japan-U.S. trade imbalance.

Trade Protectionism

The Japanese seem to think that trade deficits are no proof of fair conduct any more than trade surpluses are evidence of protectionist behavior. Fallows would have to conclude that the U.S. economy during the 1950s and 60s and many more decades prior thereto, indeed since 1893, was extremely protectionist!

The Japanese are deeply concerned over the U.S.'s recent use of this type of "results-oriented" argument. Not only does it fail to make sense but it signifies the abandoning of America's long-cherished principle of fairness by rule. In August, 1989, the Japan-U.S. Business Council published its critical comments on a report produced by its American counterpart. The ACTPN Report, entitled "Analysis of the U.S.-Japan Trade Problem," takes this results-oriented, bilateral and sectorial approach to the trade imbalance problem and attributes most of the industry-by-industry imbalances to the unfair practices of the Japan-ese.

The Japan-U.S. Business Council Report does recognize the existence of certain "barriers" in the Japanese system such as intra-company group or *keiretsu* transactions, retail price settings by manufacturers of certain consumer products and price discriminations between domestic and export markets. But it strongly disagrees with the basic thesis of the ACTPN Report for a number of reasons. First, the U.S.'s trade deficit problem is basically a macroeconomic problem caused by the country's persistent overspending. Barriers specific to industries would affect the composition of U.S. exports to Japan but not the total. In this connection, the Economic Planning Agency estimates that a reduction of U.S. federal budget deficit by 1% of GNP (or $44 billion of the total deficit of $150 billion as of 1987) will reduce the U.S. current account deficit by $21 billion. Second, Japan's imports of manufactured goods have already surpassed the $100 billion mark which the ACTPN Report regarded as the likely volume in the absence of "invisible barriers." This fact indicates that the macroeconomic effects of yen appreciation and domestic demand expansion are at work and that the nature of the invisible barriers in Japan, if any, is more like tariffs than import quotas as suggested by the Report. Third, adoption by many of this sort of results-oriented, bilateral and sectorial approach will lead to the destruction of the global system of free trade.

Fallows (1989a) pointed that the last time one nation had such an unbalanced position in world trade was the late 1940s, when the U.S. economy represented half the economic activity in the entire war-battered world. But the U.S. rapidly and deliberately opened its markets with the result that its trade surplus of 1947 amounting to 4.5% of GNP was driven down to a mere 0.5% by 1950. The Japanese consider this assessment of the historical episode lacking in fairness and objectivity. First, the period from 1947 to 1950 was a unique period in which massive aid to Western Europe was carried out under the Marshall Plan. As much as $13 billion of public funds was poured into Europe during this period. In terms of scale, it exceeded any foreign aid before or since and contributed greatly to the economic recovery of the region. But its chief motive was to strengthen Europe's resistance to communism; the economic motive was was secondary. Second, the singling out of such a short and special period does not provide a more accurate and complete picture of the performance of the U.S. economy in the postwar period. Table 10.3 summarizes the trade balances of the U.S., Germany and Japan by decade.

True, Japan appears to be the villain during the 1980s on the surface. But a closer examination of the facts tells a different story.

TABLE 10.3. Balance of Trade (Billions of U.S. Dollars)

Period	United States	Germany	Japan
1950-59	33.56	5.15	-6.35
1960-69	34.34	21.86	-5.3
1970-79	-166.31	126.06	25.76
1980-88	-856.79	367.72	480.01

Source: IMF. *International Financial Statistics.*

TABLE 10.4 Import Share of Manufactured Goods

Year	United States	Germany	Japan
1980	56.8%	58.3%	22.8%
1985	76.5	62.0	31.0
1987	79.6	73.0	44.1
1988	-	-	49.0
1989	-	-	50.3

Source: Japan 1989.   Keizai Koho Center (Japan Institute for Social and Economic Affairs), p. 35. Figures for 1988 and 1989 were obtained from the Economic Planning Agency.

First, Japan's surpluses began only in the 1970s and even after 1970, she recorded substantial deficits on the occasions of the two oil crises. Second, U.S.'s $33 billion surplus of the 1950s was far greater than Japan's $480 billion surplus of the 1980s relative to the world trade volume. For example, the world exports were $85.5 billion in 1955 and $1,784 billion in 1984. When adjusted by these figures, the $33 billion surplus of the 1950s becomes comparable to $700 billion of the 1980s. In terms of the historical-dynamic view of the world common among the Japanese, the kind of change shown in Table 10.3 is nothing out of the ordinary; it merely reminds them that development is a never-ending task.

Low Manufactured Share of Imports

The low import share of manufactured products in Japan has become a great concern to western countries which they see it as a part of unfair trade practices. As Table 10.4 shows, Japan has a distinctly lower import share of manufactured goods among the industrialized economies. In 1987 Japan exported $225 billion of manufactured goods while importing $61 billion. The corresponding figures were $191 billion against $335 billion for the U.S., and $270 billion against $161 billion for Germany.

The Japanese admit that such an imbalance exists, particularly in motor vehicles ($58 billion against $2 billion) and machinery/transportation equipment ($161 billion against $16 billion), but insist that they have been trying their best to correct it. They would like the West to appreciate their efforts in this direction as evidenced by the sharp increase in the import share of manufactured goods during the past several years. They also expect an increase in this share in the future as the neighboring NIEs increase their manufacturing capabilities.

Though willing to comply with the wishes of the West as a friendly gesture, the Japanese are not convinced of the significance of such measures as the import share of manufactured goods. First, it should vary naturally with the endowments of the economy. Japan relies heavily on imports for foodstuffs, raw materials and fuels. In 1987 Japan's net imports of foodstuffs, raw materials and fuels were $21 billion, $21 billion, and $39 billion, respectively. The corresponding figures were $4 billion, $7 billion and $39 billion for the U.S., and $11 billion, $9 billion and $18 billion for Germany. Japan's total of the three items exceeded those of the U.S. and Germany by $40 billion. This suggests that as much as $40 billion of Japan's annual trade imbalance in manufacturing may be rationalized by her poor resource endowments. Second, there is no economic theory demonstrating the desirability of a balanced trade within the manufacturing sector, especially if the imbalance is caused by the relative technological superiority of the economy over the others.

Unbalanced Growth

From the Western point of view Japan's economic growth is unbalanced. One indication of imbalance is the gap between Japan's export success and its artificially suppressed consumption at home. As supporting evidence for this statement, Fallows points out that Japanese prices generally are the highest in the world and, more to the point, that Japanese-made products are always cheaper in New York than in Tokyo. Fallows' point is that this proves Japan's capitalist development strategy of discouraging domestic absorption and promoting exports (Johnson 1982).

However, the Japanese see the situation differently. First, there are many Japanese products that are sold cheaper in Japan. (As a longtime resident of North America, I can testify that I would rather buy a wide range of Japanese products from cameras and VCRs down to food items in Japan). Second, a careful quality adjustment is necessary in order to arrive at a meaningful price comparison. This point is particularly important given the notoriously fastidious tastes of Japanese consumers who meticulously seek better quality products even at higher prices. As a result, Japanese domestic prices have a much wider range than American prices. A slightly bent cucumber fetches only a small fraction of the price of a straight one; even lunch noodles are finely graduated in quality (and reputation) and the prices range over a scale of one to five; when it comes to durables, quality differentiation is more subtle and complex, with numerous small differences in size, weight, design, capacity, speed and other features which the more practical American consumers would not appreciate. In short, top quality consumer goods sold in Japan are more sophisticated and justifiably higher priced than those sold abroad. Therefore one might conclude that the Japanese economy is a high-price, high-quality equilibrium even though some argue that high price is a reflection of an "inefficient distribution system" in which much value is actually added through the multi-stage distribution network in terms of product quality and user convenience.

The generally defensive attitude of the Japanese toward Fallows' charge must be interpreted as an admission of guilt, however. Japanese prices have always had much greater administered content than those of the West; policy makers and business leaders have tended to regulate the prices of strategically important goods to effect the type of resource allocation they want. Price cartels by major industries have been prominent throughout Japan's history; the famous Fiscal Investment and Loans Plan of the government is a prime example of such price (in this case interest rate) administration; utility rates have conventionally been set much lower for industrial users than for residential users. Government and business leaders then have trained the citizens to accept these prices without suspicion. The result is 120 million trusting, manipulatable consumers who lack the price rationality of Westerners.

Similarly, Japanese policy makers and business leaders have traditionally kept consumer loans at a minimum. Even today, the interest rates on unsecured personal loans to *sarakin* ("salarymen") stand at 30% and over (and this in an economy where the prime lending rate for corporations is as low as 4%). Elsewhere I (1989) suggested that these extra charges on consumers could be interpreted as the premium they are asked to pay for the comprehensive job and income insurance.

It is not surprising that outsiders should find the Japanese price system difficult to comprehend. One might say that the Japanese economy operates much like the fixed-price model of the economists relative to these administered prices. Although Westerners tend to equate the lack of price flexibility with lack of competition, this is not the case. Japanese firms compete fiercely in "quantities" instead. Note also that these administered prices contain various legitimate components, such as the insurance premium mentioned earlier and various "monitoring fees," which have no counterparts in the West.

In Japanese Economics, prices have always been the key policy instruments. To the Japanese, the success of a nation's developmental project hinges on the right target setting and the requisite resource allocation through price administration. This is in sharp contrast to Western Economics which holds that the prices will find the right target for you. But whether these administered prices have really been a major cause of Japan's trade imbalance is a moot point. For one thing, they have been there for the past 120 years but failed to generate trade surpluses except only recently. For another, there is little assurance that their removal would significantly increase aggregate consumer spending, let alone imports from the U.S.

Political Interest Groups

There is a growing concern that the structure of Japanese politics with growing importance of special interest politics, far from providing a brake on one-sided economic expansion, actually keeps the expansion going. Fallows (1989a) cites as evidence the lack of progress following the historic pronouncement by the Nakasone Cabinet (in the form of the Maekawa Report of 1985) of the drastic reorientation of the Japanese economy away from exports and into domestic demand and toward an improved living standard of the citizens. In Fallows' opinion, the recent Japanese political leaders have lost effective leadership over the nation's political economy, with the result that an increasing number of special-interest *zoku* politicians are allowed to pursue their self-interest without regard to the interest of Japan as a nation.

While the Japanese do not deny the growing power of *zoku* politicians, they do not consider this as a phenomenon unique to Japan. In their opinion, special-interest politics has always been more prevalent in the U.S. where many members of the Congress are overtly spokespersons for specific industries and, in some cases, for specific corporations; by comparison, the Japanese Diet members have been more nationalistic. On the other hand, the 35 years of uninterrupted ruling by the LDP certainly has enabled its members to acquire expertise in specific fields and take vested interest in them.

But what about the political clout of the *Zenno* (National Federation of Agricultural Cooperatives) in its campaign for protectionist policies, as has been singled out by Fallows? Would the Japanese government have opened up Japan's agricultural sector more had it not been for the pressure from the *Zenno-zoku* politicians? Should home-grown rice keep costing five times as much to the consumers as Californian rice and billions of dollars more a year to the government coffers? Why should Japanese food processors be required to match imported cornstarch with domestic, when the latter is priced three times as high?

The Ministry of Agriculture, Forestry and Fisheries admits that the retail price (not to mention the producer's price) is too high relative to the imputed factor cost; in this sense, the rice price is politically determined. But much of the observed international price differences is economic-technological in nature. The average Japanese farmer oper-ates on 2 acres of land as against 200-400 acres of the American farmer. The intensive margins have already been pushed to the limit. The only hope is to join many such small lots in the form of co-operatives and reap the benefit of economies of scale. In 1987 the Agricultural Policy Council estimated that at 50 to 100 acres the average cost could be reduced by 30% for rice and 40% for wheat. At present one-third of farm families have joined such co-ops. The MAFF wants to pursue this avenue of rationalization in the future. However, it is a far cry from a free trade in farm products.

The Japanese are indeed not aiming at a full-scale liberalization of Japanese agriculture. Their Shokuryo-Anpo Theory holds that foodstuffs are special, that self-sufficiency in food supply has a significant security value for the nation much like military defense, and that a 50% level of self-sufficiency is the absolute minimum. The actual level was 75% in 1983, 71% in 1987, and 70% in 1988, which makes Japan's self-sufficiency ratio already the lowest among the major industrialized economies.

Ironically, it was the U.S.'s embargo of soybeans some years ago that reminded the Japanese of the importance of food security. In particular, they are resolved to maintain rice production at all costs. Irrational as this may sound, there is even a Japanese sense of equity behind this resolve. Throughout the prewar developmental stage, the government relied heavily on the agricultural sector for savings and tax revenues; it also kept the prices of rice and other staple farm products low in order to hold down the labor cost in the infant industries. In short, the Japanese economy owed much to its agricultural sector in the first stage of development. The situation was reversed in the postwar period. Farm product prices, if anything, came to be supported by the government with the resources released from the now efficient industries; the growth of industrial real wages has been held below that of productivity, with the difference subsidizing the farmers. The MAFF is showing no sign of undoing this social compact, which means Japan's liberalization of agriculture is limited in both pace and scope.

One conspicuous feature of Japanese society is the "long-term contracts" that pervade human and business relations. These contracts, though often implicit, form the basis of mutual trust. This feature of the Japanese system poses two problems when dealing with outsiders. First, when an outsider's demand conflicts with the honoring of existing contracts, the Japanese political leader gets caught in a dilemma. Second, even when the Japanese find the outsider's demand agreeable in principle, any change must be implemented slowly to minimize the ill effects of possible breach of trust.

Lack of Abstract Principles

Japan is a highly honorable society. But Japanese society has always been short on abstract principles dictating proper treatment of those outside the network of obligations such as foreigners. "The result," continues Fallows, "is Japan's distinctive view of 'fair' competition and its seemingly clear conscience about one-sided behavior." The Japanese admit there is much truth in this statement but also experience much frustration at the negative connotation of this stereotypical judgment by Westerners.

According to the Japanese, many of their idiosyncrasies stem from their late-comer mentality. A late-comer must devise its own survival technique in a world already endowed with dominant players and rules written by them. Its survival strategy is necessarily conditioned by the historical environment of the time. The only choice open to the late-comer is over which of the many valves connecting it to the world to open and which ones to keep closed. Making this choice wisely, the Japanese have built an economic enclave of their own so as to maximize the gains from trade while retaining a degree of autonomy over it. There is little room for "abstract principles" in such maneuver. In short, the Japanese have always had a game-theoretic view of the world from a follower's standpoint and are not apologetic about it. Van Wolferen (1989b) accuses Japan of being "in the world but not of it" in this sense.

Late-comer Mentality

This late-comer mentality has bred some features of Japanese behavior which are not easily rationalizable, however. Probably the most significant of all is the Japanese' stern distinction between "us" and "them." The Japanese have lived under two distinct codes of conduct; one is the traditional code based on Japanese sense of values and honor; the other is the modern code of Western origin. By "us" is meant those people who rely on the traditional code among themselves; all others are "them." This distinction is not racial; even among the Japanese, strangers are "them" until proven trustworthy. Thus, a new Japanese firm in an industry faces as much hardship as a foreign entrant because Japanese firms like to do business on the basis of mutual trust built on years of relationship. On the other hand, if foreigners are willing to pay the entry fee, Japan can be a good place to do business, as some foreign firms (such as Citi-Bank) and many individuals have proven.

Japan's Investment Policy and Coordination

The purpose of this section is to present a version of the doctrines on which the Japanese appear to have long formed their economic policies and business strategies. Japan's investment policy and coordination epitomizes the spirit of Japanese Economics which I believe will provide some clue as to where it lies the difference between the Western approach and Japanese Economics.

Ever since the Meiji Restoration in 1868, Japan has pursued a developmental strategy in the spirit of the economics just described. Indeed, the motto of the Meiji government was *fukoku kyohei*, which literally means the pursuit of the nation's wealth and military strength. The core strategy toward this goal was industrialization. In 1870, the Ministry of Engineering was established to set up and run a variety of plants and factories in such fields as railroad, mining, telegraph, lighthouse, glass and cement, steel, ship building, and last but not least, arms production. In a word, the aim of the Ministry was to achieve an adequate level of military strength needed to defend the land in a shortest possible time.

The method employed was that of outright and complete transfer of Western technologies, followed by a more indirect method of government-guided industrialization by the private sector, with the government providing assistance to select "infant industries" including Mitsubishi's shipping business. Many of the governmental enterprises were sold to private interests often at prices much below cost. Industrialization shifted into the hands of private entrepreneurs. A sudden surge of private enterprises began in the late 1880s and, after the industrial revolution of the 1890s, the Japanese economy completed the transition from a feudalistic agrarian state to a modern capitalist state in the short span of 30 years. By 1910, finished goods exports exceeded their imports for good. See Tables 10.5 and 10.6 below.

If the industrial technology was rudimentary in the Meiji Japan, her commercial technology for external trade was nonexistent. Japan therefore had to rely entirely on foreign agents for their know-how concerning foreign exchange transactions, bond sales and shipping of cargoes. Here again, the Meiji government chose to take the matter in its own hands. It set up public corporations specializing in foreign exchanges and commerce. It further sought direct export trade by-passing the foreign agents. It also converted Mitsubishi into a first-rate shipping company by pouring governmental resources into it (including an outright gift of 13 government-owned vessels). After the first foreign exchange corporation folded, the government helped the founding of a foreign exchange bank (the Yokohama Shokin Bank) by becoming its part-owner.

But the most important element of Japan's early developmental policies was public finance. Through it a massive transfer of resources was effected from the agricultural sector to the modern industrial sector. Throughout the Meiji period (1868 - 1912), the dominant item in

Table 10.5. Japanese Exports, 1868-1877

Year	Exports (A)	Raw Silk (B)	Tea (C)	B/A	C/A	(B+C)/A
1868	15.5*	10.3*	3.6*	66.6%	23.0%	89.6%
1869	12.9	8.6	2.1	66.9	16.2	83.1
1870	14.5	7.2	4.5	49.8	31.0	80.8
1871	17.9	9.9	4.7	55.1	25.9	81.0
1872	17.0	8.2	4.2	48.1	24.8	72.9
1873	21.6	10.9	4.6	50.3	21.5	71.8
1874	19.3	6.6	7.2	34.1	37.5	71.6
1875	18.6	6.4	6.8	34.7	36.8	71.5
1876	27.7	16.2	5.4	58.4	19.6	78.0
1877	23.3	10.6	4.4	45.6	18.7	64.3

Source: Tamura, S. 1977. *Shokusankogyo (Japan's Industrialization).* Tokyo: Kyoiku-sha, table 7, p. 122. *Figures in millions of yen.

the governmental tax revenue was the land tax. In 1877, for example, the land tax accounted for 82% of the the total tax revenue and 79% of the current account revenue. In 1887, they were 40% and 30% (Ministry of Finance 1927: vol. 3). Besides the land tax, the Meiji government relied heavily on excise taxes on such basic consumption items as sake, tobacco and soy sauce. The income tax was introduced in 1887 and the business tax in 1897, but these modern direct taxes did not amount to very much for quite some time. Most of these revenues was injected into the military and other industrial sectors. The land tax after the 1873 reform played a particularly significant role in the government's modernization project. The rate was high (3% of land value), rigid (inflexible to annual variations in crops) and payable in cash (previously payable in kind). Many small-scale owner-operators were forced to sell their land and turn themselves into tenant farmers or industrial workers.

In the meantime, the government abolished the warrior class by buying out their jobs with pensions and severance payments which cost the government an average of 38% of the land tax revenues over the 1867-1876 period (Tamura 1977:93). Millions of ex-samurai members had to join the working class. In short, the Meiji government achieved the drastic resource reallocation needed for modernization not through the market system but through its coercive power as fiscal authority.

Table 10.6. Japan's Trade Balance, 1868-1940

Year	Exports	(Finished Goods)	Imports	(Finished Goods)	Net E.
1868	16	(0.2)	11	(6.5)	5
1870	15	(0.3)	34	(6.8)	-19
1875	19	(0.6)	30	(18.)	-11
1880	28	(2.9)	37	(18.)	-9
1885	37	(3.3)	29	(14.)	8
1890	57	(10.)	82	(31.)	-25
1895	136	(38.)	129	(46.)	7
1900	204	(57.)	287	(92.)	-83
1905	322	(103.)	489	(131.)	-167
1910	458	(137.)	464	(103.)	-8
1915	708	(243.)	532	(51.)	176
1920	1948	(963.)	2336	(328.)	-388
1925	2306	(878.)	2573	(349.)	-267
1930	1470	(691.)	1546	(255.)	-76
1935	2490	(1451.)	2472	(286.)	27
1940	3655	(2071.)	3453	(448.)	202

Source: *Nihon No Hyaku Nen* (One Hundred Years of Japanese Statistics). Tokyo: Kokusei-sha (1986), pp. 298-299. Figures in millions of yen.

The Japanese financial industry has always been a crucial part of the nation's developmental project. As of 1868, the industry was in a state of chaos with over 1600 local paper currencies in circulation. The new government had to finance the extraordinary fiscal demands in its initial phase as well as redeem these lapsed issues by borrowing heavily from big merchants and by printing money much of which was inconvertible notes. The government imported the American banking system in a hurry (1872) to absorb the unpopular fiduciary notes (by allowing subscription to the banks' capital with these notes up to 60%); it introduced the postal savings and money-order system (1875) again primarily for the purpose of redeeming national debt and promoting the public's savings. As well, the government instituted a stringent deflationary policy in 1881 and by 1886 was able to redeem over 20 million yen of notes with tax revenues. In 1882 the Bank of Japan was founded as the country's central bank. Although the origins of central banks were much the same elsewhere, the Bank of Japan was more the bank for the government than others. Japan was able to join the gold standard of the West in 1886 on the strength of the 350 million yen of

specie she received from China as reparation payments arising from
the Sino-Japanese War of 1894-1895.

Another feature of Japan's financial system was (and still is) the
prominence of "special banks" designed as the arms and hands of the
government's developmental project. The Yokohama Shokin Bank
opened business in 1880 as the country's first foreign exchange bank. Its
aim was to take over the foreign exchange business monopolized by a
few foreign banks. The government not only subscribed one-third of its
initial capital but gave continued assistance throughout its existence.
The bank also enjoyed a privileged status with the Bank of Japan. A
group of special banks were established in 1880 and after to promote
the public's savings. By 1897 the savings at these savings banks stood
at 25 million yen, as against 26 million yen at postal savings. The
Japan Industrial Promotion Bank (1897) and some 40 Agricultural and
Industrial Banks (1898) were founded for the purpose of making long-
term, low-interest loans to agricultural and industrial development
projects. The Hokkaido Development Bank came into being in 1901 and
took over part of the programs pursued by the government. The Industrial Bank of Japan (1902) was the last but a very significant addition
to the list of special banks within Japan. In addition, the Bank of
Taiwan (1899) and the Bank of Korea (1911) were established to
facilitate the military and economic activities in these areas. These
special banks were all partially owned by the government and served
as part of the visible hand of the state.

So far I have dwelt on the developmental policies in the Meiji
period because the policies adopted from World War II to the present
were formulated and implemented essentially in the same spirit as
those of the Meiji period. The loss in the Second World War pushed
Japan's economic development back by a few decades. Industrial capital was short, technologies were obsolete, food was scarce, inflation
was rampant, and dollar reserves were virtually nil -- a situation very
similar to that in the early 1880s. The government took a drastic
deflationary monetary/fiscal measure in 1949-50 to bring the economy
back in track, and followed it with a state-led reconstruction and
development policy package. The government designated several
kikan ("key") industries such as coal, steel, shipbuilding and textiles
and gave them preferential treatment. The financial industry, headed
by the Bank of Japan and including the new governmental banks such as
the Japan Development Bank and the Japan Export-Import Bank, were
firmly behind this national endeavor.

The core of the package has been the Fiscal Investment and Loans
Plan (FILP) formulated and administered by the Ministry of Finance in
close collaboration with the MITI. The object of FILP has been to secure

long-term, low-cost funds the private financial institutions are in-capable of supplying for key industries and other important sectors of the economy. (In the early 1960s, for example, the bulk of FILP loans were made at 4.5-6.5% interest for 15-25 years with a 3 year grace period when the official discount rate of the Bank of Japan was in the 7-8% range.) The size of FILP has also been quite significant, amounting, for example, to 15-20% of the nation's gross fixed capital formation throughout the postwar period. The main source of FILP funds has always been postal savings and the insurance premium on public life insurance administered by the post offices. But the private financial sector has also been asked to contribute its share.

As van Wolferen (1989b) and many other Westerners have complained, the Japanese decision-making process has been a mystery to outsiders. In a typical Japanese firm, the CEO is usually not the most competent member in the organization in terms of Western cri-teria; he is not the best product designer or engineer, or a superstar in sales. If he excels in "skills," he does so in "relational" or "contextual" skills, in Aoki's terminology. In other words, he knows the firm organization inside out and is the number-one expert on how to mobilize the firm resources for its prosperity. His task is more coordination than planning. From the employees' standpoint, he is the man whose judg-ment they can trust. The nature of the CEO being what it is, ideas for new products and other innovative suggestions tend to come from the bottom up (in sharp contrast to the Western organization where new products are designed by the professional researchers and production orders are issued to the shop floor downstairs). In such a setup, it is not clear who should get the credit for the success of a product.

What is true of the firm is also true of the government. It is not correct to say that the government formulates policies and tells businesses to comply. Rather, in determining the list of key industries, for example, businesses take the initiative, do the required research and coordination among the membership, and draft the list for con-sultation and authorization with the government. In this context (and in business-government relations in general), the role of the central organ called *Keidanren* (literally, the Association of Business Organ-izations) is of particular importance.

The *Keidanren* encompasses many firms in a variety of important industries and plays multiple roles as a research organ, a lobby and a self-regulator for the membership. When it draws up the list of key industries, it already has resolved any conflicts among the members and, hence, when it lobbies the government for the adoption of the list, it is acting in the interest of the business community at large. Whether or not the government adopts the list as it is, the government has a degree of assurance that the list has been drawn up through a rational process and that the list, once adopted, is easily enforceable. As a result, the government appears to possess more power and authority than it really has. By contrast, the Western policy-making process which permits random, competitive lobbies by firms looks chaotic. It puts too much burden of decision making on the government and invites resistance and dissent at the implementation stage. As a result, the government appears less competent and efficient than it really is.

The question of who holds the real power in the Japanese system has been a puzzle even to the Japanese themselves. Japanese political scientists are constantly debating it. But the average citizen accustomed to the Japanese style of politics knows that no single group among politicians, bureaucrats and big business wields too much power alone in the Japanese society and politics but that the power rests with the partnership of the three groups such that politicians control the bureaucracy, the bureaucracy control business, and business has influence over members of the LDP.

Another important feature of Japan's investment coordination is its emphasis on the financial aspect of the plan. As mentioned above, the government-sponsored FILP uses primarily public sources of funds. But it also relies on private funds through the collaboration of the financial industry. Since the plan itself is arrived at after months of detailed study of individual investment projects between government banks and borrowers (FILP is submitted annually to the Diet as an attachment to the budget), it is not just an estimate of what is to come but a readily executable plan. In reality, the government's investment coordination is not limited to FILP but extends to a significant portion of private investment. The following description of how this is done is based on my own experience as a member of the Ministry of Finance.

I still remember the great excitement I experienced when I first witnessed investment (I) being equated to savings (S), literally in front of my eyes. In a modest conference room in the Ministry of Finance, a large table occupied the middle. On one side of the table were the representatives of the dozen major industries under the supervision of the Ministry of International Trade and Industry. On the other side were the representatives of the major lending institutions. In addition, there were representatives from the Bank of Japan, academia, and consumer groups. The Minister of Finance was in the chair. The Minister first asked the borrowers to reveal their desired amounts of investment funds, and then he asked the lenders what they were willing to supply. After a few rounds of *tatonnement*, the aggregate planned I was brought into equality with the aggregate planned S at a level deemed optimal by policy-makers, at which point the meeting adjourned. This meeting was not a mere ritual; the amount of information the government obtained from it was vital for an effective policy formulation (Nagatani 1989:227-228).

Back in the early sixties, when this event took place, the Japanese economy suffered from a chronic dollar shortage. Money had to be tightly controlled. The government refrained from borrowing; it could not possibly have borrowed from the public after annulling all its wartime debt with a 100% tax in 1946. This meant that additional credit needed for growth had to come from the Bank of Japan and that the Bank rationed credit in accordance with the national policy priorities. The above episode was part of such a broader rationing scheme. But this does not mean that such investment coordination is a thing of the past. The Japanese continue to practice it if not with the same sense of urgency, because they believe that an investment plan without financial backing is no plan at all.

Can this style of investment coordination, which has several important potential merits for a national economy, be implemented in the Western system? Apart from their ideological bias against "government intervention," the Westerners' chief concern would be how to secure the compliance of borrowers and lenders. How could the government prevent the borrowers from misusing the funds? How could the government bring the notoriously unpatriotic bankers into the pact and persuade them to commit their funds at rates possibly below their global opportunity cost?

In the Japanese case, the major banks have been the center of *zaibatsu* conglomerates or *keiretsu* corporate groups from the beginning. This setup has forced them to commit to the nation's developmental endeavor. But even so, the banks had to be convinced of the rationality of such a commitment. The government thus has had to assure them enough profits through various protective measures. In a country like the United States, where the banks would rather lend to Mexico than finance domestic projects (or so I am told), how to bring the industrialists and the lenders into a socially desirable investment pact may prove to be a problem. If anything, such a pact would be easier to work out for a small region than for an entire nation.

Whither Japanese Economics?

This section synthesizes the basic tenets of which I believe are the essential elements of Japanese Economics, by way of recapitulation of the whole discussion.

Tendency Towards a Political Economy

As is clear from Adam Smith's definition of the political economy, the classical economists conceived political economy as a very pragmatic set of skills or strategies to enable a nation to get richer.

> Political economy, considered as a branch of the science of a statesman or legislator, proposes two distinct objects: first, to provide a plentiful revenue or subsistence for the people, or more properly to enable them to provide such a revenue or subsistence for themselves; and secondly, to supply the state or commonwealth with a revenue sufficient for public services. It proposes to enrich the people and the sovereign. Adam Smith (1776-1910, 1:375).

As such it was necessarily nation- and time-specific both in scope and methods. Note that Smith defined political economy in terms of ends, leaving the choice of means to achieve these ends to the ingenuities of individual nations. The Japanese have always been faithful to this classical spirit of political economy.

Western neoclassical economics, by contrast, developed in the latter half of the nineteenth century amid the world-wide euphoria over the great accomplishments of the Newtonian physics. Leon Walras, one of the founders of the new economics, objected to Smith's definition, arguing that "the distinguishing characteristic of a science is the complete indifference to consequences, good or bad, with which it carries on the pursuit of pure truth." (Walras 1954:52).

Modelled after this new science, neoclassical economics elected to stand above the mundane affairs of human life and seek universal truths within an abstractly formulated economic system. It found a strict parallel between equilibrium of the physical world and "competitive" economic equilibrium. As the physicists had shown, Nature was an optimizer, an economizer. By implication, a competitive economic equilibrium was identified as a desirable or efficient equilibrium.

The policy implications of neoclassical economics are fully summarized in this finding. The "theorem of the invisible hand" or of the "optimality of *laissez-faire*" is the name the economists have given it. It is an economics of the first best or nothing; it is an economics sans human beings. Western Economics faithful to the neoclassical tradition holds that the best developmental strategy for a nation is to keep adapting to market signals with the passive rationality of natural objects.

Game-Theoretic Perception of the World From a Late-Comer's Standpoint

To the Japanese, the world was made up of a number of dominant economies already controlling a lion's share of global resources and is governed by the rules written and enforced by them. They realized from the start that in order to survive and prosper in such a world they needed a great deal of active rationality in setting national goals and mobilizing available resources toward them within the constraints imposed from outside. Although a similar outlook was shared by the late-comers in Europe such as Germany and Russia, Japan seems to have carried out the task with greater efficiency, as evidenced by her most rapid pace of industrialization and income growth. The key to success-ful development for a late-comer lay in maintaining an adequate degree of national autonomy. Japan secured it partly by deliberately choosing the pace of opening of the economy, and partly by using prices as control variables. She also kept her external debt to a minimum for the same purpose. In short, what Japan as a late-comer aimed at was a second-best or max-min solution under a multitude of external con-straints (but with a strong sense of direction). It is not surprising that the Japanese should have found the Western economics of first-best largely irrelevant and sometimes even false (see below).

The Human or Biological, as Opposed to Physical, View of a National Economy

The Japanese regard their economy as a living thing. They constantly take the temperature, feel the pulse and check the mood of the economy for diagnostic purposes. They then write a prescription suited to the health of the economy. The Japanese define a business firm as the people who make it up namely, the shareholders, the body of quasi-permanent employees, and the management. The firm is to serve the joint interests of all these parties.

The two major implications of this biological view are the following. First, it permits the Japanese to take a much more active approach to economic management. Just as rational career planning is essential to individual lives, so the right goal setting and its efficient implementation are vital to successful economic management. In particular, the Japanese believe that economic growth does not come naturally but needs to be earned. Because of the wide-ranging positive spillover effects of growth, the growth rate determined by decentralized markets tends to be lower than what the society should really want and what the society is capable of realizing.

Second, it admonishes the Japanese of the importance of the art of organizing people with diverse interests into a coherent and cooperative whole. The Japanese believe that an equilibrium superior to a competitive equilibrium is possible with human ingenuity in incentive-setting and organization (see, e.g., Aoki 1988, for a detailed discussion on these points). They are skeptical of some of the basic tenets of Western neoclassical economics such as competitive individualism (for the myopia and social wastes arising from the competitive expenditure of efforts and rent seeking), specialization according to the principle of comparative advantage (for its failure to provide national autonomy, for its failure to evolve a broad industrial base and for its divisive political effects) and free trade (which favors the strong).

Long-Term Prosperity as the Goal of Economic Policy

Western neoclassical economists define the goal of macroeconomics as price and income stability and the search for an optimal policy formula within a simple formal model open to random shocks but which abstracts from growth, technological changes and other important trends that determine the long-term prosperity of an economy. This preoccupation with short-run by the economists, though understandable in the light of the much improved data collection and computer facilities in the recent years, is alarming for two reasons.

First, the prospect of successful stabilization policies against shocks is very dim if their track record is any indication. Second and more importantly, the preoccupation with the short run comes at the expense of the more important long-term considerations. And this fashion apparently has spread into business and government sectors. The result is a permeation of superficially scientific but myopic decision makings at all levels.

The Japanese, by contrast, have maintained their long-term perspective. In their thinking, short-run shocks are acts of God. Rather than wasting energy in outsmarting God, they would focus attention to long-term health and forget about these shocks. In this way the Japanese have been able to devote greater amounts of energy and resources to long-term diagnosis and prescription. Currently they are engaged in a comprehensive and coordinated research on a wide range of socio-economic questions with a view to building the type of economy they want in the year 2050.

Summary

Because of the number of positive externalities, economic growth, if left to individual choices, tends to fall short of the socially optimal rate. Growth tends to feed on itself; its lack tends to aggravate misery. Securing an optimal growth requires both a will and a "plan" at the economy level. Part of the differential growth performances between Japan and the U.S. since the 1970s must have been due to the difference in will and plan; while the Japanese managed to stick with their growth-oriented policy, the Americans all but abandoned it.

Experience also shows that the success of a growth policy depends crucially on the art of implementation. Reducing taxes on high income earners, for example, increases personal savings but these savings may merely result in more luxury condos or myopic business ventures. It takes much more than just a tax policy to realize and sustain an adequate growth rate for a system as a whole. It takes a sophisticated sequencing of desirable types of investment and a well-designed coordination between materials and finance.

The fact that all these ideas are alien to Western Economics is an indication that this economics has some serious flaws and that a more relevant "political economy" is on the horizon. In particular, it calls into question the conventional way of thinking among Westerners that policies are either growth-oriented or welfare-oriented and that the latter is more civil and advanced than the former. The truth is that the two are not viable alternatives because a welfare state cannot support itself without growth.

Acknowledgments

I wish to thank the following individuals for taking the time out of their busy schedule for my interviews in August 1989: Messrs. Shunji Fukinbara (Director General, Planning Bureau, Economic Planning Agency); Masahiro Hirotsu (MITI alumnus); Toshio Ohsu (Director General, Financial Bureau, MOF); Miyohei Shinohara (Professor of Economics, Tokyo International University); Masaaki Tsuchida (Director General, Banking Bureau, MOF); Satoshi Uematsu (MITI, on leave as Director General, Equipments Bureau, National Defence Agency); Yusuke Watanabe (MOF alumnus); Takashi Yoshikuni (MAFF alumnus) and Masaru Yoshitomi (Director General, Economic Research Institute, Economic Planning Agency). I am also grateful to the Japan Foundation for a grant which made my two-week visit to Japan possible. Lastly, numerous discussions on the subject with Jim

Roumasset, Chung Lee, and my colleagues Hiroshi Niida, Ashok Kotwal and Ardo Hansson have been very useful.

References

Aoki, M. 1988. *Information, Incentives, and Bargaining in, the Japanese Economy*. Cambridge: Cambridge University Press.
Emmott, B. 1989. *The Sun Also Sets*. New York: Times Books.
Fallows, J. 1989a. "Containing Japan." *Atlantic Monthly* May: 40-54.
_____. 1989b. "Getting Along with Japan." *Atlantic Monthly* December: 53-64.
Johnson, C. 1982. *MITI and the Japanese Miracle*. 1925-1975, Stanford: Stanford University Press.
Ministry of Finance. 1927. *History of Public Finance in the Meiji Period*. 15 volumes.
Morita, A., and S. Ishihara. 1989. *The Japan That Can Say "No."* Tokyo: Kobunsha.
Morrison, C. J., and W. E. Diewert. 1988. "Productivity Growth and Changes in the Terms of Trade in Japan and the U.S." UBC Department of Economics Discussion Paper 88-89.
Nagatani, K. 1989. *Political Macroeconomics*. Oxford: Oxford University Press.
Nihon No Hyaku Nen (One Hundred Years of Japanese Statistics). 1986. Tokyo: Kokusei-sha. (In Japanese).
Smith, A. 1776, 1910. *The Wealth of Nations*. London: J. M. Dent & Sons.
Tamura, S. 1977. *Shokusankogyo (Japan's Industrialization)*. Tokyo: Kyoiku-sha. (In Japanese).
van Wolferen, K. 1989a. "Why Do Japanese Intellectuals Flatter to Power?" *Chuo Koron*.
_____. 1989b. *The Enigma of Japanese Power*. New York: Alfred A. Knopf.
Walras, L. 1874, 1954. *Elements of Pure Economics*, translated by W. Jaffe. Chicago: Irwin.

Epilogue

The traditional dichotomy of government versus the market as alternative mechanisms for resource allocation tends to obscure a more fundamental question. The issue is not how much and in what spheres government planning should replace markets, but how government action can promote mutually beneficial exchange.

The classical role of government is to provide the security, infrastructure and institutional prerequisites for contractual exchange. These roles are typically described as if omnipotent government despots are eagerly awaiting the marching orders of their economist wizards. But facilitating exchange is more complicated than making a few prudent public investments. Indeed, much of the social infrastructure of exchange involves an intricate cultural and moral constitution that may have evolved over centuries or even eons.

As evidenced by the discussions of East Asia in this volume (Introduction and Part II), there are a number of pro-market government functions which extend beyond the traditional scriptures of Adam Smith. In particular, industrial conglomerates can achieve a degree of investment coordination that is not possible by means of static competitive markets. Moreover, government can play a partnership role with the private sector so that public as well as private investments are coordinated. On the other hand, the very concentration of economic and political power that facilitates coordination can wreak havoc with the workings of the invisible hand. This is the central constitutional challenge of market governance.

The key to pro-market intervention is to promote the evolution of efficiency-enhancing specialization and the alignment of individual incentives. A great variety of institutional mechanisms -- intercontract linkages, communal resource management, corporate organizations -- may contribute to the evolution of economic cooperation. Efficiency is not necessarily aided by jumping as fast as possible to private property rights and the replacement of non-market institutions by market coordination. The natural evolution of property rights in land, for example, may pass through communal organization before reaching private property. Thus, confiscatory land reform and compulsory creation of private property may interrupt efficient evolution instead of accelerating it.

For example, foreign aid and international donor lending programs that focus on the vestiges of private property and markets, such as land titles and concrete structures where farmers may sell agricultural commodities, do not necessarily promote exchange in accordance with comparative advantage. Similarly, as noted in chapter 2, replacing non-market institutions with new markets is not necessarily welfare-enhancing. On the other hand, government action may sometimes create market-enhancing mechanisms that increase the scope and extent of economic cooperation (chapter 3).

In static welfare economics, the benefit of competition is limited to the decrease in excess burden associated with constraining monopoly power. From an evolutionary perspective, however, competition plays the additional role of selecting the most efficient firms. This is why the World Bank has placed increased emphasis on reducing entry restrictions in structural adjustment lending (see chapter 6). Government subsidies, on the other hand, tend to be anti-evolutionary and work against efficient selection. Most subsidy programs are associated with excess demand for the subsidies and therefore some rationing mechanism needs to be adopted to decide who the fortunate beneficiaries will be. Not only is rent-seeking after government largesse costly in terms of the expenditures on political influence, but it results in selection based on patronage instead of productivity.

It is natural that as evolution proceeds, the scope of economic cooperation widens from village to region to nation and finally to the international level. As newly industrializing countries expand, it is initially profitable to initiate technology from abroad. At more advanced stages of development, however, failure to protect intellectual property rights deters domestic producers from inventive activity. Thus the stage is set for international agreements regarding intellectual property rights (chapters 4 and 5).

The evolutionary perspective may also have implications for the liberalization of socialist economies. Creating the preconditions for effective capitalism requires far more than getting the government out of the way. In order for decentralized decision making to become the basis of economic coordination, centralized control, via the rule of law and a uniform standard of justice, is required to call forth order out of chaos. In a frictionless world, efficient allocation does not require any particular initial distribution of property. Without an elaborate physical and legal infrastructure of exchange, however, transaction costs render property distribution important, even aside from considerations of equity. Evolutionary strategies are needed to allow the creation and selection of new organizational forms to dominate existing enterprises.

These issues involve questions beyond the scope of conventional economics. Their pursuit will illuminate the nature of economic cooperation and will infuse new vigor into the study of Economic Development.

About the Contributors

Robert E. Evenson is a Professor in the Department of Economics at the Economic Growth Center at Yale University. He has held appointments at the University of Minnesota, at the University of the Philippines, and with the Agricultural Development Council. He has conducted pioneering research on agricultural productivity growth, returns to agricultural research, and research resource allocation.

Mukesh Eswaran and Ashok Kotwal, both of the Economics Department at the University of British Columbia, have tried to probe, in earlier work, organizational questions such as why capitalists are the bosses and why the different forms of tenancy exist. Recently, they have worked on broader questions such as whether trade with North makes South poorer, and what makes poverty impervious to industrial progress.

Sumner J. La Croix is a Professor of Economics at the University of Hawaii at Manoa and has held visiting positions in New Zealand, Australia, and China. His current research focuses on the development of property rights in land, natural resources, and intellectual property in Asia and the Pacific.

Chung H. Lee is a Professor of Economics at the University of Hawaii at Manoa and a Research Associate at the Institute for Economic Development and Policy, East-West Center, Honolulu, Hawaii. He has done extensive research on East Asian economic development with a special focus on the role of government in economic development. Currently, he is engaged in comparative research on financial systems and economic development in Asia and Latin America.

Ira W. Lieberman is President and owner of LIPAM International, Inc., a consulting group that advises governments, international institutions such as the World Bank and the Inter-American Development Bank and selected private sector companies on industrial restructuring, industrial policy and competitiveness and privatization. Dr. Lieberman's publications include *Industrial Restructuring Policy and Practice* (World Bank, 1989).

Keizo Nagatani is Professor of Economics at the University of British Columbia and served in the Ministry of Finance, Japan, from 1959 to 1965. He is the author of several books including *Political Macroeconomics* (Oxford University Press, 1989). His current interests include macroeconomics and monetary theory policy issues as well as the Japanese economy.

David M. G. Newbery is the Chair of the Department of Applied Economics at the University of Cambridge, England. He has worked with the Overseas Development Institute, the World Bank, USAID and FAO and has written extensively in the area of commodity market stabilization and the economics of risk.

Louis Putterman is Professor of Economics at Brown University, where he has taught since 1980. He is the author of numerous papers on aspects of economic development in China and Tanzania, and of papers and monographs on economic organization, including *Division of Labor and Welfare: An Introduction to Economic Systems* (Oxford University Press, 1990).

Joseph E. Stiglitz is Professor of Economics at Stanford University, Senior Fellow at the Hoover Institution and at the Institute for Policy Reform, and Research Associate at the National Bureau of Economic Research. Professor Stiglitz was awarded the John Bates Clark award in 1979 and has made important contributions to the theory of market structures, to the economics of the public sector, to financial economics, to macroeconomics, to monetary economics, and to the economics of development and growth. He was one of the originators of the "economics of information" and has shown how it can provide a new perspective on long-standing economic problems.

Brian D. Wright is a Professor of Agricultural and Resource Economics at the University of California at Berkeley, and previously served on the faculty at Yale. He has published numerous academic papers in public economics, agricultural policy, trade, financial markets, research and development, market organization and behavior, antitrust theory and commodity market stabilization. Professor Wright is the author (with Jeffrey C. Williams) of a newly published book, *Storage and Commodity Markets* (Cambridge University Press).

About the Editors

Susan Barr is a practicing attorney, writer and editor whose interests include law and economics and constitutional law. She is currently revising a paper co-authored with James Roumasset entitled *Markets, Mediation and Governance: A Constitutional Perspective for Commercial Relations*, University of Hawaii Program on Conflict Resolution Working Paper 89-6.

James A. Roumasset is a Professor of Economics at the University of Hawaii at Manoa and a member of the editorial board of the Journal of Economic Behavior and Organizations. Previous appointments include the East-West Center, the World Bank, the Agricultural Development Council, the University of the Philippines, the University of Maryland, Yale University, Australia National University, and the University of California at Davis. He has published extensively in economic development, public policy, the new institutional economics, decision-making under uncertainty, and resource/environmental economics. His previous books include *Rice and Risk* (North-Holland, 1976).